WORKERS OF ALL COUNTRIES, UNITE!

THE COLLECTED WORKS

OF

JOSEF STALIN

This softcover edition published by *Iskra Books* 2022

Original Russian Edition published by the decision of the Central Committee of the Communist Party of the Soviet Union (Bolshevik) 1946. Original English Edition published by Foreign Languages Publishing House, Moscow 1954.

First published in Russian.
All rights reserved.

The moral rights of the author and the preparer have been asserted.

Iskra Books
Madison, Wisconsin
US | UK | Ireland | Canada | Australia | India | South Africa
www.peacelandbread.com/books

Iskra Books is the imprint of the *Center for Communist Studies*, an international research center dedicated to the advancement of academic and public scholarship in the field of Marxist-Leninist studies and applied communist theory.

ISBN-13: 978-1-0880-0035-9

British Library Cataloguing in Publication Data
A catalogue record for this book is available from the British Library

Library of Congress Cataloging-in-Publication Data
A catalog record for this book is available from the Library of Congress

Prepared by Iskra Books
Typesetting and Cover Design by Ben Stahnke
Printed and Distributed by IngramSpark

THE COLLECTED WORKS
OF
JOSEF STALIN

VOLUME ONE

A young Josef Stalin in 1902 at the age of 23. Born *Ioseb Besarionis dze Jughashvili*, the Georgian revolutionary would, after time in the Theological Seminary, grow to become one of the most influential revolutionaries of the Twentieth Century. The works in the present volume represent Jugashvili's earliest published revolutionary writings—written during a period in which the author found himself hiding from the *Okhrana*, organizing strikes and demonstrations, being arrested and imprisoned in Siberia, escaping through the bitter cold, rising to prominence in the RSDLP, co-editing *Proletariatis Brdzola*, and robbing banks—a revolutionary above all else.

CONTENTS

PUBLISHER'S NOTE

This edition of the English translation of J. V. Stalin's *Works* has been reproduced faithfully from the text of the 1950's English version—based on the Russian edition—prepared by the Marx-Engels-Lenin Institute of the Central Committee, C.P.S.U.

Some of J. V. Stalin's writings given in Volumes 1 and 2 of the Russian edition of the *Works* are translations from the Georgian. This is indicated at the end of each of the works concerned. Throughout the text, J. V. Stalin's own footnotes can be found, interspersed with footnotes from the original editors of the Marx-Engels-Lenin Institute of the Soviet Union. Where applicable, the editors' footnotes have been distinguished from those of the author.

Iskra Books, the imprint of the *Center for Communist Studies*, has chosen to publish the full series of the *Collected Works* due to an academic scarcity of the materials, an increasing inaccessibility of *used* copies of the original Foreign Languages Publishing House editions, and a growing scholarly and practical interest in the writings and ideas of one of the Twentieth Century's most impactful socialist heads of state.

Stalin's *Works* are both accessible and important, and deserve to be studied not only as world-historical and practical applications of the development of Marxist-Leninist political theory, but—especially in an era where the rise of hegemonic imperialism and the decay of capitalism lead to an increasing global fascism—also as political-theoretical texts in their own right; as the core theoretical works underpinning extant socialist state governance, policy, legislation, and practice.

Editors, Iskra Books

PREPARER'S NOTE

Having not been published since 1954, the book you hold in your hands is the first of sixteen volumes of the *Collected Works* of Josef Stalin—the principled Soviet leader who helped take the country from a feudal state to an industrialized one, defeated the Nazis, and synthesized the political theory of Marxism-Leninism. Many words—both positive and negative—have been written about the man they called "The Man of Steel," yet, good or bad, one thing is certain: without Stalin, the contemporary world would be a very different place.

As I write this in 2022, the world is on the brink of a Third World War, the decline of capitalism has sharpened the contradictions of both class and state, and a virulent pandemic continues to rage across the globe. Stalin lived through similar conditions; and, because of this, his writings still speak to us in the present day. His writings also showcase his wit and his charm, his revolutionary fervor, and his engagement with the masses during a time when the whole world seemed to be in upheaval. Now, in our own time of upheaval, it is critical that contemporary organizers, scholars, and theorists have easy and financially accessible access to Stalin's writings.

This project is entirely a labor of love. No profit is being made from these books, and their publication is a collective effort—our goal is simply to get these volumes printed and distributed amongst the workers of the world.

March 12, 2022

FOREIGN LANGUAGES PUBLISHING HOUSE
PREFACE

The present collection of the works of J. V. Stalin is published by decision of the Central Committee of the Communist Party of the Soviet Union (Bolsheviks).

Hitherto only part of Comrade Stalin's works has been published in separate collections. His articles and speeches of the period immediately before October 1917 were collected in the book *On the Road to October*, which appeared in two editions in 1925. In 1932 the collection *The October Revolution* was published, containing articles and speeches on the Great October Socialist Revolution. Works on the national question went into the collection *Marxism and the National and Colonial Question*, which has appeared in several editions. The articles and speeches of 1921-1927, dealing mainly with internal Party questions and the rout of the opposition groups that were hostile to the Party, constituted a separate collection entitled *On the Opposition*, which was published in 1928. In addition, there are other collections in which are compiled J. V. Stalin's articles and speeches on definite subjects, such as, for example, the collections: *On Lenin, Articles and Speeches on the Ukraine, The Peasant Question, The Young Communist League*, and others.

At different times several collections were published containing works by both V. I. Lenin and J. V. Stalin, such as, *1917—Selected Writings and Speeches, The Defence of the Socialist Motherland, A Collection of Works for the Study of the History of the C.P.S.U.(B.)*. in three volumes, Lenin-Stalin—selected works in one volume, *On Party Affairs, On Socialist Emulation, On Labour*, and others.

The most widely distributed collection of the works of Comrade Stalin up to this point has been the book *Problems of Leninism*, which has gone through eleven editions. With every new edition the contents of this book underwent considerable change: nearly every edition included new works and, at the same time, in order to keep the book to its previous size, the author deleted certain works from it. Comrade Stalin's speeches, reports and Orders of the Day delivered during the Patriotic War the Soviet people waged against the German fascist invaders are collected in the book *On the Great Patriotic War of the Soviet Union*, which has gone through five editions.

However, a large number of J. V. Stalin's works, written before and after the October Revolution, were not reprinted and, hitherto, not collected after their publication in newspapers and magazines. Moreover, there are articles and letters by Comrade Stalin which have not been published before.

This is a first attempt to collect and publish in one edition nearly all the works of J. V. Stalin.

Volume 1 contains the works of J. V. Stalin written from 1901 to April 1907.

Volume 2 includes works written from 1907 to 1913.

Volume 3 consists of works of the period of preparation for the Great October Socialist Revolution (March-October 1917). These are mainly articles that were published in *Pravda*.

Volume 4 (November 1917-1920) includes works written in the first months of the existence of the Soviet government and in the period of foreign military intervention and civil war.

The next three Volumes—5, 6 and 7—contain works of the period of the Soviet state's transition to the peaceful work of rehabilitating the national economy (1921-1925). Volume 5 contains works written from 1921 up to the death of V. I. Lenin (January 1924). Volume 6 includes works of 1924. Volume 7 contains works written in 1925.

J. V. Stalin's works of the period of the struggle for the socialist industrialisation of the country (1926-1929) constitute Volumes 8, 9, 10, 11 and 12. Volumes 8 and 9 contain articles, speeches, reports, etc., made during 1926; Volumes 10 and 11, those of 1927; and Volume 12, those of the period of 1928-1929.

Volume 13 contains works of the period 1930-1933, dealing mainly with questions concerning the collectivisation of agriculture and the further development of socialist industrialisation.

Volume 14 contains works covering the period 1934-1940, dealing with the struggle to complete the building of socialism in the U.S.S.R., with the creation of the new Constitution of the Soviet Union, and with the struggle for peace in the situation prevailing at the opening of the Second World War.

Volume 15 consists of J. V. Stalin's work, *History of the C.P.S.U.(B.)*, *Short Course*, which appeared in a separate edition in 1938.

Volume 16 contains works of the period of the Soviet Union's Great Patriotic War, including J. V. Stalin's reports, speeches, and Orders of the Day on the anniversaries of the Great October Socialist Revolution, addresses to the people in connection with the rout and surrender of Germany and Japan, and other documents

All the works in the respective volumes are arranged in chronological order according to the time at which they were written or published. Each volume is furnished with a preface, brief explanatory notes, and a biographical chronicle. Dates until the adoption of the New Style calendar (up to February 14, 1918) are given in Old Style; those after that are given in New Style.

The texts of Comrade Stalin's works are given in their original form except in a few instances where the author has introduced slight changes of a purely stylistic character.

Marx-Engels-Lenin Institute
of the C.P., C.P.S.U.(B.)

PREFACE TO VOLUME ONE

Volume 1 includes the works of J. V. Stalin written from 1901 to April 1907, the period when he conducted his revolutionary activities mainly in Tiflis.

In this period the Bolsheviks, under the leadership of V. I. Lenin, were laying the foundations of the Marxist-Leninist Party, of its ideology and principles of organisation.

In this period Comrade Stalin, combating various anti-Marxist and opportunist trends, created Leninist-*Iskra* Bolshevik organisations in Transcaucasia and directed their activities. In his works he substantiated and vindicated the fundamental principles of the Marxist-Leninist doctrine.

Only a small part of J. V. Stalin's works included in Volume 1 were published in Russian. Most of them were published in Georgian newspapers and pamphlets. The majority of these appear in Russian for the first time.

The archives of the Caucasian Union Committee of the Russian Social-Democratic Labour Party, and some of the publications issued by the Transcaucasian Bolshevik organisations, in which works of J. V. Stalin were published, have not been found to this day. In particular, the *Programme of Studies for Marxist Workers' Circles* (1898) and *Credo* (1904) are still missing.

Volume 1 of the present edition does not contain all the works of J. V. Stalin written from 1901 to April 1907.

Marx-Engels-Lenin Institute
of the C.P., C.P.S.U.(B.)

JOSEF STALIN'S PREFACE TO
VOLUME ONE

The works comprising Volume 1 were written in the early period of the author's activities (1901-1907), when the elaboration of the ideology and policy of Leninism was not yet completed. This partly applies also to Volume 2 of the *Works*.

To understand and properly appraise these works, they must be regarded as the works of a young Marxist not yet moulded into a finished Marxist-Leninist. It is natural therefore that these works should bear traces of some of the propositions of the old Marxists which afterwards became obsolete and were subsequently discarded by our Party. I have in mind two questions: the question of the agrarian programme, and the question of the conditions for the victory of the socialist revolution.

As is evident from Volume 1 (see articles "The Agrarian Question"), at that time the author maintained that the landlords' lands should be distributed among the peasants as the peasants' private property. At the Party's Unity Congress, at which the agrarian question was discussed, the majority of the Bolshevik delegates engaged in practical Party work supported the distribution point of view, the majority of the

Mensheviks stood for municipalisation, Lenin and the rest of the Bolshevik delegates stood for the nationalisation of the land. In the course of the controversy around these three drafts, when it became evident that the prospect of the congress accepting the draft on nationalisation was hopeless, Lenin and the other nationalisers at the congress voted with the distributors.

The distributors advanced three arguments against nationalisation:

a) that the peasants would not accept the nationalisation of the land-lords' lands, because they wanted to obtain those lands as their private property; b) that the peasants would resist nationalisation, because they would regard it as a measure to abolish the private ownership of the land which they already privately owned; c) that even if the peasants' objection to nationalisation could be overcome, we Marxists should not advocate nationalisation, because, after the victory of the bourgeois-democratic revolution, the state in Russia would not be a socialist, but a bourgeois state, and the possession by the bourgeois state of a large fund of nationalised land would inordinately strengthen the bourgeoisie to the detriment of the interests of the proletariat.

In this the distributors proceeded from the premise that was accepted among Russian Marxists, including the Bolsheviks, that after the victory of the bourgeois-democratic revolution there would be a more or less long interruption in the revolution, that between the victorious bourgeois revolution and the future socialist revolution there would be an interval, during which capitalism would have the opportunity to develop more freely and powerfully and embrace agriculture too; that the class struggle would become more intense and more widespread, the proletariat's class would grow in numbers, the proletariat's class consciousness and organisation would rise to the proper level, and that only after all this could the period of the socialist revolution set in.

It must be observed that the premise that a long interval would set in between the two revolutions was not opposed by anybody at the congress; both the advocates of nationalisation and distribution on the one hand, and the advocates of municipalisation on the other, were of the opinion that the agrarian programme of Russian Social-Democracy should facilitate the further and more powerful development of capitalism in Russia.

Did we Bolshevik practical workers know that Lenin at that time held the view that the bourgeois revolution in Russia would grow into the socialist revolution, that he held the view of uninterrupted revolution? Yes, we did. We knew it from his pamphlet entitled *Two Tactics* (1905), and also from his celebrated article "The Attitude of Social-Democracy Towards the Peasant Movement" of 1905, in which he stated that "we stand for uninterrupted revolution" and that "we shall not stop halfway." But because of our inadequate theoretical training, and because of our neglect, characteristic of practical workers, of theoretical questions, we had not studied the question thoroughly enough and had failed to understand its great significance. As we know, for some reason Lenin did not at that time develop the arguments following from the theory of the growing over of the bourgeois revolution into the socialist revolution, nor did he use them at the congress in support of nationalisation.

Was it not because he believed that the question was not yet ripe, and because he did not expect the majority of the Bolshevik practical workers at the congress to be sufficiently equipped to understand and accept the theory that the bourgeois revolution must grow into the socialist revolution that he refrained from advancing these arguments?

It was only some time later, when Lenin's theory that the bourgeois revolution in Russia must grow into the socialist revolution became the guiding line of the Bolshevik Party, that disagreements on the agrarian question vanished in the Party; for it became evident that in a country like Russia—where the specific conditions of development had prepared the ground for the growth of the bourgeois revolution into the socialist revolution—the Marxist party could have no other agrarian programme than that of land nationalisation.

The second question concerns the problem of the victory of the socialist revolution. As is evident from Volume 1 (see articles *Anarchism or Socialism?*), at that time the author adhered to the thesis, current among Marxists, that one of the major conditions for the victory of the socialist revolution is that the proletariat must become the majority of the population, that, consequently, in those countries where the proletariat does not yet constitute the majority of the population owing to the inadequate development of capitalism, the victory of socialism is impossible.

This thesis was taken as generally accepted among Russian Marxists, including the Bolsheviks, as well as among the Social-Democratic parties of other countries. The subsequent development of capitalism in Europe and America, however, the transition from pre-imperialist capitalism to imperialist capitalism and, finally, Lenin's discovery of the law of the uneven economic and political development of different countries, showed that this thesis no longer corresponded to the new conditions of development, that the victory of socialism was quite possible in individual countries where capitalism had not yet reached the highest point of development and the proletariat did not yet constitute the majority of the population, but where the capitalist front was sufficiently weak to be breached by the proletariat. Lenin's theory of the socialist revolution thus arose in 1915-1916. As is well known, Lenin's theory of the socialist revolution proceeds from the thesis that the socialist revolution will be victorious not necessarily in those countries where capitalism is most developed, but primarily in those countries where the capitalist front is weak, where it is easier for the proletariat to breach that front, where capitalism has reached, say, only the medium stage of development.

This is all the comment the author wishes to make on the works collected in Volume 1.

J. Stalin
January 1946

1901-1907

FROM THE EDITORS[1]

Convinced that for intelligent Georgian readers the publication of a free periodical is an urgent question; convinced that this question must be settled today and that further delay can only damage the common cause; convinced that every intelligent reader will welcome such a publication and will render it every assistance, we, a group of Georgian revolutionary Social-Democrats, are meeting this want in the endeavour to satisfy the readers' wishes as far as it lies in our power. We are issuing the first number of the first Georgian free newspaper *Brdzola*.[2]

To enable the reader to form a definite opinion about our publication and, in particular, about ourselves, we shall say a few words.

The Social-Democratic movement has not left untouched a sin-

---

1 Leading article in the illegal Social-Democratic newspaper *Brdzola* (*The Struggle*).

2 **Original editors' note**: *Brdzola* (*The Struggle*)—the first illegal Georgian newspaper issued by the Leninist-*Iskra* group of the Tiflis Social-Democratic organisation. It was founded on the initiative of J. V. Stalin. The newspaper was launched as a result of the struggle that had been waged since 1898 by the revolutionary minority in the first Georgian Social-Democratic organisation known as the Messameh Dassy (J. V. Stalin, V. Z. Ketskhoveli and A. G. Tsulukidze) against the opportunist majority (Jordania and others) on the question of instituting an underground revolutionary Marxist press. *Brdzola*, was printed in Baku at an underground printing plant that had been organised by V. Z. Ketskhoveli, J. V. Stalin's closest colleague, on the instructions of the revolutionary wing of the Tiflis Social-Democratic organisation. He was also responsible for the practical work of issuing the newspaper. The leading articles in *Brdzola*, on questions concerning the programme and tactics of the revolutionary Marxist party were written by J. V. Stalin. Four numbers of *Brdzola*, were issued: No. 1, in September 1901; No. 2-3, in November-December 1901; and No. 4, in December 1902. The best Marxist newspaper in Russia next to *Iskra*, *Brdzola* urged that there was an inseverable connection between the revolutionary struggle that was being waged by the Transcaucasian proletariat and the revolutionary struggle waged by the working class all over Russia. Propagating the theoretical principles of revolutionary Marxism, *Brdzola*, like Lenin's *Iskra*, urged that the Social-Democratic organisations must proceed to take up mass political agitation and the political struggle against the autocracy, and advocated the Leninist idea of the hegemony of the proletariat in the bourgeois-democratic revolution. In its fight against the "Economists," *Brdzola*, urged the necessity of creating a united revolutionary party of the working class and exposed the liberal bourgeoisie, nationalists and opportunists of all shades. Commenting on the appearance of No. 1 of *Brdzola*, Lenin's *Iskra* stated that it was an event of extreme importance.

gle corner of the country. It has not avoided that corner of Russia which we call the Caucasus, and with the Caucasus, it has not avoided our Georgia. The Social-Democratic movement in Georgia is a recent phenomenon, it is only a few years old; to be more precise, the foundations of that movement were laid only in 1896. Here, as everywhere else, our activities at first did not extend beyond the bounds of secrecy. Agitation and wide propaganda in the form that we have been witnessing lately were impossible and, willy-nilly, all efforts were concentrated in a few circles. This period has now passed. Social-Democratic ideas have spread among the masses of the workers, and activities have also overflowed the narrow bounds of secrecy and have spread to a large section of the workers. The open struggle has started. This struggle has confronted the pioneer Party workers with many questions of a kind that have been in the background hitherto and have not urgently called for explanation. The first question that has arisen in all its magnitude is: what means have we at our command to enlarge the area of the struggle? In words, the answer to this question is very simple and easy; in practice it is quite different.

It goes without saying that for the organised Social-Democratic movement the principal means is the extensive propaganda of and agitation for revolutionary ideas. But the conditions under which the revolutionary is obliged to operate are so contradictory, so difficult, and call for such heavy sacrifices, that often both propaganda and agitation become impossible in the form that the initial stage of the movement requires. Studying in circles with the aid of books and pamphlets becomes impossible, first, because of police persecution, and secondly, because of the very way this work is organised. Agitation wanes with the very first arrests. It becomes impossible to maintain contact with the workers and to visit them often; and yet the workers are expecting explanations of numerous questions of the day. A fierce struggle is raging around them; all the forces of the government are mustered against them; but they have no means of critically analysing the present situation, they have no information about the actual state of affairs, and often a slight setback at some neighbouring factory is enough to cause revolutionary-minded workers to cool off, to lose confidence in the future, and the leader is obliged to start drawing them into the work anew.

In most cases, agitation with the aid of pamphlets which provide answers only to certain definite questions has little effect. It becomes necessary to create a literature that provides answers to questions of the day. We shall not stop to prove this commonly-known truth. In the Georgian labour movement the time has already arrived when a periodical becomes one of the principal means of revolutionary activity.

For the information of some of our uninitiated readers we deem it necessary to say a few words about the legally printed newspapers. We would deem it a great mistake if any worker regarded such a newspaper, irrespective of the conditions under which it was published or of the trend it pursued, as the mouthpiece of his, the worker's, interests. The government, which "takes care" of the workers, is in a splendid position as far as such newspapers are concerned. A whole horde of officials, called censors, are attached to them, and it is their special function to watch them and to resort to red ink and scissors if even a single ray of truth breaks through. Circular after circular comes flying to the committee of censors ordering: "Don't pass anything concerning the workers; don't publish anything about this or that event; don't permit the discussion of such and such a subject," and so on and so forth. Under these conditions, it is, of course, impossible for a newspaper to be run properly; and in vain will the worker seek in its columns, even between the lines, for information on and a correct appraisal of matters that concern him. If anybody were to believe that a worker can gain any benefit from the rare lines that appear in this or that legally printed newspaper casually mentioning matters concerning him, and let through by the butchering censors only by mistake, we would have to say that he who placed his hopes on such fragments and attempted to build up a system of propaganda on such snippets would display lack of understanding.

We repeat that we are saying this only for the information of a few uninitiated readers.

And so, a Georgian free periodical is something the Social-Democratic movement needs very urgently. The only question now is how to run such a publication; by what should it be guided, and what should it give the Georgian Social-Democrats.

From the point of view of the onlooker, the question of the existence of a Georgian newspaper in general, and the question of its content and trend in particular, may seem to settle themselves naturally and simply: the Georgian Social-Democratic movement is not a separate, exclusively Georgian, working-class movement with its own separate programme; it goes hand in hand with the entire Russian movement and, consequently, accepts the authority of the Russian Social-Democratic Party—hence it is clear that a Georgian Social-Democratic newspaper should be only a local organ that deals mainly with local questions and reflects the local movement. But behind this reply lurks a difficulty which we cannot ignore and which we shall inevitably encounter. We refer to the language difficulty. While the Central Committee of the Russian Social-Democratic Party is able to explain all general questions with the aid of the all-Party newspaper and leave it to the regional committees to deal only with local questions, the Georgian newspaper finds itself in a difficulty as regards content. The Georgian newspaper must simultaneously play the part of an all-Party and of a regional, or local organ. As the majority of Georgian working-class readers cannot freely read the Russian newspaper, the editors of the Georgian newspaper have no right to pass over those questions which the all-Party Russian newspaper is discussing, and should discuss. Thus, the Georgian newspaper must inform its readers about all questions of principle concerning theory and tactics. At the same time it must lead the local movement and throw proper light on every event, without leaving a single fact unexplained, and providing answers to all questions that excite the local workers. The Georgian newspaper must link up and unite the Georgian and Russian militant workers The newspaper must inform its readers about everything that interests them at home, in Russia and abroad.

Such, in general, is our view of what the Georgian newspaper should be.

A few words about the content and trend of the newspaper.

We must demand that as a Social-Democratic newspaper it should devote attention mainly to the militants workers. We think it superfluous to say that in Russia, and everywhere, the revolutionary proletariat alone is destined by history to liberate mankind and bring the world happiness. Clearly, only the working-class movement stands on solid ground, and it alone is free from all sorts of utopian fairy tales. Consequently, the newspaper, as the organ of the Social-Democrats, should lead the working-class movement, point the road for it, and safeguard it from error. In short, the primary duty of the newspaper is to be as close to the masses of the workers as possible, to be able constantly to influence them and serve as their conscious and guiding centre.

As, however, in the conditions prevailing in Russia today, it is possible that other elements of society besides the workers may come out as the champions of "freedom," and as this freedom is the immediate goal of the militant workers of Russia, it is the duty of the newspaper to afford space for every revolutionary movement, even one outside the labour movement. We say "afford space" not only for casual information, or simply news. No! The newspaper must devote special attention to the revolutionary movement that goes on, or will arise, among other elements of society. It must explain every social phenomenon and thereby influence every one who is fighting for freedom. Hence, the newspaper must devote special attention to the political situation in Russia, weigh up all the consequences of this situation, and on the widest possible basis raise the question of the necessity of waging a political struggle.

We are convinced that nobody will quote our words as proof that we advocate establishing connection and compromising with the bourgeoisie. The proper appraisal, the exposure of the weaknesses and errors of the movement against the existing system, even if it proceeds among the bourgeoisie, cannot cast the stain of opportunism on the Social-Democrats. The only thing here is not to forget Social-Democratic principles and revolutionary methods of fighting. If we measure every movement with this yardstick, we shall keep free of all Bernsteinian delusions.

Thus, the Georgian Social-Democratic newspaper must provide plain answers to all questions connected with the working-class movement, explain questions of principle, explain theoretically the role the working class plays in the struggle, and throw the light of scientific socialism upon every phenomenon the workers encounter.

At the same time, the newspaper must serve as the representative of the Russian Social-Democratic Party and give its readers timely information about all the views on tactics held by Russian revolutionary Social-Democracy. It must inform its readers about how the workers in other countries live, what they are doing to improve their conditions, and how they are doing it, and issue a timely call to the Georgian workers to enter the battle-field. At the same time, the newspaper must not leave out of account, and without Social-Democratic criticism, a single social movement.

Such is our view of what a Georgian newspaper should be.

We cannot deceive either ourselves or our readers by promising to carry out these tasks in their entirety with the forces at present at our command. To run the newspaper as it really ought to be run we need the aid of our readers and sympathisers. The reader will note that the first number of *Brdzola* suffers from numerous defects, but defects which can be rectified, if only our readers give us their assistance. In particular, we emphasise the paucity of home news. Being at a distance from home we are unable to watch the revolutionary movement in Georgia and provide timely information and explanation concerning questions of that movement. Hence we must receive assistance from Georgia. Whoever wishes to assist us also with literary contributions will undoubtedly find means of establishing direct or indirect contact with the editors of *Brdzola*.

We call upon all Georgian militant Social-Democrats to take a keen interest in the fate of *Brdzola*, to render every assistance in publishing and distributing it, and thereby convert the first free Georgian newspaper *Brdzola* into a weapon of the revolutionary struggle.

Brdzola (The Struggle), No. 1
September 1901
Unsigned
Translated from the Georgian

THE RUSSIAN SOCIAL-DEMOCRATIC PARTY AND ITS IMMEDIATE TASKS

I

Human thought was obliged to undergo considerable trial, suffering and change before it reached scientifically elaborated and substantiated socialism. West-European Socialists were obliged for a long time to wander blindly in the wilderness of utopian (impossible, impracticable) socialism before they hewed a path for themselves, investigated and established the laws of social life, and hence, mankind's need for socialism. Since the beginning of the last century Europe has produced numerous brave, self-sacrificing and honest scientific workers who tried to explain and decide the question as to what can rid mankind of the ills which are becoming increasingly intense and acute with the development of trade and industry. Many storms, many torrents of blood swept over Western Europe in the struggle to end the oppression of the majority by the minority, but sorrow remained undispelled, wounds remained unhealed, and pain became more and more unendurable with every passing day. We must regard as one of the principal reasons for this the fact that utopian socialism did not investigate the laws of social life; it soared higher and higher above life, whereas what was needed was firm contact with reality. The utopians set out to achieve socialism as an immediate object at a time when the ground for it was totally unprepared in real life—and what was more deplorable because of its results—the utopians expected that socialism would be brought into being by the powerful of this world who, they believed, could easily be convinced of the correctness of the socialist ideal (Robert Owen, Louis Blanc, Fourier and others). This outlook completely obscured from view the real labour movement and the masses of the workers, the only *natural* vehicle of the socialist ideal. The utopians could not understand this. They wanted to establish happiness on earth by legislation, by declarations, without the assistance of the people (the workers). They paid no particular attention to the labour movement and often even denied its importance. As a consequence, their theories remained mere theories which failed to affect the masses of the workers, among whom, quite independently of these theories, matured the great idea proclaimed in the middle of the last century by that genius, *Karl Marx*: *"The emancipation of the working class must be the act of the working class itself. . . . Workingmen of all countries, unite!"*

These words brought out the truth, now evident even to the "blind," that what was needed to bring about the socialist ideal was the independent action of the workers and their amalgamation into an organised force, irrespective of nationality and country. It was necessary to establish this truth—and this was magnificently performed by *Marx* and his friend *Engels*—in order to lay firm foundations for the mighty Social-Democratic Party, which today towers like inexorable fate over the European bourgeois system, threatening its destruction and the erection on its ruins of a socialist system.

In Russia the evolution of the idea of socialism followed almost the same path as that in Western Europe. In Russia, too, Socialists were obliged for a long time to wander blindly before they reached Social-Democratic consciousness—scientific socialism. Here, too, there were Socialists and there was a labour movement, but they marched independently of each other, going separate ways: the Socialists towards utopian dreams (*Zemlya i Volya, Narodnaya Volya*[1]), and the labour movement towards spontaneous revolts. Both operated in the same period—seventies-eighties—ignorant of each other. The Socialists had no roots among the working population and, consequently, their activities were abstract, futile. The workers, on the other hand, lacked leaders, organisers, and, consequently, their movement took the form of disorderly revolts. This was the main reason why the heroic struggle that the Socialists waged for socialism remained fruitless, and why their legendary courage was shattered against the solid wall of autocracy. The Russian Socialists established contact with the masses

---

1 *Zemlya i Volya*—Land and Freedom; *Narodnaya Volya*—People's Will.—Tr.

of the workers only at the beginning of the nineties. They realised that salvation lay only in the working class, and that this class alone would bring about the socialist ideal. Russian Social-Democracy now concentrated all its efforts and attention upon the movement that was going on among the Russian workers at that time. Still inadequately class conscious, and ill-equipped for the struggle, the Russian workers tried gradually to extricate themselves from their hopeless position and to improve their lot somehow. There was no systematic organisational work in that movement at the time, of course; the movement was a spontaneous one.

And so, Social-Democracy set to work upon this unconscious, spontaneous and unorganised movement. It tried to develop the class consciousness of the workers, tried to unite the isolated and sporadic struggles of individual groups of workers against individual masters, to combine them in a common class struggle, in order that it might become the struggle of the Russian working *class* against the oppressing class of Russia; and it tried to give this struggle an organised character.

In the initial stages, Social-Democracy was unable to spread its activities among the masses of the workers and it, therefore, confined its activities to propaganda and agitation circles. The only form of activity it engaged in at that time was to conduct study circles. The object of these circles was to create among the workers themselves a group that would subsequently be able to lead the movement. Therefore, these circles were made up of advanced workers—only chosen workers could attend them.

But soon the study-circle period passed away. Social-Democracy soon felt the necessity of leaving the narrow confines of the circles and of spreading its influence among the broad masses of the workers. This was facilitated by external conditions. At that time the spontaneous movement among the workers rose to an exceptional height. Who of you does not remember the year when nearly the whole of Tiflis was involved in this spontaneous movement? Unorganised strikes at the tobacco factories and in the railway workshops followed one after another. Here, it happened in 1897-98; in Russia it happened somewhat earlier. Timely assistance was needed, and Social-Democracy hastened to render that assistance. A struggle started for a shorter working day, for the abolition of fines, for higher wages, and so forth. Social-Democracy well knew that the development of the labour movement could not be restricted to these petty demands, that these demands were not the goal of the movement, but only a means of achieving the goal. Even if these demands were petty, even if the workers themselves in individual towns and districts were now fighting separately, that fight itself would teach the workers that complete victory would be achieved only when the entire working class launched an assault against its enemy as a united, strong and organised force. This fight would also show the workers that in addition to their immediate enemy, the capitalist, they have another, still more vigilant foe—the organised force of the entire bourgeois class, the present capitalist *state*, with its armed forces, its courts, police, prisons and gendarmerie. If even in Western Europe the slightest attempt of the workers to improve their condition comes into collision with the bourgeois power, if in Western Europe, where human rights have already been won, the workers are obliged to wage a direct struggle against the authorities, how much more so must the workers in Russia, in their movement, inevitably come into collision with the *autocratic power*, which is the vigilant foe of every labour movement, not only because this power protects the capitalists, but also because, as an autocratic power, it cannot resign itself to the independent action of social classes, particularly to the independent action of a class like the working class, which is more oppressed and downtrodden than other classes. That is how Russia Social-Democracy perceived the course of the movement, and it exerted all its efforts to spread these ideas among the workers. Herein lay its strength, and this explains its great and triumphant development from the very outset, as was proved by the great strike of the workers in the St. Petersburg weaving mills in 1896.

But the first victories misled and turned the heads of certain weaklings. Just as the Utopian Socialists in their time had concentrated their attention exclusively on the ultimate goal and, dazzled by it, totally failed to see, or denied, the real labour movement that was developing under their very eyes, so certain Russian Social-Democrats, on the contrary, devoted all their attention exclusively to the spontaneous labour movement, to its everyday needs. At that time (five years ago), the class consciousness of the Russian workers was extremely low. The Russian workers were only just awakening from their age-long sleep, and their eyes, accustomed to darkness, failed, of course, to register all that was happening in a world that had become revealed to them for the first time. Their needs were not great, and so their demands were not great. The Russian workers still went no further than to demand slight increases in wages or a reduction of the working day. That it was necessary to change the existing system, that it was necessary to abolish private property, that it was necessary to organise a socialist system—of all this the masses of the Russian workers had no inkling. They scarcely dared to think about abolishing the slavery in which the entire Russian people were submerged under the autocratic regime, to think about freedom for the people, to think about the people taking part in the government of the country. And so, while one section of Russian Social-Democracy deemed it its duty to carry its socialist ideas into the labour movement, the other part, absorbed in the economic struggle—the struggle for partial improvements in the conditions of the workers (as for example, reduction of the working day and higher wages)—was prone to forget entirely its great duty and its great ideals.

Echoing their like-minded friends in Western Europe (called Bernsteinians), they said: "For us the movement is everything—the final aim is nothing." They were not in the least interested in what the working class was fighting for so long as it fought. The so-called farthing policy developed. Things reached such a pass that, one fine day, the St. Petersburg newspaper *Rabochaya Mysl*[2] announced. "Our political programme is a ten-hour day and the restitution of the holidays that were abolished by the law of June 2"[3] (!!!).[4]

Instead of leading the spontaneous movement, instead of imbu-

---

2 **Original editor**: *Rabochaya Mysl (Workers' Thought)*—a newspaper which openly advocated the opportunist views of the "Economists." Published from October 1897 to December 1902. Sixteen issues appeared.

3 **Original editor**: The Law of June 2, 1897, fixed the working day for workers in industrial enterprises and railway workshops at 11 1/2 hours, and also reduced the number of holidays for the workers.

4 It must be stated that lately the St. Petersburg League of Struggle, and the editorial board of its newspaper, renounced their previous, exclusively economic, trend, and are now trying to introduce the idea of the political struggle into their activities.

ing the masses with Social-Democratic ideals and guiding them towards the achievement of our final aim, this section of the Russian Social-Democrats became a blind instrument of the movement; it blindly followed in the wake of the inadequately educated section of the workers and limited itself to formulating those needs and requirements of which the masses of the workers were conscious at the time. In short, it stood and knocked at an open door, not daring to enter the house. It proved incapable of explaining to the masses of the workers either the final aim—socialism, or even the immediate aim—the overthrow of the autocracy; and what was still more deplorable, it regarded all this as useless and even harmful. It looked upon the Russian workers as children and was afraid of frightening them with such daring ideas. Nor is this all: in the opinion of a certain section of Social-Democracy, it was not necessary to wage a revolutionary struggle to bring about socialism; all that was needed, in their opinion, was the economic struggle—strikes and trade unions, consumers' and producers' co-operative societies, and there you have socialism. It regarded as mistaken the doctrine of the old international Social-Democracy that a change in the existing system and the complete emancipation of the workers were impossible until political power had passed into the hands of the proletariat (the dictatorship of the proletariat). In its opinion there was nothing new in socialism and, strictly speaking, it did not differ from the existing capitalist system: it could easily fit into the existing system, every trade union and even every co-operative store or producers' co-operative society was already a "bit of socialism," they said. They imagined that by means of this absurd patching of old clothes they could make new garments for suffering mankind! But most deplorable of all, and in itself unintelligible to revolutionaries, is the fact that this section of the Russian Social-Democrats have expanded the doctrine of their West-European teachers (Bernstein and Co.) to such a degree that they brazenly state that political freedom (freedom to strike, freedom of association, freedom of speech, etc.) is compatible with *tsarism* and, therefore, a political struggle as such, the struggle to overthrow the autocracy, is quite superfluous because, if you please, the economic struggle alone is enough to achieve the aim, it is enough for strikes to occur more often—despite government prohibition—for the government to tire of punishing the strikers, and in this way freedom to strike and to hold meetings will come of its own accord.

Thus, these alleged "Social-Democrats" argued that the Russian workers should devote all their strength and energy entirely to the: economic struggle and should refrain from pursuing all sorts of "lofty ideals." In practice, their actions found expression in the view that it was their duty to conduct only *local* activities in this or that town. They displayed no interest in the organisation of a Social-Democratic workers' *party* in Russia; on the contrary, they regarded the organisation of a party as a ridiculous and amusing game which would hinder them in the execution of their direct "duty"—to wage the economic struggle. Strikes and more strikes, and the collection of kopeks for strike funds—such was the alpha and omega of their activities.

You will no doubt think that since they have whittled down their tasks to such a degree, since they have renounced Social-Democratism, these worshippers of the spontaneous "movement" would have done a great deal, at least for that movement. But here, too, we are deceived. The history of the St. Petersburg movement convinces us of this. Its splendid development and bold progress in the early stages, in 1895-97, was succeeded by blind wandering and, finally, the movement came to a halt. This is not surprising: all the efforts of the "Economists" to build up a stable organisation for the economic struggle invariably came up against the solid wall of the government and were always shattered against it. The frightful regime of police persecution destroyed all possibility of any kind of industrial organisation. Nor did the strikes bear any fruit, because out of every hundred strikes, ninety-nine were strangled in the clutches of the police; workers were ruthlessly ejected from St. Petersburg and their revolutionary energy was pitilessly sapped by prison walls and Siberian frosts. We are profoundly convinced that this check (relative of course) to the movement was due not only to external conditions, the police regime; it was due no less to the check in the development of the very ideas, of the class consciousness of the workers, and, hence, to the waning of their revolutionary energy.

Although the movement was developing, the workers could not widely understand the lofty aims and content of the struggle because the banner under which the Russian workers had to fight was still the old faded rag with its farthing motto of the economic struggle; consequently, the workers were bound to wage this struggle with reduced energy, reduced enthusiasm, reduced revolutionary striving, for great energy is engendered only for a great aim.

But the danger that threatened this movement as a result of this would have been greater had not our conditions of life, day by day and with increasing persistence, pushed the Russian workers towards the direct political struggle. Even a small simple strike brought the workers right up against the question of our lack of political rights, brought them into collision with the government and the armed forces, and glaringly revealed how inadequate the economic struggle was by itself. Consequently, despite the wishes of these "Social-Democrats," the struggle, day by day, increasingly assumed a distinctly political character. Every attempt of the awakened workers openly to express their discontent with the existing economic and political conditions under which the Russian workers are groaning today, every attempt to free themselves from this yoke, impelled the workers to resort to demonstrations of a kind in which the economic aspect of the struggle faded out more and more. The First of May celebrations in Russia laid the road to political struggle and to political demonstrations. And to the only weapon they possessed in their struggle in the past—the strike—the Russian workers added a new and powerful weapon—the political demonstration, which was tried for the first time during the great Kharkov May Day rally in 1900.

Thus, thanks to its internal development, the Russian labour movement proceeded from *propaganda* in study circles and the economic struggle by means of strikes to *political struggle* and *agitation*.

This transition was markedly accelerated when the working class saw in the arena of the struggle elements from other social classes in Russia, marching with firm determination to win political freedom.

II

The working class is not the only class that is groaning under the yoke of the tsarist regime. The heavy fist of the autocracy is also crushing other social classes. Groaning under the yoke are the Russian peasants, wasted from constant starvation, impoverished by the unbearable burden of taxation and thrown to the mercy of the grasping bourgeois traders and the "noble" landlords. Groaning under the yoke are the little people in the towns, the minor employees in government and private offices, the minor officials—in general, that numerous lower class of the urban population whose existence is as insecure as that of the working class, and which has every reason to be discontented with its social conditions. Groaning under the yoke is that section of the petty bourgeoisie and even of the middle bourgeoisie which cannot resign itself to the tsar's knout and lash; this applies especially to the educated section of the bourgeoisie, the so-called representatives of the liberal professions (teachers, physicians, lawyers, university and high-school students). Groaning under the yoke are the oppressed nations and religious communities in Russia, including the Poles, who are being driven from their native land and whose most sacred sentiments are being outraged, and the Finns, whose rights and liberties, granted by history, the autocracy is arrogantly trampling underfoot. Groaning under the yoke are the eternally persecuted and humiliated Jews who lack even the miserably few rights enjoyed by other Russian subjects —the right to live in any part of the country they choose, the right to attend school, the right to be employed in government service, and so forth. Groaning are the Georgians, Armenians, and other nations who are deprived of the right to have their own schools and be employed in government offices, and are compelled to submit to the shameful and oppressive policy of *Russification* so zealously pursued by the autocracy. Groaning are the many millions of Russian non-conformists who wish to believe and worship in accordance with the dictates of their conscience and not with the wishes of the orthodox priests. Groaning are . . . but it is impossible to enumerate all the oppressed, all who are persecuted by the Russian autocracy. They are so numerous that if they were all aware of this, and were aware who their common enemy is, the despotic regime in Russia would not exist another day. Unfortunately, the Russian peasantry is still downtrodden by agelong slavery, poverty and ignorance; it is only just awakening, it does not yet know who its enemy is. The oppressed nations in Russia cannot even dream of liberating themselves by their own efforts so long as they are opposed not only by the Russian government, but even by the Russian people, who have not yet realised that their common enemy is the autocracy. There remain the working class, the little people among the urban population, and the educated section of the bourgeoisie.

But the bourgeoisie of all countries and nations is very skillful in reaping the fruits of another's victory, very skillful in getting others to pull its chestnuts out of the fire. It never wishes to jeopardise its own relatively privileged position in the struggle against the powerful foe, the struggle which, as yet, it is not so easy to win. Although it is discontented, its conditions of life are tolerable and, therefore, it gladly yields to the working class, and to the common people in general, the right to offer their backs to the Cossacks' whips and the soldiers' bullets, to fight at the barricades, and so forth. It "sympathises" with the struggle and at best expresses "indignation" (under its breath) at the cruelty with which the brutal enemy is quelling the popular movement. It is afraid of revolutionary action and resorts to revolutionary measures itself only at the last moment of the struggle, when the enemy's impotence is evident. This is what the experience of history teaches us: only the working class, and the people generally, who in the struggle have nothing to lose but their chains, they, only they, constitute a genuine revolutionary force. And Russia's experience, although still meagre, confirms this ancient truth taught by the history of all revolutionary movements.

Of the representatives of the privileged class only a section of the students have displayed determination to fight to the end for the satisfaction of their demands. But we must not forget that this section, too, of the students consists of sons of these same oppressed citizens, and that, until they have plunged into the sea of life and have occupied a definite social position, the students, being young intellectuals, are more inclined than any other category to strive for ideals which call them to fight for freedom.

Be that as it may, at the present time the students are coming out in the "social" movement almost as leaders, as the vanguard. The discontented sections of different social classes are now rallying around them. At first the students tried to fight with a weapon borrowed from the workers—the strike. But when the government retaliated to their strikes by passing the brutal law ("Provisional Regulations"[4]) under which students who went on strike were drafted into the army, the students had only one weapon left—to demand assistance from the Russian public and to pass from strikes to *street demonstrations*. And that is what the students did. They did not lay down their arms; on the contrary, they fought still more bravely and resolutely. Around them rallied the oppressed citizens, a helping hand was offered them by the working class, and the movement became powerful, a menace to the government. For two years already, the government of Russia has been waging a fierce but fruitless struggle against the rebellious citizens with the aid of its numerous troops, police and gendarmes.

The events of the past few days prove that political demonstrations cannot be defeated. The events in the early days of December in Kharkov, Moscow, Nizhni-Novgorod, Riga and other places show that public discontent is now manifesting itself consciously, and that the discontented public is ready to pass from silent protest to revolutionary action. But the demands of the students for freedom of education, for non-interference in internal university life, are too narrow for :the broad social movement. To unite all the participants in this movement a banner is needed, a banner that will be understood and cherished by all and will combine all demands. *Such a banner is one inscribed: Overthrow the autocracy.* Only on the ruins of the autocracy will it be possible to build a social system that will be based on government by the people and ensure *freedom* of education, *freedom* to strike, *freedom* of speech, *freedom* of religion, *freedom* for nationalities, etc., etc. Only such a system will provide the people with means to protect themselves against all oppressors, against the grasping merchants and capitalists, the clergy and the nobility; only such a system will open a free road to a better future, to the unhindered struggle for the establishment of the socialist system.

The students cannot, of course, wage this stupendous struggle by their own efforts alone; their weak hands cannot hold this heavy banner. To hold this banner stronger hands are needed, and under present conditions this strength lies only in the united forces of the working people. Hence, the working class must take the all-Russian banner out of the weak hands of the students and, inscribing on it the slogan: "Down with the autocracy! Long live a democratic constitution!", lead the Russian people to freedom. We must be grateful to the students for the lesson they have taught us: they showed how enormously important political demonstrations are in the revolutionary struggle.

Street demonstrations are interesting in that they quickly draw large masses of the people into the movement, acquaint them with our demands at once and create extensive favourable soil in which we can boldly sow the seeds of socialist ideas and of political freedom. Street demonstrations give rise to street agitation, to the influence of which the backward and timid section of society cannot help yielding.[5] A man has only to go out into the street during a demonstration to see courageous fighters, to understand what they are fighting for, to hear free voices calling upon everybody to join the struggle, and militant songs denouncing the existing system and exposing our social evils. That is why the government fears street demonstrations more than anything else. That is why it threatens with dire punishment not only the demonstrators, but also the "curious onlookers." In this curiosity of the people lurks the chief danger that threatens the government: the "curious onlooker" of today will be a demonstrator tomorrow and rally new groups of "curious onlookers" around himself. And today there are tens of thousands of such "curious onlookers" in every large town. Russians no longer run into hiding, as they did before, on hearing of disorders taking place somewhere or other ("I'd better get out of the way in case I get into trouble," they used to say); today they flock to the scene of the disorders and evince "curiosity": they are eager to know why these disorders are taking place, why so many people offer their backs to the lash of the Cossacks' whip.

In these circumstances, the "curious onlookers" cease to listen indifferently to the swish of whips and sabres. The "curious onlookers" see that the demonstrators have assembled in the streets to express their wishes and demands, and that the government retaliates by beatings and brutal suppression. The "curious onlookers" no longer run away on hearing the swish of whips; on the contrary, they draw nearer, and the whips can no longer distinguish between the "curious on-

---

5 Under the conditions at present prevailing in Russia illegally printed books and agitation leaflets reach each inhabitant with enormous difficulty. Although the effects of the distribution of such literature are considerable, in most cases it covers only a minority of the population.

lookers" and the "rioters." Now, conforming to "complete democratic equality" the whips play on the backs of all, irrespective of sex, age and even class. Thereby, the whip lash is rendering us a great service, for it is hastening the revolutionisation of the "curious onlookers." It is being transformed from an instrument for taming into an instrument for rousing the people.

Hence, even if street demonstrations do not produce direct results for us, even if the demonstrators are still too weak today to compel the government immediately to yield to the popular demands—the sacrifices we make in street demonstrations today will be compensated a hundredfold. Every militant who falls in the struggle, or is torn out of our ranks, rouses hundreds of new fighters. For the time being we shall be beaten more than once in the street; the government will continue to emerge victorious from street fighting again and again; but these will be Pyrrhic victories. A few more victories like these—and the defeat of absolutism is inevitable. The victories it achieves today are preparing its defeat. And we, firmly convinced that that day will come, that that day is not far distant, risk the lash in order to sow the seeds of political agitation and socialism.

The government is no less convinced than we are that street agitation spells its death warrant, that within another two or three years the spectre of a *people's revolution* will loom before it. The other day the government announced through the mouth of the Governor of Yekaterinoslav Gubernia that it "will not hesitate to resort to extreme measures to crush the slightest attempt at a street demonstration." As you see, this statement smacks of bullets, and perhaps even of shells, but we think that bullets are no less potent than whips as a means of rousing discontent. We do not think that the government will be able even with the aid of such "extreme measures" to restrain political agitation for long and hinder its development. We hope that revolutionary Social-Democracy will succeed in adjusting its agitation to the new conditions which the government will create by resorting to these "extreme measures." In any case, Social-Democracy must watch events vigilantly, it must quickly apply the lessons taught by these events, and skilfully adjust its activities to the changing conditions.

But to be able to do this, Social-Democracy must have a strong and compact organisation, to be precise, a *party organisation*, that is unit-ed not only in name, but also in its fundamental principles and tactical views. Our task is to work to create this strong party that is armed with firm principles and impenetrable secrecy.

The *Social-Democratic Party* must take advantage of the new street movement that has commenced, it *must take the banner of Russian democracy into its own hands and lead it to the victory that all desire!*

Thus, there is opening up before us a period of *primarily political struggle*. Such a struggle is inevitable for us because, under present po-litical conditions, the economic struggle (strikes) cannot produce sub-stantial results. Even in free countries the strike is a two-edged sword: even there, although the workers possess the means of fighting—po-litical freedom, strongly organised labour unions and large funds—strikes often end in the defeat of the workers. In our country, however, where strikes are a crime punishable by arrest and are suppressed by armed force, where all labour unions are prohibited, strikes acquire the significance only of a *protest*. For the purpose of protest, however, demonstrations are far more powerful weapons. In strikes the forces of the workers are dispersed; the workers of only one factory, or of a few factories and, at best, of one trade, take part; the organisation of a general strike is a very difficult matter even in Western Europe, but in our country it is quite impossible. In street demonstrations, however, the workers unite their forces at once.

All this shows what a narrow view is taken by those "Social-Dem-ocrats" who want to confine the labour movement to the economic struggle and industrial organisation, to leave the political struggle to the "intelligentsia," to the students, to society, and assign to the work-ers only the role of an *auxiliary* force. History teaches that under such circumstances the workers will merely pull the chestnuts out of the fire for the bourgeoisie. The bourgeoisie, as a rule, gladly utilise the muscular arms of the workers in the struggle against autocratic gov-ernment, and when victory has been achieved they reap its fruits and leave the workers empty-handed; If this happens in our country, the workers will gain nothing from this struggle. As regards the students and other dissidents among the public—they, after all, also belong to the bourgeoisie. It will be sufficient to give them a harmless, "plucked constitution" that grants the people only the most insignificant rights, for all these dissidents to sing a different song: they will begin to extol the "new" regime. The bourgeoisie live in constant dread of the "red spectre" of communism, and in all revolutions they try to put a stop to things when they are only just beginning. After receiving a tiny concession in their favour they, terrified by the workers, stretch out a hand of conciliation to the government and shamelessly betray the cause of freedom.[6]

The working class alone is a reliable bulwark of genuine democracy. It alone finds it impossible to compromise with the autocracy for the sake of a concession, and it will not allow itself to be lulled by sweet songs sung to the accompaniment of the constitutional lute.

Hence the question as to whether the working class will succeed in taking the lead in the general democratic movement, or whether it will drag at the tail of the movement in the capacity of an auxiliary force of the "intelligentsia," i.e., the bourgeoisie, is an extremely important one for the cause of democracy in Russia. In the former case, the overthrow of the autocracy will result in a broad *democratic constitution*, which will grant equal rights to the workers, to the downtrodden peasantry and to the capitalists. In the latter case, we shall have that "plucked constitution," which will be able, no less than absolutism, to trample upon the demands of the workers and will grant the *people* the mere shadow of freedom.

But in order to be able to play this leading role, the working class must organise in an *independent political party*. If it does that, no betrayal or treachery on the part of its temporary ally—"society"—will have any terrors for it in the struggle against absolutism. The moment this "society" betrays the cause of democracy, the working class itself will lead that cause forward by its own efforts—the independent political party will give it the necessary strength to do so.

Brdzola (The Struggle), No. 2-3, November-December 1901
Unsigned; Translated from the Georgian

---

6 Here, of course, we do not mean that section of the intelligentsia which is already renouncing its class and is fighting in the ranks of the Social-Democrats. But such intellectuals are only exceptions, they are "white ravens."

THE SOCIAL-DEMOCRATIC VIEW ON THE NATIONAL QUESTION

I

Everything changes ... Social life changes, and with it the "national question" changes, too. At different periods different classes enter the arena, and each class has its own view of the "national question." Consequently, in different periods the "national question" *serves different interests* and assumes different shades, according to *which* class raises it, and *when*.

For instance, we had the so-called "*national question*" *of the nobility*, when—after the "annexation of Georgia to Russia"—the Georgian nobility, realising how disadvantageous it was for them to lose the old privileges and power they had enjoyed under the Georgian kings, and regarding the status of "mere subjects" as being derogatory to their dignity wanted the "*liberation of Georgia.*" *Their aim was to place the Georgian kings and the Georgian nobility at the head of "Georgia," and thus place the destiny of the Georgian people in their hands! That was feudal-monarchist "nationalism."* This "movement" left no visible trace in the life of the Georgians; not a single fact sheds glory on it, if we leave out of account isolated conspiracies hatched by Georgian nobles against the Russian rulers in the Caucasus. A slight touch from the events of social life to this already feeble "movement" was enough to cause it to collapse to its foundations. Indeed, the development of commodity production, the abolition of serfdom, the establishment of the Nobles' Bank, the intensification of class antagonisms in town and country, the growth of the poor peasants' movement, etc.—all this dealt a mortal blow to the Georgian nobility and, with it, to "*feudal-monarchist nationalism.*" The Georgian nobility split into two groups. One renounced all "nationalism" and stretched forth its hand to the Russian autocracy with the object of obtaining soft jobs, cheap credit and agricultural implements, the government's protection against the rural "rebels," etc. The other, the weaker section of the Georgian nobility; struck up a friendship with the Georgian bishops and archimandrites, and thus found under the protecting wing of clericalism a sanctuary for the "nationalism" which is being hounded by realities. This group is working zealously to restore ruined Georgian churches (that is the main item in its "programme"!)—"the monuments of departed glory"—and is reverently waiting for a miracle that will enable it to achieve its *feudal-monarchist* "aspirations."

Thus, in the last moments of its existence, feudal-monarchist nationalism has assumed a clerical form.

Meanwhile, our contemporary social life has brought the *national question of the bourgeoisie* to the fore. When the young Georgian bourgeoisie realised how difficult it was to contend with the free competition of "foreign" capitalists, it began, through the mouths of the Georgian National-Democrats, to prattle about an *independent Georgia*. The Georgian bourgeoisie wanted to fence off the Georgian market with a tariff wall, to drive the "foreign" bourgeoisie from this market by force, artificially raise prices, and by means of "patriotic" tricks of this sort to achieve success in the money-making arena.

This was, and is, the aim of the nationalism of the Georgian bourgeoisie. Needless to say, to achieve this aim, strength was required— but only the proletariat possessed this strength. Only the proletariat could infuse life into the emasculated "patriotism" of the bourgeoisie. It was necessary to win over the proletariat—and so the "National-Democrats" appeared on the scene. They spent a great deal of ammunition in the endeavour to refute scientific socialism, decried the Social-Democrats and advised the Georgian proletarians to desert them, lauded the Georgian proletariat and urged it to strengthen in one way or another the Georgian bourgeoisie "in the interests of the workers themselves." They pleaded incessantly with the Georgian proletarians: Don't ruin "Georgia" (or the Georgian bourgeoisie?), forget "internal differences," make friends with the Georgian bourgeoisie, etc. But all in vain! The honeyed words of the bourgeois publicists failed to lull the Georgian proletariat! The merciless attacks of the

Georgian Marxists and, particularly, the powerful class actions which welded Russian, Armenian, Georgian and other proletarians into a single socialist force, dealt our *bourgeois nationalists* a crushing blow and drove them from the battle-field.

Since our fugitive patriots were unable to assimilate socialist views, they were obliged, "in order to rehabilitate their tarnished names," "at least to change their colour," at least to deck themselves in socialist garb. And indeed, an illegal . . . bourgeois-nationalist—"socialist," if you please—organ suddenly appeared on the scene, Sakartvelo![1] That was how they wanted to seduce the Georgian workers! But it was too late! The Georgian workers had learned to distinguish between black and white, they easily guessed that the bourgeois nationalists had "changed only the colour" but not the substance of their views, that *Sakartvelo was socialist only in name.* They realised this and made a laughing-stock of these "saviours" of Georgia! The hopes of the Don Quixotes of *Sakartvelo* were dashed to the ground!

On the other hand, our economic development is gradually building a bridge between the advanced circles of the Georgian bourgeoisie and "Russia"; it is connecting these circles with "Russia" both economically and politically, thereby cutting the ground from under the feet of already tottering bourgeois nationalism. This is another blow to bourgeois nationalism!

A new class has entered the arena—the *proletariat*—and, with it, a new "national question," has arisen—*"the national question" of the proletariat.* And the "national question" raised by the proletariat differs from the "national question" of the nobility and of the bourgeoisie to the same degree that the proletariat differs from the nobility and the bourgeoisie.

Let us now discuss this "nationalism."

---

1 **Original editor:** *Shkartvelo* (Georgia)—a newspaper published by a group of Georgian nationalists abroad which became the core of the bourgeois-nationalist party of the Social-Federalists. The newspaper was published in Paris in the Georgian and French languages, and ran from 1903 to 1905.

The party of the Georgian Federalists (formed in Geneva in April 1904) consisted of the Sakartvelo group, as well as of Anarchists, Socialist-Revolutionaries and National-Democrats. The principal demand of the Federalists was national autonomy for Georgia within the Russian landlord-bourgeois. state. During the period of reaction they became avowed enemies of the revolution.

What is the Social-Democratic view of the "national question"?

The proletariat of all Russia began to talk about the struggle long ago. As we know, the goal of every struggle is victory. But if the proletariat is to achieve victory, *all* the workers, *irrespective of nationality*, must be united. Clearly, the demolition of national barriers and close unity between the Russian, Georgian, Armenian, Polish, Jewish and other proletarians is a necessary condition for the victory of the proletariat of all Russia.

That is in the interests of the proletariat of all Russia.

But the Russian autocracy, the bitterest enemy of the proletariat of all Russia, is constantly counteracting the efforts to unite the proletarians. It brutally persecutes the national cultures, the languages, customs and institutions of the "alien" nationalities in Russia. It deprives them of their essential civil rights, oppresses them in every way, hypocritically sows distrust and hostility among them and incites them to bloody collisions. This shows that its sole object is to sow discord among the nations that inhabit Russia, to intensify national strife among them, to reinforce national barriers in order more successfully to disunite the proletarians, more successfully to split the entire proletariat of Russia into small national groups and in this way bury the class consciousness of the workers, their class unity.

That is in the interests of Russian reaction; such is the policy of the Russian autocracy.

Obviously, sooner or later, the interests of the proletariat of all Russia inevitably had to come into collision with the tsarist autocracy's reactionary policy. That is what actually happened and what brought up the "national question" in the Social-Democratic movement.

How are the national barriers that have been raised between the nations to be demolished? How is national isolation to be eliminated in order to draw the proletarians of all Russia closer together and to unite them more closely?

That is the substance of the "national question" in the Social-Democratic movement.

Divide up into separate national parties and establish a "loose federation" of these parties—answer the *Federalist* Social-Democrats.

That is just what the Armenian Social-Democratic Labour Organisation[2] is talking about all the time.

As you see, we are advised not to unite into one all-Russian party with a single directing centre, but to divide up into several parties with several directing centres—all in order to strengthen class unity! We want to *draw together* the proletarians of the different nations. What should we do? Divide the proletarians from one another and you will achieve your aim! answer the Federalist Social-Democrats. We want to unite the proletarians in one party. What should we do? Split up the proletarians of all Russia into separate parties and you will achieve your aim! answer the Federalist Social-Democrats. We want to demolish national barriers. What measures shall we take? Reinforce the national barriers with organisational barriers and you will achieve your aim! they reply. And all this advice is offered to us, the proletarians of all Russia, who are fighting under the same political conditions, and against a common enemy! In short, we are told: Act so as to please your enemies and bury your common goal with your own hands!

But let us agree with the Federalist Social-Democrats for a moment, let us follow them and see where they will lead us! It has been said: "Pursue the liar to the threshold of the lie."

Let us assume that we have taken the advice of our Federalists and have formed separate national parties. What would be the results?

This is not difficult to see. Hitherto, while we were *Centralists*, we concentrated our attention mainly on the *common* conditions of the proletarians, on the *unity* of their interests, and spoke of their "national distinctions" only in so far as these did not contradict their *common* interests; hitherto, our major question was: in what way do the proletarians of the different nationalities of Russia resemble each oth-

---

2 **Original editor**: The Armenian Social-Democratic Labour Organisation was formed by Armenian National-Federalist elements soon after the Second Congress of the Russian Social-Democratic Labour Party. V. I. Lenin noted the close connection between this organisation and the Bund. In a letter to the members of the Central Committee of the Party dated September 7 (New Style), 1905, he wrote: "*This is a creature of the Bund*, nothing more, invented especially for the purpose of fostering Caucasian Bundism. . . . The Caucasian comrades are all opposed to this gang of pen-pushing disruptors" (see Lenin, *Works*, 4th Russ. ed., Vol. 34, p. 290).

er, what have they in common?—for our object was to build a single centralised party of the workers of the whole of Russia on the basis of these common interests. Now that "we" have become Federalists, our attention is engaged by a different major question, namely: in what way do the proletarians of the different nationalities of Russia differ from one another, what are the distinctions between them?—for our object is to build separate national parties on the basis of "national distinctions." Thus, "national distinctions," which are of minor importance for the Centralist, become, for the Federalist, the foundation of national parties.

If we follow this path further we shall, sooner or later, be obliged to conclude that the "national" and, perhaps, some other "distinctions" of, say, the Armenian proletarians are the same as those of the Armenian bourgeoisie; that the Armenian proletarian and the Armenian bourgeois have the same customs and character; that they constitute one people, one indivisible "nation."[3] From this it is not a far

3 The Armenian Social-Democratic Labour Organisation has just taken this laudable step. In its "Manifesto" it emphatically declares that "the proletariat (Armenian) cannot be separated from society (Armenian): the united (Armenian) proletariat must be the most intelligent and the strongest organ of the Armenian people"; that "the Armenian proletariat, united in a socialist party, must strive to mould Armenian social opinion, that the Armenian proletariat will be a true son of its tribe," etc. (see Clause 3 of the "Manifesto" of the Armenian Social-Democratic Labour Organisation).

In the first place, it is difficult to see why "the Armenian proletariat cannot be separated from Armenian society," when actually this "separation" is taking place at every step. Did not the united Armenian proletariat "separate" from Armenian society when, in 1900 (in Tiflis), it declared war against the Armenian bourgeoisie and bourgeois-minded Armenians?! What is the Armenian Social-Democratic Labour Organisation itself, if not a class organisation of Armenian proletarians who have "separated" from the other classes in Armenian society? Or, perhaps the Armenian Social-Democratic Labour Organisation is an organisation that represents all classes!? And can the militant Armenian proletariat confine itself to "moulding Armenian social opinion"? Is it not its duty to march forward, to declare war upon this "social opinion," which is bourgeois through and through, and to infuse a revolutionary spirit into it? The facts say that it is its duty to do so. That being the case, it is self-evident that the "Manifesto" should have drawn its readers' attention not to "moulding social opinion," but to the struggle against it, to the necessity of revolutionising it—that would have been a more correct description of the duties of the "socialist proletariat." And, lastly, can the Armenian proletariat be "a true son of its tribe," if one section of this tribe—the Armenian bourgeoisie—sucks its blood like a vampire, and another section—the Armenian clergy—in addition to sucking the blood of the workers, is systematically engaged in corrupting their minds? All these questions are plain and inevitable, if we look at things from the standpoint of the class struggle. But the authors of the "Manifesto" fail to see these questions, because they look at things from the Federalist-nationalistic standpoint they have borrowed from the Bund (the Jewish Workers' Union).* In general, it seems as though the authors of the "Manifesto" have set out to ape the Bund in all things. In their "Manifesto" they also introduced Clause 2 of the resolution of the Fifth Congress of the Bund:

cry to "common ground for joint action," on which the bourgeois and the proletarian must stand and join hands as members of the same "nation." The hypocritical policy of the autocratic tsar may appear as "additional" proof in support of such friendship, whereas talk about class antagonisms may appear as "misplaced doctrinairism." And then somebody's poetic fingers will "more boldly" touch the narrow-national strings that still exist in the hearts of the proletarians of the different nationalities in Russia and make them sound in the proper key. Credit (confidence) will be granted to chauvinistic humbug, friends will be taken for enemies, enemies for friends—confusion will ensue, and the class consciousness of the proletariat of all Russia will wane.

Thus, thanks to the Federalists, instead of *breaking down the national barriers* we shall *reinforce* them with organisational barriers; instead of *stimulating* the class consciousness of the proletariat we shall *stultify*

"The Bund's Position in the Party." They describe the Armenian Social-Democratic Labour Organisation as the sole champion of the interests of the Armenian proletariat (see Clause 3 of the above-mentioned "Manifesto"). The authors of the "Manifesto" have forgotten that for several years now the Caucasian Committees of our Party** have been regarded as the representatives of the Armenian (and other) proletarians in the Caucasus, that they are developing class consciousness in them by means of oral and printed propaganda and agitation in the Armenian language, and are guiding them in their struggle, etc., whereas the Armenian Social-Democratic Labour Organisation came into being only the other day. They have forgotten all this and, no doubt, will forget many other things for the sake of faithfully copying the Bund's organisational and political views.

* **Original editors**: *The Bund*—the General Jewish Workers' Union of Lithuania, Poland and Russia, a Jewish petty-bourgeois opportunist organisation, was formed in October 1897 at a congress in Vilno. It carried on its activities chiefly among the Jewish artisans. It joined the Russian Social-Democratic Labour Party at the latter's First Congress in 1898, "as an autonomous organisation independent only in matters specifically concerning the Jewish proletariat." The Bund was a centre of nationalism and separatism in the Russian working-class movement. Its bourgeois-nationalist stand was sharply criticised by Lenin's *Iskra*. The Caucasian *Iskra*-ists whole-heartedly supported V. I. Lenin in his struggle against the Bund.

** **Original editors**: This refers to the Party Committees which at the First Congress of the Social-Democratic Labour Organisations in the Caucasus held in Tiflis in March 1903 united to form the Caucasian Union of the Russian Social-Democratic Labour Party. Represented at the congress were the organisations of Tiflis, Baku, Batum, Kutais, Guria, and other districts. The congress approved the political line pursued by Lenin's *Iskra*, adopted the programme drafted by *Iskra* and *Zarya* for guidance, and drew up and endorsed the Rules for the Union. The First Congress of the Caucasian Union laid the foundation for the international structure of the Social-Democratic Organisations in the Caucasus. The congress set up a directing Party body known as the Caucasian Union Committee of the R.S.D.L.P. to which J. V. Stalin was elected in his absence, as at that time he was confined in the Batum prison. After his flight from exile and return to Tiflis in the beginning of 1904, J. V. Stalin became the head of the Caucasian Union Committee of the R.S.D.L.P.

it and subject it to a dangerous strain. And the autocratic tsar "will rejoice in his heart," for he would never have obtained such unpaid assistants as we would be for him.

Is that, then, what we have been striving for?

And, lastly, at a time when we need a single, flexible, centralised party, whose Central Committee should be able to rouse the workers of the whole of Russia at a moment's notice and lead them in a decisive onslaught upon the autocracy and the bourgeoisie, we are offered a monstrous "federal league" broken up into separate parties! Instead of a sharp weapon, they hand us a rusty one and assure us: With this you will more speedily wipe out your mortal enemies!

That is where the Federalist Social-Democrats are leading us!

But since our aim is not to "reinforce national barriers," but to break them down; since we need not a rusty, but a sharp weapon to uproot existing injustice; since we want to give the enemy cause not for rejoicing but for lamentation, and want to make him bite the dust, it is obviously our duty to turn our backs on the Federalists and find a better means of solving the "national question."

II

So far we have discussed the way the "national question" should not be solved. Let us now discuss the way this question should be solved, i.e., the way it has been solved by the Social-Democratic Labour Party.[4]

To begin with, we must bear in mind that the Social-Democratic Party which functions in Russia called itself *Rossiiskaya* (and not *Russkaya*).[5] Obviously, by this it wanted to convey to us that it will gather under its banner not only Russian proletarians, but the proletarians of *all the nationalities* in Russia, and, consequently, that it will do everything

---

4 It will not be amiss to point out that the following is a comment on the clauses of our Party programme which deal with the national question.

5 The adjective *Rossiiskaya* was applied to the whole land of Russia with all its different nationalities. *Russkaya* applies more specifically to the Russian people. In English both are rendered by the word Russian.—Tr.

to break down the *national barriers* that have been raised to separate them.

Further, our Party has dispelled the fog which enveloped the "national question" and which lent it an air of mystery; it has divided this question into its separate elements, has lent each element the character of a class demand, and has expounded them in its programme in the form of separate clauses. Thereby it has clearly shown us that, *taken by themselves*, the so-called "national interests" and "national demands" are of no particular value; that these "interests," and "demands" deserve our attention only in so far as they stimulate, or can stimulate, the proletariat's class consciousness, its class development.

The Russian Social-Democratic Labour Party has thereby clearly mapped the path it has chosen and the position it has taken in solving the "national question."

What are the elements of the "national question"?

What do Messieurs the Federalist Social-Democrats demand?

1) *"Civil equality for the nationalities in Russia?"*

You are disturbed by the civil inequality that prevails in Russia? You want to restore to the nationalities in Russia the civil rights taken away by the government and therefore you demand civil equality for these nationalities? But are we opposed to *this* demand. We are perfectly aware of the great importance of civil rights for the proletarians. Civil rights are a weapon in the struggle; to take away civil rights means taking away a weapon; and who does not know that unarmed proletarians cannot fight well? It is necessary for the proletariat of all Russia, however, that the proletarians of all the nationalities inhabiting Russia should fight well; for, the better these proletarians fight, the greater will be their class consciousness, and the greater their class consciousness, the closer will be, the class unity of the proletariat of all Russia. Yes, we know all this, and that is why we are fighting, and will go on fighting with, all our might, for the civil equality of the nationalities in Russia! Read Clause 7 of our Party programme, where the Party speaks of "complete equality of rights for all citizens, irrespective of sex, religion, race or *nationality*," and you will see that the Russian Social-Democratic Labour Party sets out to achieve these demands.

What else do the Federalist Social-Democrats demand?

2) "Freedom of language for the nationalities in Russia?"

You are disturbed by the fact that the proletarians of the "alien" nationalities in Russia are practically forbidden to receive education in their own languages, or to speak their own languages in public, state and other institutions? Yes, it is something to be disturbed about! Language is an instrument of development and struggle. Different nations have different languages. The interests of the proletariat of all Russia demand that the proletarians of the different nationalities inhabiting Russia shall have full right to use *the language* in which it is easiest for them to receive education, in which they can best oppose their enemies at meetings or in public, state and other institutions. *That* language is the *native language*. They ask: Can we keep silent when the proletarians of the "alien" nationalities are deprived of their native language? Well, and what does our Party programme say to the proletariat of all Russia on this point? Read Clause 8 of our Party programme, in which our Party demands "the right of the population to receive education in their native languages, this right to be ensured by the establishment of schools for this purpose at the expense of the state and of local government bodies; the right of every citizen to speak at meetings in his native language; the introduction of the native language on a par with the official state language in all local public and state institutions"— read all this, and you will see that the Russian Social-Democratic Labour Party sets out to achieve this demand as well.

What else do the Federalist Social-Democrats demand?

3) "Self-government for the nationalities in Russia?"

By that you want to say that the same laws cannot be applied in the same way in the various localities of the Russian state which differ from one another in specific conditions of life and composition of the population? You want these localities to have the right to adapt the *general* laws of the state to their own specific conditions? If that is the case, if that is what you mean by your demand, you should formulate it properly; you should dispel the nationalistic fog and confusion and call a spade a spade. And if you follow this advice you will see for yourselves that we have no objection to such a demand. We have no doubt at all that the various localities of the Russian state which differ from one another in specific conditions of life and composition of the population, cannot all apply the state constitution in the same way, that such localities must be granted the right to put into effect the general state constitution in such a way as will benefit them most and contribute to the fuller development of the political forces of the people. This is in the class interests of the proletariat of all Russia. And if you re-read Clause 3 of our Party programme, in which our Party demands "wide local self-government; regional self-government for those localities which are differentiated by their special conditions of life and the composition of their population," you will see that the Russian Social-Democratic Labour Party first dispelled the nationalistic fog which enveloped this demand and then set out to achieve it.

4) You point to the tsarist autocracy, which is brutally persecuting the "national culture" of the "alien" nationalities in Russia, which is violently interfering in their internal life and oppressing them in every way, which has barbarously destroyed (and goes on destroying) the cultural institutions of the Finns, has robbed Armenia of her national property, etc.? You demand guarantees against the robber violence of the autocracy? But are we blind to the violence which the tsarist autocracy is perpetrating? And have we not always fought against this violence?! Everyone today clearly sees how the present Russian government oppresses and strangles the "alien" nationalities which inhabit Russia. It is also beyond all doubt that this policy of the government is day after day corrupting the class consciousness of the all-Russian proletariat and exposing it to a dangerous strain. Consequently, we shall always and everywhere fight the tsarist government's corrupting policy. Consequently, we shall always and everywhere defend against the autocracy's police violence not only the useful, but even the useless institutions of these nationalities; for the interests of the proletariat of all Russia suggest to us that only the nationalities themselves have the right to abolish or develop this or that aspect of their national culture. But read Clause 9 of our programme. Is not this the purport of Clause 9 of our Party programme, which, incidentally, has caused much argument among both our enemies and our friends?

But here we are interrupted with the advice to stop talking about

Clause 9. But why? we ask. "Because," we are told, this clause of our programme "fundamentally contradicts" Clauses 3, 7 and 8 of the same programme; because, if the nationalities are granted the right to arrange all their national affairs according to their own will (see Clause 9), there should be no room in thisprogramme for Clauses 3, 7 and 8; and, vice versa, if these clauses are left in the programme, Clause 9 must certainly be deleted from the programme. Undoubtedly, *Sakartvelo*[6] means something of the same sort when it asks with its characteristic levity: "Where is the logic in saying to a nation, 'I grant you regional self-government,' and reminding it at the same time that it has the right to arrange all its national affairs as it sees fit?" (see *Sakartvelo*, No. 9). "Obviously," a logical contradiction has crept into the programme; "obviously," one or several clauses must be deleted from the programme if this contradiction is to be eliminated! Yes, this must "certainly" be done, for, as you see, logic itself is protesting through the medium of the illogical *Sakartvelo*.

This calls to mind an ancient parable. Once upon a time there lived a "learned anatomist." He possessed "everything" a "real" anatomist requires: a degree, an operating room, instruments and inordinate pretensions. He lacked only one minor detail—knowledge of anatomy. One day he was asked to explain the connection between the various parts of a skeleton that were lying scattered on his anatomical table. This gave our "celebrated savant" an opportunity to show off his skill. With great pomp and solemnity he set to "work." Alas and alack, the "savant" did not know even the ABC of anatomy and was entirely at a loss as to how the parts should be put together so as to produce a complete skeleton!

The poor fellow busied himself for a long time, perspired copiously, but all in vain! Finally, when nothing had come of all his efforts and he had got everything mixed up, he seized several parts of the skeleton, flung them into a far corner of the room and vented his philosophic ire on certain "evil-minded" persons, who, he alleged, had placed spurious parts of a skeleton on his table. Naturally, the specta-

---

6 We are referring here to *Sakartvelo* for the sole purpose of better explaining the contents of Clause 9. The object of the present article is to criticise the Federalist Social-Democrats, and not the *Sakartvelo*-ists, who differ radically from the former (see Chapter I.)

tors made fun of this "learned anatomist."

A similar "misadventure" has befallen *Sakartvelo*. It took it into its head to analyse our Party programme; but it turns out that *Sakartvelo* has no idea of what our programme is, nor of how it ought to be analysed; it has not grasped the connection that exists between the various clauses of this programme or the significance of each clause. So it "philosophically" gives us the following advice: I cannot understand such and such clauses of your programme, therefore (?!) they must be deleted.

But I do not want to make fun of *Sakartvelo*, which is a laughing-stock already; as the saying goes: don't hit a man when he is down! On the contrary, I am even prepared to help it and explain our programme to it, but on condition that 1) it confesses its ignorance, 2) listens to me with attention, and 3) keeps on good terms with logic.[7]

The point is as follows. Clauses 3, 7 and 8 of our programme arose out of the idea of *political centralism*.

When inserting these clauses in its programme the Russian Social-Democratic Labour Party was guided by the consideration that what is called the "final" solution of the "national question," i.e., the "emancipation" of the "alien" nationalities in Russia, is, speaking generally, impossible so long as the bourgeoisie retains political power. There are two reasons for this: first, present-day economic development is gradually building a bridge between the "alien nationalities" and "Russia," it is creating increasing intercourse between them, and thereby engendering friendly feeling among the leading circles of the bourgeoisie of these nationalities, thus removing the ground for their "national-emancipation" aspirations; second, *speaking generally*, the proletariat will not support the so-called "national-emancipation" movement, for up till now, every *such* movement has been conducted in the interests of the bourgeoisie, and has corrupted and crippled the class consciousness of the proletariat. These considerations gave rise to the idea of *political centralism*, on which Clauses 3, 7 and 8 of our Party

---

7 I deem it necessary to inform the readers that from its very first issues *Sakartvelo* declared war upon logic as fetters which must be combated. No attention need be paid to the fact that *Sakartvelo* often speaks in the name of logic; it does so only because of its characteristic levity and forgetfulness.

programme are based.

But this, as has been said above, is the *general* view.

It does not, however, preclude the possibility that economic and political conditions may arise under which the advanced bourgeois circles among the "alien" nationalities will want "national emancipation."

It may also happen that such a movement will prove to be favourable for the development of the class consciousness of the proletariat.

How should our Party act in such cases?

It is precisely with such possible cases in view that Clause 9 was included in our programme; it is precisely in anticipation of such possible circumstances that the nationalities are accorded a right which will prompt them to strive to arrange their national affairs in accordance with their own wishes (for instance, to "emancipate themselves" completely, to secede).

Our Party, the party whose aim is to lead the militant proletariat of the whole of Russia, must be prepared for such contingencies in the life of the proletariat and, accordingly, had to insert such a clause in its programme.

That is how every prudent, far-sighted party ought to act.

It seems, however, that this interpretation of Clause 9 fails to satisfy the "savants" of *Sakartvelo*, and also some of the Federalist Social-Democrats. They demand a "precise" and "straightforward" answer to the question: is "national independence" advantageous or disadvantageous to the proletariat?[8]

This reminds me of the Russian metaphysicians of the fifties of the last century who pestered the dialecticians of those days with the question: is rain good or bad for the crops? and demanded a "precise" answer. It was not difficult for the dialecticians to prove that this way of presenting the question was totally unscientific; that such questions must be answered differently at different times; that during a drought rain is beneficial, whereas in a rainy season more rain is useless and even harmful; and that, consequently, to demand a "precise" answer to

---

8 See the article by "Old (i.e., old-fashioned!) Revolutionary" in *Sakartvelo*, No. 9.

such a question is obviously stupid.

But *Sakartvelo* has learned nothing from such examples.

Bernstein's followers demanded of the Marxists an equally "precise" answer to the question: are co-operatives (i.e., consumers' and producers' co-operative societies) useful or harmful to the proletariat? It was not difficult for the Marxists to prove that this way of presenting the question was pointless; they explained very simply that everything depends on time and place; that where the class consciousness of the proletariat has reached the proper level of development and the proletarians are united in a single, strong political party, cooperatives may be of great benefit to the proletariat, if the party itself undertakes to organise and direct them. On the other hand, where these conditions are lacking, the co-operatives are harmful to the proletariat, for they breed small-shopkeeper tendencies and craft insularity among the workers, and thereby corrupt their class consciousness.

But the *Sakartvelo*-ists have learned nothing even from this example. They demand more insistently than ever: is national independence useful or harmful to the proletariat? Give us a precise answer!

But we see that the circumstances which may give rise to and develop a "national-emancipation" movement among the bourgeoisie of the "alien" nationalities do not yet exist, nor, for that matter, are they really inevitable in the future—we have only assumed them as a possibility. Furthermore, it is impossible to tell at present what the level of the class consciousness of the proletariat will be at that particular moment, and to what extent this movement will then be useful or harmful to the proletariat! Hence, we may ask, on what basis can one build[9] a "precise" answer to this question? From what premises can it be deduced? And is it not stupid to demand a "precise" answer under such circumstances?

Obviously, we must leave it to the "alien" nationalities to decide that question themselves; our task is to win for them the right to do so. Let the nationalities themselves decide, when this question faces them, whether "national independence" is useful or harmful to them,

---

9 Messrs. the *Sakartvelo*-ists always build their demands on sand and cannot conceive of people who are capable of finding firmer ground for their demands!

and, if useful—in what form to exercise it. They alone can decide this question!

Thus, Clause 9 grants the "alien" nationalities the right to arrange their national affairs in accordance with their own wishes. And that same clause imposes on us the duty to see to it that the wishes of these nationalities are really Social-Democratic, that these wishes spring from the class interests of the proletariat; and for this we must educate the proletarians of these nationalities in the Social-Democratic spirit, subject some of their reactionary "national" habits, customs and institutions to stern Social-Democratic criticism—which, however, will not prevent us from defending these habits, customs and institutions against police violence.

Such is the underlying idea of Clause 9.

It is easy to see what a profound logical connection there is between this clause of our programme and the principles of the proletarian class struggle. And since ourentire programme is built on these principles, the logical connection between Clause 9 and all the other clauses of our Party programme is self-evident.

It is precisely because dull-witted *Sakartvelo* cannot assimilate such simple ideas that it is styled a "wise" organ of the press.

What else remains of the "national question"?

5) *"Defence of the national spirit and its attributes?"*

But what is this "national spirit and its attributes"? Science, through the medium of dialectical materialism, proved long ago that there is no such thing as a "national spirit" and that there cannot be. Has anyone refuted this view of dialectical materialism? History tells us that no one has refuted it. Hence, we must agree with this view of science, and, together with science, reiterate that there is no such thing as a "national spirit," nor can there be. And since this is the case, since there is no such thing as a "national spirit," it is self-evident that defence of what does not exist is a logical absurdity, which must inevitably lead to corresponding historical (undesirable) consequences. It is becoming only for *Sakartvelo*—"organ of the revolutionary party of Georgian Social-Federalists" (see *Sakartvelo*, No. 9)[10] to utter such "philosophical" absurdities.

*   *   *

That is how matters stand with the national question.

As is evident, our Party divided this question into several parts, distilled its vital juices from it, injected them into the veins of its programme, and thereby showed how the "national question" should be solved in the Social-Democratic movement in such a way as to destroy national barriers to their foundations, while not departing from our principles for a moment.

The question is: Where is the need for separate national parties? Or, where is the Social-Democratic "basis," on which the organisational and political views of the Federalist Social-Democrats are supposed to be built? No such "basis" is to be seen—it does not exist. The Federalist Social-Democrats are floating in mid-air.

---

10 What is this "party," which bears such a strange name? *Sakartvelo* informs us (see Supplement No. 1 to *Sakartvelo*, No. 10) that "in the spring of this year Georgian revolutionaries: Georgian Anarchists, supporters of *Sakartvelo*, Georgian Social-Revolutionaries, gathered abroad and . . . united . . . in a 'party' of Georgian Social-Federalists.". . . Yes, Anarchists, who despise all politics heart and soul, Social-Revolutionaries who worship politics, and the *Sakartvelo*-ists, who repudiate all terrorist and anarchist measures—and it turns out that this motley and mutually-negating crowd united to form . . . a "party"! As ideal a patchwork as anyone could ever imagine! Here's a place where one won't find it dull! Those organisers who assert that people must have common principles in order to unite in a party are mistaken! Not common principles, but absence of principles is the basis on which a "party" must be built, says this motley crowd. Down with "theory" and principles—they are only slaves' fetters! The sooner we free ourselves of them the better—philosophises this motley crowd. And, indeed, the moment these people freed themselves of principles they forthwith, at one stroke, built . . . a house of cards—I beg your pardon—the "party of Georgian Social-Federalists." So it turns out that "seven men and a boy" can form a "party" at any time, whenever they get together. Can one refrain from laughing when these ignoramuses, these "officers" without an army, philosophise like this: the Russian Social-Democratic Labour Party "is anti-socialist, reactionary," etc.; the Russian Social-Democrats are "chauvinists"; the Caucasian Union of our party "slavishly" submits to the Central Committee of the Party,* etc. (see the resolutions of the First Conference of the Georgian Revolutionaries). Nothing better could be expected of the archeological fossils of the Bakunin era: the fruit is typical of the tree that bore it, goods are typical of the factory that produced them.

* I must observe that some abnormal "individuals" regard the co-ordinated action of the various sections of our Party as "slavish submission." It is all due to weak nerves, the physicians say.

They have two ways of getting out of this uncomfortable position. Either they must entirely abandon the standpoint of the revolutionary proletariat and accept the principle of reinforcing the national barriers (opportunism in the shape of federalism); or they must renounce all federalism in party organisation, boldly raise the banner of demolition of national barriers, and rally to the united camp of the Russian Social-Democratic Labour Party.

Proletariatis Brdzola
(The Proletarian Struggle), No. 7
September 1, 1904
Unsigned
Translated from the Georgian

A LETTER FROM KUTAIS[1]

What we need here now is *Iskra*[2] (although it has no sparks, we need it: at all events it contains news, the devil take it, and we must thoroughly know the enemy), beginning with No. 63. We very much need Bonch-Bruyevich's[3] publications: *The Fight for the Congress, To the Party* (isn't this the Declaration of the 22?[4]), *Our Misunderstand-*

---

1 **Original editor**: J. V. Stalin's two letters from Kutais were found among the correspondence of V. I. Lenin and N. K. Krupskaya with the Bolshevik organisations in Russia. He wrote these letters while he was in Kutais in September-October 1904, and they were addressed to his comrade in revolutionary activity in Transcaucasia, M. Davitashvili, who at that time lived in Leipzig, Germany, and was a member of the Leipzig group of Bolsheviks. In his reminiscences, D. Suliashvili, another member of the Leipzig group of Bolsheviks, wrote the following about one of these letters: "Soon after, Mikhail Davitashvili received a letter from Joseph Stalin who was in Siberia. In the letter he spoke enthusiastically and admiringly of Lenin and the revolutionary Bolshevik theses Lenin advanced; he wished Lenin success and good health and called him a 'mountain eagle.' We forwarded the letter to Lenin. Soon we received an answer from him to be forwarded to Stalin. In his letter he called Stalin a 'fiery Colchian'" (see D. Suliashvili, *Reminiscences About Stalin*. Magazine Mnatobi, No. 9, 1935, p. 163, in Georgian). The Georgian originals of J. V. Stalin's letters have not been found.

2 **Original editor**: This refers to the new, Menshevik *Iskra* (*The Spark*). After the Second Congress of the R.S.D.L.P., the Mensheviks, with the assistance of Plekhanov, seized *Iskra* and utilised it in their struggle against V. I. Lenin and the Bolsheviks. In its columns they began openly to advocate their opportunist views. The Menshevik *Iskra* ceased publication in October 1905.

3 **Original editor**: In the autumn of 1904, after the Mensheviks had seized *Iskra*, V. D. Bonch-Bruyevich, on V. I. Lenin's instructions, organized a publishing house with the object of publishing "Party literature, particularly literature in defence of the principles of the majority at the Second Party Congress." The Party Council and the Central Committee, which at that time were controlled by the Mensheviks, did all in their power to hinder the publication and distribution of Bolshevik literature. In this connection a conference of Caucasian Bolshevik Committees held in November 1904 adopted a resolution "On the Literature of the Majority" which said: "The conference calls upon the Central Committee to supply the Party Committees with the literature issued by the Bonch-Bruyevich and Lenin group together with other Party literature explaining the disagreements in the Party." At the end of December 1904 these publishing activities passed to the newspaper *Vperyod* (*Forward*), organised by V. I. Lenin.

4 **Original editor**: The Declaration of the 22 was the appeal "To the Party," written

ings, on the *quintessence of socialism* and on *strikes* by Ryadovoi (if issued), Lenin's pamphlet against Rosa and Kautsky,[5] Minutes of the Congress of the League,[6] *One Step Forward*[7] (this can be put aside if you can't send it now). We need everything new that's published, from simple declarations to large pamphlets, which in any way deals with the struggle now going on within the Party.

I have read Galyorka's pamphlet *Down With Bonapartism*. It's not bad. It would have been better had he struck harder and deeper with his hammer. His jocular tone and pleas for mercy, rob his blows of strength and weight, and spoil the reader's impression. These defects are all the more glaring for the reason that the author evidently understands our position well, and explains and elaborates certain questions excellently. A man who takes up our position must speak with a firm and determined voice. In this respect Lenin is a real mountain eagle.

I have also read Plekhanov's articles in which he analyses *What Is To Be Done?*[8] This man has either gone quite off his head, or else is moved by hatred and enmity. I think both causes operate. I think that

---

by V. I. Lenin. It was adopted at the conference of Bolsheviks held under Lenin's guidance in Switzerland in August 1904. The pamphlet *To the Party* which is mentioned in J. V. Stalin's letter contained, in addition to the appeal "To the Party," the resolutions of the Riga and Moscow committees, and also of the Geneva group of Bolsheviks, associating themselves with the decisions of the conference of the twenty-two Bolsheviks. The appeal "To the Party" became the Bolsheviks' programme of struggle for the convocation of the Third Congress. Most of the committees of the R.S.D.L.P. expressed solidarity with the decisions of the Bolshevik conference. In September 1904 the Caucasian Union Committee, and the Tiflis and Imeretia-Mingrelia Committees, associated themselves with the Declaration of the 22 and launched a campaign for the immediate convocation of the Third Congress of the Party.

5 **Original editor**: V. I. Lenin's article "One Step Forward, Two Steps Back" was written in September 1904 in answer to an article by Rosa Luxemburg entitled "The Organisational Problems of Russian Social-Democracy," published in Iskra, No. 69, and in Neue Zeit, Nos. 42, 43, and also in reply to a letter by K. Kautsky published in *Iskra*, No. 66. Lenin intended to have his article published in *Neue Zeit*, but the editors of that magazine sympathised with the Mensheviks and refused to publish it.

6 **Original editor**: *The Minutes of the Second Ordinary Congress of the League of Russian Revolutionary Social-Democrats Abroad*, published by the League in Geneva, in 1904.

7 **Original editor**: V. I. Lenin's book *One Step Forward, Two Steps Back* was written in February-May 1904 and appeared on May 6 (19) in that year (see Works, 4th Russ. ed., Vol. 7, pp. 185-392).

8 This refers to V. I. Lenin's book *What Is To Be Done?* (see Works, 4th Russ. ed., Vol. 5, pp. 319-494).

Plekhanov has fallen behind the *new problems*. He imagines he has the old opponents before him, and he goes on repeating in the old way: "social consciousness is determined by social being," "ideas do not drop from the skies." As if Lenin said that Marx's socialism would have been possible under slavery and serfdom. Even schoolboys know now that "ideas do not drop from the skies." The point is, however, that we are now faced with quite a different issue. We assimilated this general formula long ago and the time has now come to analyse this general problem. What interests us now is how separate ideas are worked up into a system of ideas (the theory of socialism), how separate ideas, and hints of ideas, link up into one harmonious system—the theory of socialism, and who works and links them up. Do the masses give their leaders a programme and the principles underlying the programme, or do the leaders give these to the masses? If the masses themselves and their spontaneous movement give us the theory of socialism, then there is no need to take the trouble to safeguard the masses from the pernicious influence of revisionism, terrorism, Zubatovism and anarchism: "the spontaneous movement engenders socialism *from itself.*" If the spontaneous movement does *not* engender the theory of socialism from itself (don't forget that Lenin is discussing the theory of socialism), then the latter is engendered *outside of* the spontaneous movement, from the observations and study of the spontaneous movement by men who are equipped with up-to-date knowledge. Hence, the theory of socialism is worked out "quite independently of the growth of the spontaneous movement," in spite of that movement in fact, and is then *introduced* into that movement *from outside, correcting* it in conformity with its content, i.e., in conformity with the objective requirements of the proletarian class struggle.

The conclusion (practical deduction) to be drawn from this is as follows: we must raise the proletariat to a consciousness of its true class interests, to a consciousness of the socialist ideal, and not break this ideal up into small change, or adjust it to the spontaneous movement. Lenin has laid down the theoretical basis on which this practical deduction is built. It is enough to accept this theoretical premise and no opportunism will get anywhere near you. Herein lies the significance of Lenin's idea. I call it Lenin's, because nobody in Russian literature has expressed it with such clarity as Lenin. Plekhanov believes that he is still living in the nineties, and he goes on chewing what has already been chewed eighteen times over—twice two make four. And he is not ashamed of having talked himself into repeating Martynov's ideas. . . .

You are no doubt familiar with the Declaration of the 22. . . . There was a comrade here from your parts who took with him the resolutions of the Caucasian Committees in favour of calling a special congress of the Party.

You are wrong in thinking that the situation is hopeless—only the Kutais Committee wavered, but I succeeded in convincing them, and after that they began to swear by Bolshevism. It was not difficult to convince them: the two-faced policy of the Central Committee became obvious thanks to the Declaration, and after fresh news was received, there could be no further doubt about it. It (the C.C.) will break its neck, the local and Russian comrades will see to that. It has got everybody's back up.

Written in September-October 1904
Published for the first time
Translated from the Georgian

A LETTER FROM KUTAIS

(FROM THE SAME COMRADE)

I am late with this letter, don't be angry. I have been busy all the time. All that you sent I have received (Minutes of the League; *Our Misunderstandings* by Galyorka and Ryadovoi; *Sotsial-Demokrat*, No 1; *Iskra*, the last issues). I liked Ryadovoi's idea ("A Conclusion"). The article against Rosa Luxemburg is also good. These ladies and gentlemen—Rosa, Kautsky, Plekhanov, Axel-rod, Vera Zasulich and the others, being old acquaintances, have evidently worked out some kind of family tradition. They cannot "betray" one another; they defend one another as the members of a clan in a patriarchal tribe used to defend one another without going into the guilt or innocence of the kinsman. It is this family feeling, this feeling of "kinship" that has prevented Rosa from studying the crisis in the Party objectively (of course, there are other reasons, for example, inadequate knowledge of the facts, foreign spectacles, etc.). Incidentally, this explains certain unseemly actions on the part of Plekhanov, Kautsky and others.

Everybody here likes Bonch's publications as masterly expositions of the Bolsheviks' position. Galyorka would have done well if he had dealt with the substance of Plekhanov's articles (*Iskra*, Nos. 70, 71). The fundamental idea in Galyorka's articles is that Plekhanov once said one thing and is now saying another, that he is contradicting himself. How very important! As if this were new! This is not the first time he is contradicting himself. He may even be proud of it and regard himself as the living embodiment of the "dialectical process." It goes without saying that inconsistency is a blotch on the political physiognomy of a "leader," and it (the blotch) should undoubtedly be noted. But that is not what we are discussing (in Nos. 70, 71); we are discussing an important question of theory (the question of the relation between being and consciousness) and of tactics (the relation between the led and the leaders). In my opinion, Galyorka should have shown that Plekhanov's theoretical war against Lenin is quixotic to the utmost degree, tilting at windmills, for in his pamphlet Lenin, with the utmost consistency, adheres to K. Marx's proposition concerning the *origin* of consciousness. And Plekhanov's war on the question of tactics is a manifestation of utter confusion, characteristic of the "individual" who is passing over to the camp of the opportunists. Had Plekhanov formulated the question clearly, for example, in the following shape: "who formulates the programme, the leaders or the led?" or: "who raises whom to an understanding of the programme, the leaders the led, or vice versa?" or: "perhaps it is undesirable that the leaders should raise the masses to an understanding of the programme, tactics and principles of organisation?" The simplicity and tautology of these questions provide their own solution, and had Plekhanov put them to himself as clearly as this, he, perhaps, would have been deterred from his intention and would not have come out against Lenin with such fireworks. But since Plekhanov did not do that, i.e., since he confused the issue with phrases about "heroes and the mob," he digressed in the direction of *tactical opportunism.* To confuse the issue is characteristic of opportunists.

Had Galyorka dealt with the substance of these and similar questions he would have done much better, in my opinion. Perhaps you will say that this is Lenin's business; but I cannot agree with this, because the views of Lenin that are criticised are not Lenin's private property, and their misinterpretation is a matter that concerns other members of the Party no less than Lenin. Lenin, of course, could perform this task better than anybody else. . . .

We already have resolutions in favour of Bonch's publications. Perhaps we shall have the money too. You have probably read the resolutions "in favour of peace" in No. 74 of *Iskra.* The resolutions passed by the *Imeretia-Mingrelia* and *Baku Committees* were not mentioned, because they said nothing about "confidence" in the C.C. The September resolutions, as I wrote you, insistently demanded the convocation of the congress. We shall see what happens, i.e., we shall see what the results of the meetings of the Party Council[1] show. Have you received the six rubles? You will receive some more within the next few days. Don't forget to send with that fellow the pamphlet *A Letter to a Comrade*[2]— many here have not yet read it. Send also the next number of the *Sotsial-Demokrat*.

Kostrov[3] has sent us another letter in which he talks about the spiritual and the material (one would think he was talking about cotton material). That ass doesn't realise that his audience are not the readers of *Kvali*.[4] What does he care about organisational questions?

A new issue (the 7th) of *The Proletarian Struggle (Proletariatis Brdzola)*[5]

---

1 **Original editor**: In conformity with the Rules adopted at the Second Congress of the R.S.D.L.P., the Party Council was the supreme body of the Party. It consisted of five members: two appointed by the Central Committee, two by the Central Organ, and the fifth elected by the congress. The main function of the Council was to co-ordinate and unite the activities of the Central Committee and the Central Organ. Soon after the Second Congress of the R.S.D.L.P. the Mensheviks obtained control of the Party Council and converted it into an instrument of their factional struggle. The Third Congress of the R.S.D.L.P. abolished the multiple centre system in the Party and set up a single Party centre in the shape of the Central Committee, which was divided into two sections—one functioning abroad, and the other in Russia. In conformity with the Rules adopted at the Third Congress, the editor of the Central Organ was appointed by the Central Committee from among its members.

2 **Original editor**: V. I. Lenin's pamphlet *A Letter to a Comrade on Our Organisational Tasks*, with a Preface and Postscript by the author, was published in Geneva, in 1904, by the Central Committee of the R.S.D.L.P. (see Works, 4th Russ. ed., Vol. 6, pp. 205-24).

3 **Original editor**: Kostrov—pseudonym of N. Jordania. He also signed himself An.

4 **Original editor**: *Kvali (The Furrow)*—a weekly newspaper published in the Georgian language, an organ of the liberal-nationalist trend. In the period of 1893-97 it placed its columns at the disposal of the young writers of the Messameh Dassy. At the end of 1897 the newspaper passed into the hands of the majority in Messameh Dassy (N . Jordania and others) and became a mouthpiece of "legal Marxism." After the Bolshevik and Menshevik groups arose within the R.S.D.L.P. *Kvali* became the organ of the Georgian Mensheviks. The newspaper was suppressed by the government in 1904.

5 **Original editor**: Proletariatis Brdzola (*The Proletarian Struggle*)—an illegal Georgian newspaper, the organ of the Caucasian Union of the R.S.D.L.P., published from April-May 1903 to October 1905, and suppressed after the issue of the twelfth number. J. V. Stalin became its chief editor on his return from exile in 1904. The editorial board included also A. G. Tsulukidze, S. G. Shaumyan, and others. The leading articles were written by J . V. Stalin. *Proletariatis Brdzola* was the successor to *Brdzola*. The First Congress of the Caucasian Union of the R.S.D.L.P. decided to combine *Brdzola* with *Proletariat*, the Armenian Social-Democratic newspaper, and issue a joint organ in three languages: Georgian (*Proletariatis Brdzola*), Armenian (*Proletariati Kriv*) and Russian (*Borba Proletariata*). The contents of the newspapers were the same in all three languages. The numbering of the respective newspapers was continued

has appeared. Incidentally, it contains an article of mine against organisational and political federalism.[6] I'll send you a copy if I can.

Written in October 1904
Published for the first time
Translated from the Georgian

---

from their preceding issues. *Proletariatis Brdzola* was the third largest illegal Bolshevik newspaper (after *Vperyod* and *Proletary*) and consistently advocated the ideological, organisational and tactical principles of the Marxist party. The editorial board of *Proletariatis Brdzola* maintained close contact with V. I. Lenin and with the Bolshevik centre abroad. When the announcement of the publication of *Vperyod* appeared in December 1904, the Caucasian Union Committee formed a group of writers to support that newspaper. In answer to an invitation of the Union Committee to contribute to *Proletariatis Brdzola*, V. I. Lenin, in a letter dated December 20 (New Style), 1904, wrote: "Dear Comrades. I have received your letter about *The Proletarian Struggle*. I shall try to write myself and pass on your request to the comrades on the editorial board" (see Lenin, *Works*, 4th Russ. ed., Vol. 34, p. 240). *Proletariatis Brdzola* regularly reprinted in its columns articles and information from Lenin's *Iskra*, and later from *Vperyod* and *Proletary*. The newspaper published articles by V. I. Lenin. *Proletary* often published favourable reviews and comments on *Proletariatis Brdzola* and also reprinted articles and correspondence from it. No. 12 of *Proletary* noted the issue of No. 1 of *Borba Proletariata* in Russian. The comment concluded as follows: "We shall have to deal with the contents of this interesting newspaper again. We heartily welcome the expansion of the publishing activities of the Caucasian Union and wish it further success in reviving the Party spirit in the Caucasus."

6 **Original editor**: This refers to J. V. Stalin's article "The Social-Democratic View of the National Question" (present volume, p. 31).

THE PROLETARIAN CLASS
AND THE PROLETARIAN PARTY
(CONCERNING PARAGRAPH ONE OF THE PARTY RULES)

The time when people boldly proclaimed "Russia, one and indivisible," has gone. Today even a child knows that there is no such thing as Russia "one and indivisible," that Russia long ago split up into two opposite classes, the bourgeoisie and the proletariat. Today it is no secret to anyone that the struggle between these two classes has become the axis around which our contemporary life revolves.

Nevertheless, until recently it was difficult to notice all this, the reason being that hitherto we saw only individual groups in the arena of the struggle, for it was only individual groups in individual towns and parts of the country that waged the struggle, while the proletariat and the bourgeoisie, as classes, were not easily discernible. But now towns and districts have united, various groups of the proletariat have joined hands, joint strikes and demonstrations have broken out—and before us has unfolded the magnificent picture of the struggle between the two Russias—bourgeois Russia and proletarian Russia. Two big armies have entered the arena—the army of proletarians and the army of the bourgeoisie—and the struggle between these two armies embraces the whole of our social life.

Since an army cannot operate without leaders, and since every army has a vanguard which marches at its head and lights up its path, it is obvious that with these armies there had to appear corresponding groups of leaders, corresponding parties, as they are usually called.

Thus, the picture presents the following scene: on one side there is the bourgeois army, headed by the liberal party; on the other, there is the proletarian army, headed by the Social-Democratic Party; each army, in its class struggle, is led by its own party.[1]

We have mentioned all this in order to compare the proletarian party with the proletarian class and thus briefly to bring out the general features of the Party.

The foregoing makes it sufficiently clear that the proletarian party, being a fighting group of leaders, must, firstly, be considerably smaller than the proletarian class with respect to membership; secondly, it must be superior to the proletarian class with respect to its understanding and its experience; and, thirdly, it must be a united organisation.

In our opinion, what has been said needs no proof, for it is self-evident that, so long as the capitalist system exists, with its inevitably attendant poverty and backwardness of the masses, the proletariat as a whole cannot rise to the desired level of class consciousness, and, consequently, there must be a group of class-conscious leaders to enlighten the proletarian army in the spirit of socialism, to unite and lead it in its struggle. It is also clear that a party which has set out to lead the *fighting* proletariat must not be a chance conglomeration of individuals, but a united centralised *organisation*, so that its activities can be directed according to a single plan.

Such, in brief, are the general features of our Party.

Bearing all this in mind, let us pass to the main question: Whom can we call a Party member? Paragraph One of the Party Rules, which is the subject of the present article, deals with precisely this question.

And so, let us examine this question.

Whom, then, can we call a member of the Russian Social-Democratic Labour Party—i.e., what are the duties of a Party member?

Our Party is a Social-Democratic Party. This means that it has its own programme (the immediate and the ultimate aims of the movement), its own tactics (methods of struggle), and its own organisational principle (form of association). *Unity* of programmatic, tactical and organisational views is the basis on which our Party is built. Only

---

1 We do not mention the other parties in Russia, because there is no need to deal with them in examining the questions under discussion.

the *unity* of these views can unite the Party members in *one* centralised party. If unity of views collapses, the Party collapses. Consequently, only one who fully accepts the Party's programme, tactics and organisational principle can be called a Party member. Only one who has adequately studied and has fully accepted our Party's programmatic, tactical and organisational views can be in the ranks of our Party and, thereby, in the ranks of the leaders of the proletarian army.

But is it enough for a Party member merely to *accept* the Party's programme, tactics and organisational views? Can a person like that be regarded as a true leader of the proletarian army? Of course not! In the first place, everybody knows that there are plenty of windbags in the world who would readily "accept" the Party's programme, tactics and organisational views, but who are incapable of being anything else than windbags. It would be a desecration of the Party's Holy of Holies to call a windbag like that a Party member (i.e., a leader of the proletarian army)! Moreover, our Party is not a school of philosophy or a religious sect. Is not our Party a *fighting* party? Since it is, is it not self-evident that our Party will not be satisfied with a platonic *acceptance* of its programme, tactics and organisational views, that it will undoubtedly demand that its members should *apply* the views they have accepted? Hence, whoever wants to be a member of our Party cannot rest content with merely accepting our Party's programmatic, tactical and organisational views, but must set about applying these views, putting them into effect.

But what does applying the Party's views mean for a Party member? When can he apply these views? Only when he is fighting, when he is marching with the whole Party at the head of the proletarian army. Can the struggle be waged by solitary, scattered individuals? Certainly not! On the contrary, people first unite, first they organise, and only then do they go into battle. If that is not done, all struggle is fruitless. Clearly, then, the Party members, too, will be able to fight and, consequently, apply the Party's views, only if they unite in a compact *organisation*. It is also clear that the more compact the organisation in which the Party members unite, the better will they be able to fight, and, consequently, the more fully will they apply the Party's programme, tactics and organisational views. It is not for nothing that our Party is called an *organisation* of leaders and not a conglomeration of individuals. And, if our Party is an *organisation* of leaders, it is obvious that only those can be regarded as members of this Party, of this organisation, who work in this organisation and, therefore, deem it their duty to merge their wishes with the wishes of the Party and to act in unison with the Party.

Hence, to be a Party member one must apply the Party's programme, tactics and organisational views; to apply the Party's views one must fight for them; and to fight for these views one must work in a Party organisation, work in unison with the Party. Clearly, to be a Party member one must belong to one of the Party organisations.[2] Only when we join one of the Party organisations and thus merge our personal interests with the Party's interests can we become Party members, and, consequently, real leaders of the proletarian army.

If our Party is not a conglomeration of individual windbags, but an *organisation* of leaders which, through its Central Committee, is worthily leading the proletarian army forward, then all that has been said above is self-evident.

The following must also be noted.

Up till now our Party has resembled a hospitable patriarchal family, ready to take in all who sympathise. But now that our Party has become a centralised *organisation*, it has thrown off its patriarchal aspect and has become in all respects like a *fortress*, the gates of which are opened only to those who are worthy. And that is of great importance to us. At a time when the autocracy is trying to corrupt the class consciousness of the proletariat with "trade unionism," nationalism, clericalism and the like, and when, on the other hand, the liberal intelligentsia is persistently striving to kill the political independence of the proletariat and to impose its tutelage upon it—at such a time we must be extremely vigilant and never forget that our Party is a *fortress*, the gates of which are opened only to those who have been tested.

---

2 Just as every complex organism is made up of an incalculable number of extremely simple organisms, so our Party, being a complex and general organisation, is made up of numerous district and local bodies called Party organisations, provided they have been endorsed by the Party congress or the Central Committee. As you see, not only committees are called Party organisations. To direct the activities of these organisations according to a single plan there is a Central Committee, through which these local Party organisations constitute one large centralised organisation.

We have ascertained two essential conditions of Party membership (acceptance of the programme and work in a Party organisation). If to these we add a third condition, namely, that a Party member must render the Party financial support, then we shall have all the conditions that give one right to the title of Party member.

Hence, a member of the Russian Social-Democratic Labour Party is one who accepts the programme of this Party, renders the Party financial support, and *works in one of the Party organisations*.

That is how Paragraph One of the Party Rules, drafted by Comrade Lenin,[3] was formulated.

The formula, as you see, springs entirely from the view that our Party is a centralised *organisation* and not a *conglomeration* of individuals.

Therein lies the supreme merit of this formula.

But it appears that some comrades reject Lenin's formula on the grounds that it is "narrow" and "inconvenient," and propose their own formula, which, it must be supposed, is neither "narrow" nor "inconvenient." We are referring to Martov's[4] formula, which we shall now analyse.

Martov's formula is: "A member of the R.S.D.L.P. is one who accepts its programme, supports the Party financially and renders it regular personal assistance under the direction of one of its organisations." As you see, this formula omits the third essential condition of Party membership, namely, the duty of Party members *to work* in one of the Party *organisations*. It appears that Martov regards this definite and essential condition as superfluous, and in his formula he has substituted for it the nebulous and dubious "personal assistance under the direction of one of the Party organisations." It appears, then, that one can be a member of the Party without belonging to any Party organisation (a fine "party," to be sure!) and without feeling obliged to submit to the Party's will (fine "Party discipline," to be sure!). Well, and how can the Party "regularly" direct persons who do not belong to any Party

---

3 Lenin is the outstanding theoretician and practical leader of revolutionary Social-Democracy.

4 Martov is one of the editors of *Iskra*.

organisation and, consequently, do not feel absolutely obliged to submit to Party discipline?

That is the question that shatters Martov's formula of Paragraph One of the Party Rules, and it is answered in masterly fashion in Lenin's formula, inasmuch as the latter definitely stipulates that a third and indispensable condition of Party membership is *that one must work in a Party organisation.*

All we have to do is to throw out of Martov's formula the nebulous and meaningless "personal assistance under the direction of one of the Party organisations." With this condition eliminated, there remain only two conditions in Martov's formula (acceptance of the programme and financial support), which, by themselves, are utterly worthless, since every windbag can "accept" the Party programme and support the Party financially—but that does not in the least entitle him to Party membership.

A "convenient" formula, we must say!

We say that real Party members cannot possibly rest content with merely accepting the Party programme, but must without fail strive to apply the programme they have accepted. Martov answers: You are too strict, for it is not so very necessary for a Party member to apply the programme he has accepted, once he is willing to render the Party financial support, and so forth. It looks as though Martov is sorry for certain windbag "Social-Democrats" and does not want to close the Party's doors to them.

We say, further, that inasmuch as the application of the programme entails fighting, and that it is impossible to fight without unity, it is the duty of every prospective Party member to join one of the Party organisations, merge his wishes with those of the Party and, in unison with the Party, lead the fighting proletarian army, i.e., he must organise in the well-formed detachments of a centralised party. To this Martov answers: It is not so very necessary for Party members to organise in well-formed detachments, to unite in organisations; fighting single-handed is good enough.

What, then, is our Party? we ask. A chance conglomeration of individuals, or a united organisation of leaders? And if it is an organisation of leaders, can we regard as a member one who does not belong to it and, consequently, does not consider it his bounden duty to submit to its discipline? Martov answers that the Party is not an organisation, or, rather, that the Party is an *unorganised* organisation (fine "centralism," to be sure!)!

Evidently, in Martov's opinion, our Party is not a centralised organisation, but a conglomeration of local organisations and individual "Social-Democrats" who have accepted our Party programme, etc. But if our Party is not a centralised organisation it will not be a fortress, the gates of which can be opened only for those who have been tested. And, indeed, to Martov, as is evident from his formula, the Party is not a fortress but a banquet, which every sympathiser can freely attend. A little knowledge, an equal amount of sympathy, a little financial support and there you are—you have full right to count as a Party member. Don't listen—cries Martov to cheer up the frightened "Party members"—don't listen to those people who maintain that a Party member must belong to one of the Party organisations and thus subordinate his wishes to the wishes of the Party. In the first place, it is hard for a man to accept these conditions; it is no joke to subordinate one's wishes to those of the Party! And, secondly, as I have already pointed out in my explanation, the opinion of those people is mistaken. And so, gentlemen, you are welcome to . . .the banquet!

It looks as though Martov is sorry for certain professors and high-school students who are loth to subordinate their wishes to the wishes of the Party, and so he is forcing a breach in our Party fortress through which these estimable gentlemen may smuggle into our Party. He is opening the door to opportunism, and this at a time when thousands of enemies are assailing the class consciousness of the proletariat!

But that is not all. The point is that Martov's dubious formula makes it possible for opportunism to arise in our Party from another side.

Martov's formula, as we know, refers only to the acceptance of the programme; about tactics and organisation it contains not a word; and yet, unity of organisational and tactical views is no less essential for Party unity than unity of programmatic views. We may be told that nothing is said about this even in Comrade Lenin's formula. True, but there is no need to say anything about it in Comrade Lenin's formula. Is it not self-evident that one who works in a Party organisation and, consequently, fights in unison with the Party and submits to Party discipline, cannot pursue tactics and organisational principles other than the Party's tactics and the Party's organisational principles? But what would you say of a "Party member" who has accepted the Party programme, but does not belong to any Party organisation? What guarantee is there that such a "member's" tactics and organisational views will be those of the Party and not some other? That is what Martov's formula fails to explain! As a result of Martov's formula we would have a queer "party," whose "members" subscribe to the same programme (and that is questionable!), but differ in their tactical and organisational views! What ideal variety! In what way will our Party differ from a banquet?

There is just one question we should like to ask: What are we to do with the ideological and practical centralism that was handed down to us by the Second Party Congress and which is radically contradicted by Martov's formula? Throw it overboard? If it comes to making a choice, it will undoubtedly be more correct to throw Martov's formula overboard.

Such is the absurd formula Martov presents to us in opposition to Comrade Lenin's formula!

We are of the opinion that the decision of the Second Party Congress, which adopted Martov's formula, was the result of thoughtlessness, and we hope that the Third Party Congress will not fail to rectify the blunder of the Second Congress and adopt Comrade Lenin's formula. We shall briefly recapitulate: The proletarian army entered the arena of the struggle. Since every army must have a vanguard, this army also had to have such a vanguard. Hence the appearance of a group of proletarian leaders — the Russian Social-Democratic Labour Party. As the vanguard of a definite army, this Party must, firstly, be armed with its own programme, tactics and organisational principle; and, secondly, it must be a united organisation. To the question—who can be called a member of the Russian Social-Democratic Labour Party? — this Party can have only one answer: one who accepts the Party programme, supports the Party financially and works in one of the Party organisations.

It is this obvious truth that Comrade Lenin has expressed in his splendid formula.

Proletariatis Brdzola
(*The Proletarian Struggle*), No. 8,
January 1, 1905
Unsigned
Translated from the Georgian

WORKERS OF THE CAUCASUS,
IT IS TIME TO TAKE REVENGE!

The tsar's battalions are dwindling, the tsar's navy is perishing, and now Port Arthur has shamefully surrendered—thus the senile decrepitude of the tsarist autocracy is once again revealed. . . .

Inadequate food and the absence of any kind of sanitary measures whatsoever, are causing infectious diseases to spread among the troops. These unbearable conditions are still further aggravated by the absence of anything like decent housing and clothing. Worn and weary, the soldiers are dying like flies. And this is after tens of thousands have been killed by bullets! . . . All this is causing unrest and discontent among the troops. The soldiers are awakening from their torpor, they are beginning to feel that they are human, they no longer blindly obey the orders of their superiors, and often greet their upstart officers with whistling and threats.

This is what an officer writes to us from the Far East:

"I did a foolish thing! On the insistence of my superior I recently delivered a speech to the men. No sooner did I begin to talk about the necessity of standing fast for tsar and country than the air was filled with whistling, curses and threats. . . . I hastened to put the greatest possible distance between myself and the infuriated mob. . . ."

Such is the situation in the Far East!

Add to this the unrest among the reservists in Russia, their revolutionary demonstrations in Odessa, Yekateri-noslav, Kursk, Penza and other cities, and the protests of the new recruits in Guria, Imeretia, Kartalinia and in south and north Russia, note that the demonstrators are undaunted either by prison or bullets (recently, in Penza, several reservists were shot for demonstrating), and you will easily understand what the Russian soldiers are thinking. . . .

The tsarist autocracy is losing its main prop—its "reliable troops"!

On the other hand, the tsar's treasury is becoming more depleted every day. Defeat follows defeat. The tsarist government is gradually losing the confidence of foreign states. It is barely able to obtain the money it needs, and the time is not far distant when it will be deprived of all credit! "Who will pay us when you are overthrown, and your fall is undoubtedly imminent," such is the answer that is given to the utterly discredited tsarist government! And the people, the dispossessed, starving people, what can they give the tsarist government when they have nothing to eat themselves?!

And so, the tsarist autocracy is losing its second main prop—its rich treasury, and credit which keeps it filled!

Meanwhile, the industrial crisis is becoming more acute every day; factories and mills are closing down and millions of workers are demanding bread and work. Hunger is afflicting the tormented poor of the countryside with renewed force. The waves of popular anger rise higher and higher and dash against the tsarist throne with increasing force, shaking the decrepit tsarist autocracy to its foundations. . . .

The besieged tsarist autocracy is casting its old skin like a snake, and while discontented Russia is preparing to launch a decisive assault, it is putting aside (pretending to put aside!) its *whip* and, disguising itself in sheep's clothing, is proclaiming a *policy of conciliation*!

Do you hear, comrades? It is asking us to forget the swish of whips and the whizz of bullets, the hundreds of our hero-comrades who have been killed, their glorious shades which are hovering around us and whispering to us: "Avenge us!"

The autocracy is brazenly offering us its bloodstained hands and is counselling conciliation! It has published some sort of an "Imperial Ukase"[1] in which it promises us some sort of "freedom.". . . The old

---

1 **Original editor:** This *ukase* of Tsar Nicholas II, dated December 12, 1904, was published in the newspapers together with a special government communique on December 14, 1904. While promising certain minor "reforms," the ukase proclaimed the inviolability of the autocratic power and breathed threats not only against the revolutionary workers and peasants, but also against the liberals who had dared to

brigands! They think they can feed the millions of starving Russian proletarians with words! They hope with words to satisfy the many millions of impoverished and tormented peasants! With promises they would drown the weeping of bereaved families—victims of the war! Miserable wretches! They are the drowning clutching at a straw! . . .

Yes, comrades, the throne of the tsarist government is being shaken to its foundations! The government which is using the taxes it has squeezed out of us to pay our executioners—ministers, governors, uyezd chiefs and prison chiefs, police officers, *gendarmes and spies*; the government which is compelling the soldiers torn from our midst— our brothers and sons—to shed our blood; the government which is doing all in its power to support the landlords and employers in their daily struggle against us; the government which has bound us hand and foot and has reduced us to the position of rightless slaves; the government which has brutally trampled upon and mocked at our human dignity—our Holy of Holies—it is this government which is tottering and feeling the ground slipping from under its feet!

It is time to take revenge! It is time to avenge our valiant comrades who were brutally murdered by the tsar's bashi-bazouks in Yaroslavl, Dombrowa, Riga, St. Petersburg, Moscow, Batum, Tiflis, Zlatoust, Tikho-retskaya, Mikhailovo, Kishinev, Gomel, Yakutsk, Guria, Baku and other places! It is time to call the government to book for the tens of thousands of innocent and unfortunate men who have perished on the battle-field in the Far East. It is time to dry the tears of their wives and children! It is time to call the government to book for the suffering and humiliation, for the shameful chains in which it has kept us for so long! It is time to put an end to the tsarist government and to clear the road for ourselves to the socialist system! It is time to *destroy* the tsarist government!

And we will *destroy* it.

In vain are Messieurs the Liberals trying to save the tottering throne of the tsar! In vain are they stretching out a helping hand to the tsar! They are begging for charity from him and trying to win his favour for

---

submit timid constitutional demands to the government. As V. I. Lenin expressed it, Nicholas II's ukase was "a slap in the face for the liberals."

their "draft constitution"[2] so as, by means of *petty* reforms, to lay a road for themselves to political domination, to transform the tsar into their instrument, to substitute the autocracy of the bourgeoisie for the autocracy of the tsar and then systematically to strangle the proletariat and the peasantry! But in vain! It is already too late, Messieurs Liberals! Look around and see what the tsarist government has given you, examine its "Imperial Ukase": a tiny bit of "freedom" for "rural and urban institutions," a tiny "guarantee" against "restriction of the rights of private persons," a tiny bit of "freedom" of the "printed word" and a big warning about the "unfailing preservation of the inviolability of the fundamental laws of the empire," about "taking effective measures to preserve the full force of the law, a most important pillar of the throne in the autocratic state"! . . . Well? You had barely time to digest the ridiculous "order" of the ridiculous tsar when "warnings" began to pour down upon the newspapers like hail, a series of gendarme and police raids commenced, and even peaceful banquets were prohibited! The tsarist government itself took care to prove that in its miserly promises it would go no further than mere words.

On the other hand, the outraged masses of the people are preparing for *revolution* and not for conciliation with the tsar. They stubbornly adhere to the proverb: "Only the grave can straighten the hunchback." Yes, gentlemen, vain are your efforts! The Russian revolution is inevitable. It is as inevitable as the rising of the sun! Can you prevent the sun from rising? *The main force in this revolution is the urban and-rural proletariat, its banner-bearer is the Social-Democratic Labour Party*, and not you, Messieurs Liberals! Why do you forget this obvious "trifle"?

The storm, the harbinger of the dawn, is already rising. Only yesterday, or the day before, the proletariat of the Caucasus, from Baku to Batum, unanimously expressed its contempt for the tsarist autocracy. There can be no doubt that this glorious effort of the Caucasian proletarians will not fail to have its effect on the proletarians in other parts of Russia. Read also the innumerable resolutions passed by workers expressing profound contempt for the tsarist government, listen to the

---

2 This "draft constitution" was drawn up by a group of members of the liberal League of Emancipation in October 1904 and was issued in pamphlet form under the title: The Fundamental State Law of the Russian Empire. Draft of a Russian Constitution, Moscow 1904.

low but powerful murmuring in the countryside—and you will convince yourselves that Russia is a loaded gun with the hammer cocked ready to go off at the slightest shock. Yes, comrades, the time is not far distant when the Russian revolution will hoist sail and "sweep from the face of the earth" the vile throne of the despicable tsar!

Our vital duty is to be ready for that moment. Let us prepare then, comrades! Let us sow the good seed among the broad masses of the proletariat. Let us stretch out our hands to one another and *rally around the Party Committees*! We must not forget for a moment that *only the Party Committees can worthily lead us, only they* will light up our road to the "promised land" called the socialist world! The party which has opened our eyes and has pointed out our enemies to us, which has organised us in a formidable army and has led us to fight our foes, which has stood by us amidst joy and sorrow and has always marched ahead of us—is the Russian Social-Democratic Labour Party! It, and it *alone*, will lead us in future!

A Constituent Assembly elected on the basis of universal, equal, direct and secret suffrage—this is what we must fight for now!

Only such an Assembly will give us the *democratic republic* which we need so urgently in our struggle for socialism.

Forward then, comrades! When the tsarist autocracy is tottering, our duty is to prepare for the decisive assault! It is time to take revenge!

Down With the Tsarist Autocracy!

Long Live the Popular Constituent Assembly!

Long Live the Democratic Republic!

Long Live the Russian Social-Democratic Labour Party!

January 1905
Reproduced from the manifesto printed
on January 8, 1905 at the underground
(Aviabar) printing plant of the Caucasian
Union of the R.S.D.L.P.
Signed: *Union Committee*

LONG LIVE

INTERNATIONAL FRATERNITY!

Citizens! The revolutionary proletarian movement is growing—and national barriers are collapsing! The proletarians of the different nationalities in Russia are uniting in a single international army, the individual streams of the proletarian movement are merging in one general revolutionary flood. The waves of this flood are rising higher and higher and dashing against the tsarist throne with increasing force—and the decrepit tsarist government is tottering. Neither prisons nor penal servitude, nor gallows—nothing can stop the proletarian movement: it is continuously growing!

And so, to bolster up its throne the tsarist government is inventing "new" methods. It is sowing enmity among the nationalities of Russia, it is inciting them against one another; it is trying to break up the general proletarian movement into petty movements and to incite them *against one another*; it is organising pogroms against the Jews, Armenians, etc. And the purpose of all this is to separate the nationalities of Russia from one another by means of fratricidal war and, by enfeebling them, to vanquish them one by one without difficulty!

Divide and rule—such is the policy of the tsarist government. That is what it is doing in the cities of Russia (remember the pogroms in Gomel, Kishinev and other towns), and it is doing the same in the Caucasus. What infamy! It is buttressing its despicable throne with the blood and the corpses of citizens! The groans of the dying Armenians and Tatars in Baku; the tears of wives, mothers and children; the blood, the innocent blood of honest but unenlightened citizens; the frightened faces of fugitive, defenceless people fleeing from death; wrecked homes, looted shops and the frightful, unceasing whizz of bullets—that is what the tsar—the murderer of honest citizens—is bolstering up his throne with.

Yes, citizens! It is they, the agents of the tsarist government, who incited the politically unenlightened among the Tatars against the peaceful Armenians! It is they, the flunkeys of the tsarist government, who distributed arms and ammunition among them, disguised policemen and Cossacks in Tatar clothing and hurled them against the Armenians! For two months, they—the servants of the tsar—prepared this fratricidal war—and at last they achieved their barbarous object. Curses and death on the head of the tsarist government!

Now these miserable slaves of the miserable tsar are trying to foment a fratricidal war among us, here in Tiflis! They are demanding your blood, they want to divide and rule over you! But be vigilant, you Armenians, Tatars, Georgians and Russians! Stretch out your hands to one another, unite more closely, and to the attempts of the government to divide you answer unanimously: Down with the tsarist government!

Long live the fraternity of the peoples!

Stretch out your hands to one another and, having united, rally around the proletariat, the real gravedigger of the tsarist government which is the sole culprit in the Baku massacres.

Let your cry be:

Down With National Strife!

Down With the Tsarist Government!

Long Live the Fraternity of the Peoples!

Long Live the Democratic Republic!

February 13 , 1905
Reproduced from the manifesto printed
at the printing plant of the Tiflis
Committee of the R.S.D.L.P.
Signed: *Tiflis Committee*

TO CITIZENS:
LONG LIVE THE RED FLAG!

G reat hopes and great disappointment! Instead of national enmity—mutual love and confidence! Instead of a fratricidal
pogrom—a huge demonstration against tsarism, the culprit in the
pogroms! The hopes of the tsarist government have collapsed: the
attempt to incite the different nationalities in Tiflis against one another
has failed! . . .

The tsarist government has long been trying to incite the proletarians against one another, has long been trying to break up the
general proletarian movement. That is why it organised the pogroms
in Gomel, Kishinev and other places. It provoked a fratricidal war in
Baku with the same object. At last, the gaze of the tsarist government rested on Tiflis. Here, in the middle of the Caucasus, it intended
to enact a bloody tragedy and then to carry it to the provinces! No
small matter: to incite the nationalities of the Caucasus against one
another and to drown the Caucasian proletariat in its own blood! The
tsarist government rubbed its hands with glee. It even distributed a
leaflet calling for a massacre of Armenians! And it hoped for success.
But suddenly, on February 13, as if to spite the tsarist government, a
crowd numbering many thousands of Armenians, Georgians, Tatars,
and Russians assembles in the enclosure of the Vanque Cathedral and
takes a vow of mutual support "in the struggle against the devil who is
sowing strife among us." Complete unanimity. Speeches are delivered
calling for "unity." The masses applaud the speakers. Our leaflets are
distributed (3,000 copies). The masses eagerly take them. The temper
of the masses rises. In defiance of the government they decide to assemble again next day in the enclosure of the same cathedral in order

once again to "vow to love one another."

February 14. The entire cathedral enclosure and the adjacent streets are packed with people. Our leaflets are distributed and read quite openly. The crowds split up into groups and discuss the contents of the leaflets. Speeches are delivered. The temper of the masses rises. They decide to march in demonstration past the Zion Cathedral and the Mosque, to "vow to love one another," to halt at the Persian Cemetery to take the vow once again and then disperse. The masses put their decision into execution. On the way, near the Mosque and in the Persian Cemetery, speeches are delivered and our leaflets are distributed (on this day 12,000 were distributed). The temper of the masses rises higher and higher. Pent-up revolutionary energy breaks through to the surface. The masses decide to march in demonstration through Palace Street and Golovinsky Prospect and only then to disperse. Our committee takes advantage of the situation and immediately organises a small leading core. This core, headed by an advanced worker, takes the central position—and an improvised red flag flutters right in front of the Palace. The banner-bearer, carried shoulder high by demonstrators, delivers an emphatically political speech during which he first of all asks the comrades not to be dismayed by the absence of a Social-Democratic appeal on the flag. "No, no," answer the demonstrators, "it is inscribed in our hearts!" He then goes on to explain the significance of the Red Flag, criticises the preceding speakers from the Social-Democratic viewpoint, exposes the half-heartedness of their speeches, urges the necessity of abolishing tsarism and capitalism, and calls upon the demonstrators to fight under the Red Flag of Social-Democracy. "Long live the Red Flag!" the masses shout in response. The demonstrators proceed towards the Vanque Cathedral. On the way they halt three times to listen to the banner-bearer. The latter again calls upon the demonstrators to fight against tsarism and urges them to take a vow to rise in revolt as unanimously as they are demonstrating now. "We swear!" the masses shout in response. The demonstrators then reach the Vanque Cathedral and after a minor skirmish with Cossacks, disperse.

Such was the "demonstration of eight thousand Tiflis citizens."

That is how the citizens of Tiflis retaliated to the hypocritical policy of the tsarist government. That is how they took revenge on the despicable government for the blood of the citizens of Baku. Glory and honour to the citizens of Tiflis!

In face of the thousands of Tiflis citizens who assembled under the Red Flag and several times pronounced sentence of death on the tsarist government, the despicable flunkeys of the despicable government were compelled to retreat. They called off the pogrom.

But does that mean, citizens, that the tsarist government will not try to organise pogroms in future? Far from it! As long as it continues to exist, and the more the ground slips from under its feet, the more often will it resort to pogroms. The only way to eradicate *pogroms* is to abolish the tsarist autocracy.

You cherish your own lives and the lives of your dear ones, do you not? You love your friends and kinsmen and you want to abolish pogroms, do you not? Know then, citizens, that pogroms and the bloodshed that accompanies them will be abolished only when tsarism is abolished!

First of all you must strive to overthrow the tsarist autocracy!

You want to abolish *all* national enmity, do you not? You are striving for the complete solidarity of peoples, are you not? Know then, citizens, that all national strife will be abolished only when inequality and capitalism are abolished!

The ultimate aim of your striving must be—the triumph of socialism!

But who-will sweep the disgusting tsarist regime from the face of the earth, who will rid you of pogroms?—The proletariat, led by Social-Democracy.

And who will destroy the capitalist system, who will establish international solidarity on earth?—The proletariat, led by Social-Democracy.

The proletariat, and only the proletariat, will win freedom and peace for you.

Therefore, unite around the proletariat and rally under the flag of

Social-Democracy!

Rally Under the Red-Flag, Citizens!

Down With the Tsarist Autocracy!

Long Live the Democratic Republic!

Down With Capitalism!

Long Live Socialism!

Long Live the Red Flag!

February 15, 1905
Reproduced from the manifesto printed
at the printing plant of the Tiflis
Committee of the R.S.D.L.P.
Signed: *Tiflis Committee*

BRIEFLY ABOUT DISAGREEMENTS
IN THE PARTY[1]

"Social-Democracy is a combination of the working-class movement with socialism."

Karl Kautsky

Our "Mensheviks" are really too tiresome! I am referring to the Tiflis "Mensheviks." They heard that there are disagreements in the Party and so they began harping: whether you like it or not we shall talk about disagreements, always and everywhere; whether you like it or not we shall abuse the "Bolsheviks" right and left! And so they are hurling abuse for all they are worth, as if they are possessed. At all the crossroads, among themselves and among strangers, in short, wherever they happen to be, they howl one thing: beware of the "majority," they are strangers, infidels! Not content with the "habitual" field, they have carried the "case" into the legally published literature, thereby proving to the world once again . . . how tiresome they are.

What has the "majority" done? Why is our "minority" so "wrathful"?

---

1 **Original editor:** J. V. Stalin's pamphlet *Briefly About the Disagreements in the Party* was written at the end of April 1905 in reply to articles by N. Jordania: "Majority or Minority?" in the *Social-Democrat*, "What Is a Party?" in Mogzauri, and others. News of the appearance of this pamphlet soon reached the Bolshevik centre abroad. On July 18, 1905, N. K. Krupskaya wrote to the Caucasian Union Committee of the R.S.D.L.P. requesting that copies of the pamphlet be sent to the centre. The pamphlet was widely circulated among the Bolshevik organisations in Transcaucasia. From it the advanced workers learned of the disagreements within the Party and of the stand taken by the Bolsheviks headed by V. I. Lenin. The pamphlet was printed at the underground printing press of the Caucasian Union of the R.S.D.L.P. in Avlabar in May 1905, in the Georgian language, and in June it was printed in the Russian and Armenian languages, each in 1,500-2,000 copies.

Let us turn to history.

The "majority" and "minority" first came into being at the Second Party Congress (1903). That was the congress at which our scattered forces were to have united in one powerful party. We Party workers placed great hopes in that congress. At last!—we exclaimed joyfully— we, too, shall be united in one party, we, too, shall be able to work according to a single plan! . . . It goes without saying that we had been active before that, but our activities were scattered and unorganised. It goes without saying that we had made attempts to unite before that; it was for this purpose that we convened the First Party Congress (1898), and it even looked as if we had "united," but this unity existed in name only: the Party still remained split up into separate groups; our forces still remained scattered and had yet to be united. And so the Second Party Congress was to have mustered our scattered forces and united them in one whole. We were to have formed a united party.

Actually it turned out, however, that our hopes had been to some degree premature. The congress failed to give us a single and indivisible party; it merely laid the foundation for such a party. The congress did, however, clearly reveal to us that there are two trends within the Party: the *Iskra* trend (I mean the old *Iskra*),[2] and the trend of its opponents. Accordingly, the congress split up into two sections: into a "majority" and a "minority." The former joined the *Iskra* trend and rallied around that paper; the latter, being opponents of *Iskra*, took the opposite stand.

Thus, *Iskra* became the banner of the Party "majority," and *Iskra's* stand became the stand of the "majority."

What path did *Iskra* take? What did it advocate?

To understand this one must know the conditions under which it entered the historical field.

---

2 **Original editor**: *Iskra* (*The Spark*)—the first all-Russian illegal Marxist newspaper, founded by V. I. Lenin in 1900. The first issue of Lenin's *Iskra* appeared on December 11 (24), 1900, in Leipzig, after which it was published in Munich, London (from April 1902), and, beginning with the spring of 1903, in Geneva. Groups and committees of the R.S.D.L.P. supporting the Lenin-*Iskra* line were organised in a number of towns of Russia, including St. Petersburg and Moscow. In Transcaucasia the ideas propagated by *Iskra* were upheld by the illegal newspaper *Brdzola*, the organ of Georgian revolutionary Social-Democracy. (On the role and significance of *Iskra* see the *History of the C.P.S.U.(B.), Short Course*, Moscow 1952, pp. 55-68.)

Iskra started publication in December 1900. That was the time when a crisis began in Russian industry. The industrial boom, which was accompanied by a number of economic strikes (1896-98), gradually gave way to a crisis. The crisis grew more acute day by day and became an obstacle to economic strikes. In spite of that, the working-class movement hewed a path for itself and made progress; the individual streams merged in a single flood; the movement acquired a class aspect and gradually took the path of the political struggle. The working-class movement grew with astonishing rapidity. . . . But there was no sign of an advanced detachment, no Social-Democracy[3] which would have introduced socialist consciousness into the movement, would have combined it with socialism, and, thereby, would have lent the proletarian struggle a Social-Democratic character.

What did the "Social-Democrats" of that time (they were called "Economists") do? They burned incense to the spontaneous movement and light-heartedly reiterated: socialist consciousness is not so very necessary for the working-class movement, which can very well reach its goal without it; the main thing is the movement. The movement is everything—consciousness is a mere trifle. *A movement without socialism*—that was what they were striving for.

In that case, what is the mission of Russian Social-Democracy? Its mission is to be an obedient tool of the spontaneous movement, they asserted. It is not our business to introduce socialist consciousness into the working-class movement, it is not our business to lead this movement—that would be fruitless coercion; our duty is merely to watch the movement and take careful note of what goes on in social life—we must drag at the tail of the spontaneous movement.[4]

---

3 Social-Democracy is the advanced detachment of the proletariat. Every militant Social-Democrat, whether industrial worker or intellectual, belongs to this detachment.

4 Our Social-Democrat* has developed a passion for "criticism" (see No. 1, "Majority or Minority?") but I must observe that it does not correctly describe the "Economists" and Rabocheye Delo-ists (they scarcely differ from each other). It is not that they "ignored political questions," but that they dragged at the tail of the movement and repeated what the movement suggested to them. At one time only strikes took place, and so they preached the economic struggle. The period of demonstrations came (1901), blood was shed, disillusionment was rife, and the workers turned to terrorism in the belief that that would save them from the tyrants, and so the "Economists-Rabocheye Delo-ists" also joined the general chorus and pompously declared: The time has come to resort to terrorism, to attack the prisons, liberate our com-

In short, *Social-Democracy* was depicted as *an unnecessary burden* on the movement.

Whoever refuses to recognise Social-Democracy must also refuse to recognise the Social-Democratic Party.

That is precisely why the "Economists" so persistently reiterated that a proletarian political party could not exist in Russia. Let the liberals engage in the political struggle, it is more fitting for them to do so, said the "Economists." But what must we Social-Democrats do? We must continue to exist as separate circles, each operating isolatedly in its own corner.

Not a Party, but a circle! they said.

Thus, on the one hand, the working-class movement grew and stood in need of a guiding advanced detachment; on the other hand, "Social-Democracy," represented by the "Economists," instead of taking the lead of the movement, abnegated itself and dragged at the tail of the movement.

It was necessary to proclaim for all to hear the idea that a spontaneous working-class movement without socialism means groping in the dark, and, even if it ever does lead to the goal, who knows how long it will take, and at what cost in suffering; that, consequently, socialist consciousness is of enormous importance for the working-class movement.

It was also necessary to proclaim that it is the duty of the vehicle of this consciousness, Social-Democracy, to imbue the working-class movement with socialist consciousness; to be always at the head of the

---

rades and so forth (see "A Historic Turn," Rabocheye Delo.** As you see, this does not at all mean that they "ignored political questions." The author has borrowed his "criticism" from Martynov, but it would have been more useful had he familiarised himself with history.

* **Original editor:** *Social-Democrat*—the illegal newspaper published in the Georgian language in Tiflis by the Caucasian Mensheviks from April to November 1905. It was edited by N. Jordania. The first number appeared as "the organ of the Tiflis Committee of the R.S.D.L.P.," but in the subsequent issues it called itself "the organ of the Caucasian Social-Democratic Labour Organisations."

** **Original editor:** *Rabocheye Delo (The Workers' Cause)*—a magazine published in Geneva at irregular intervals from 1899 to 1902, by the Union of Russian Social-Democrats Abroad ("Economists").

movement and not to be a mere observer of the spontaneous working-class movement, not to drag at its tail.

It was also necessary to express the idea that it is the direct duty of Russian Social-Democracy to muster the separate advanced detachments of the proletariat, to unite them in one party, and thereby to put an end to disunity in the Party once and for all.

It was precisely these tasks that *Iskra* proceeded to formulate.

This is what it said in its programmatic article (see *Iskra*, No. 1): "Social-Democracy is a combination of the working-class movement with socialism,"[5] i.e., the movement without socialism, or socialism standing aloof from the movement, is an undesirable state of affairs which Social-Democracy must combat. But as the "Economists-*Rabocheye Delo*-ists" worshipped the spontaneous movement, and as they belittled the importance of socialism, *Iskra* stated: "Isolated from Social-Democracy, the working-class movement becomes petty and inevitably becomes bourgeois." Consequently, it is the duty of Social-Democracy "to point out to this movement its ultimate aim and its political tasks, and to guard its political and ideological independence."

What are the duties of Russian Social-Democracy?

"From this," continues *Iskra*, "automatically emerges the task which it is the mission of Russian Social-Democracy to fulfil: to imbue the masses of the proletariat with the ideas of socialism and with political consciousness and to organise a revolutionary party that will be inseverably connected with the spontaneous working-class movement,"—i.e., it must always be at the head of the movement, and its paramount duty is to unite the Social-Democratic forces of the working-class movement in one party.

That is how the editorial board of *Iskra*[6] formulated its programme.

Did *Iskra* carry out this splendid programme?

---

5 **Original editor:** See V. I. Lenin, Works, 4th Russ. ed., Vol. 4, p. 343.

6 The editorial board of Iskra then consisted of six members: Plekhanov, Axelrod, Zasulich, Martov, Starover* and Lenin.

*   Starover—the pseudonym of A. N. Potresov.

Everybody knows how devotedly it put these extremely important ideas into practice. That was clearly demonstrated to us by the Second Party Congress, at which the majority, numbering 35 votes, recognised *Iskra* as the central organ of the Party.

Is it not ridiculous, after that, to hear certain pseudo-Marxists "berate" the old *Iskra*?

This is what the Menshevik Social-Democrat writes about *Iskra*:

"It (*Iskra*) should have analysed the ideas of 'Economism,' rejected its fallacious views and accepted its correct ones, and directed it into a new channel. . . . *But that did not happen*. The fight against 'Econom ism' gave rise to another extreme: the economic struggle was belittled and treated with disdain; supreme importance was attached to the political struggle. *Politics without economy* (it ought to be: "without economics")—such is the new trend" (see *Social-Democrat*, No . 1, "Majority or Minority?").

But when, where, in what country did all this happen, highly esteemed "critic"? What did Plekhanov, Axelrod, Zasulich, Martov and Starover do? Why did they not turn *Iskra* to the "true" path? Did they not constitute the majority on the editorial board? And where have you yourself been up to now, my dear sir? Why did you not warn the Second Party Congress? It would not then have recognised *Iskra* as the central organ.

But let us leave the "critic."

The point is that *Iskra* correctly emphasised the "urgent questions of the day"; it took the path I spoke about above and devotedly carried out its programme.

Iskra's stand was still more distinctly and convincingly formulated by Lenin, in his splendid book *What Is To Be Done?*

Let us deal with this book.

The "Economists" worshipped the *spontaneous* working-class movement; but who does not know that the spontaneous movement is a movement without socialism, that it "is trade unionism,"[7] which

---

7 Lenin, What Is To Be Done?, p. 18.

refuses to see anything beyond the limits of capitalism. Who does not know that the working-class movement without socialism means marking time within the limits of capitalism, wandering around private property, and, even if this ever does lead to the social revolution, who knows how long it will take, and at what cost in suffering? Does it make no difference to the workers whether they enter the "promised land" in the near future or after a long period of time; by an easy or by a difficult road? Clearly, whoever extols the *spontaneous* movement and worships it, whether he wishes to or not, digs a chasm between socialism and the working-class movement, belittles the importance of socialist ideology and expels it from life, and, whether he wishes to or not, subordinates the workers to bourgeois ideology; for he fails to understand that "Social-Democracy is a combination of the working-class movement with socialism,"[8] that "*all* worship of the spontaneity of the working-class movement, *all* belittling of the role of 'the conscious element,' of the role of Social-Democracy, *means, quite irrespective of whether the belittler wants to or not, strengthening the influence of bourgeois ideology over the workers.*"[9]

To explain this in greater detail: In our times only two ideologies can exist: bourgeois and socialist. The difference between them is, among other things, that the former, i.e., bourgeois ideology, is much older, more widespread and more deep-rooted in life than the latter; that one encounters bourgeois views everywhere, in one's own and in other circles, whereas socialist ideology is only taking its first steps, is only just hewing a road for itself. Needless to say, as regards the spread of ideas, bourgeois ideology, i.e., trade-unionist consciousness, spreads far more easily and embraces the *spontaneous* working-class movement far more widely than socialist ideology, which is only taking its first steps. That is all the more true for the reason that, even as it is, the *spontaneous* movement—the movement without socialism—"leads to its becoming subordinated to bourgeois ideology."[10] And subordination to bourgeois ideology means ousting socialist ideology, because

8 Kautsky, The Erfurt Programme, published by the Central Committee, p. 94.

9 Lenin, What Is To Be Done?, p. 16.

10 Lenin, What Is To Be Done?, p 28.

one is the negation of the other.

We shall be asked: But surely the working class gravitates towards socialism? Yes, it gravitates towards socialism. *If it did not, the activities of Social-Democracy would be fruitless.* But it is also true that this gravitation is counteracted and hindered by another—gravitation towards bourgeois ideology.

I have just said that our social life is impregnated with bourgeois ideas and, consequently; it is much easier to spread bourgeois ideology than socialist ideology. It must not be forgotten that meanwhile the bourgeois ideologists are not asleep; they, in their own way, disguise themselves as Socialists and are tireless in their efforts to subordinate the working class to bourgeois ideology. If, under these circumstances, the Social-Democrats, too, like the "Economists," go woolgathering and drag at the tail of the spontaneous movement (and the working-class movement is spontaneous when Social-Democracy behaves that way), then it is self-evident that the spontaneous working-class movement will proceed along that beaten path and submit to bourgeois ideology until, of course, long wanderings and sufferings compel it to break with bourgeois ideology and strive for the social revolution.

It is this that is called gravitating towards bourgeois ideology.

Here is what Lenin says:

"The working class spontaneously gravitates towards socialism, but the more widespread (and continuously revived in the most diverse forms) bourgeois ideology nevertheless spontaneously imposes itself upon the working class still more."[11] This is precisely why the *spontaneous* working-class movement, while it is *spontaneous*, while it is not yet combined with socialist consciousness—becomes subordinated to bourgeois ideology and gravitates towards such subordination.[12] *If that were not the case, Social-Democratic criticism, Social-Democratic propaganda, would be superfluous, and it would be unnecessary to "combine the working-class movement with socialism."*

It is the duty of Social-Democracy to *combat* this gravitation to-

---

11 Lenin, What Is To Be Done?, p. 29.

12 Ibid., p. 28.

wards bourgeois ideology and to stimulate the other gravitation—gravitation towards socialism. Some day, of course, after long wanderings and sufferings, the spontaneous movement would come into its own, would arrive at the gates of the social revolution, without the aid of Social-Democracy, because "the working class *spontaneously* gravitates towards socialism."[13] But what is to happen in the meantime, what shall we do in the meantime? Fold our arms across our chests as the "Economists" do and leave the field to the Struves and Zubatovs? Renounce Social-Democracy and thereby help bourgeois, trade-unionist ideology to predominate? Forget Marxism and not "combine socialism with the working-class movement"?

No! Social-Democracy is the advanced detachment of the proletariat,[14] and its duty is always to be at the head of the proletariat; its duty is "to *divert* the working-class movement from this spontaneous, trade-unionist tendency to come under the wing of the bourgeoisie, and to bring it under the wing of revolutionary Social-Democracy."[15] The duty of Social-Democracy is to imbue the spontaneous working-class movement with socialist consciousness, to combine the working-class movement with socialism and thereby lend the proletarian struggle a Social-Democratic character.

It is said that in some countries the working *class* itself worked out the socialist ideology (scientific socialism) and will itself work it out in other countries too, and that, therefore, it is unnecessary to introduce socialist consciousness into the working-class movement from without. But this is a profound mistake. To be able to work out the theory of scientific socialism one must stand at the head of science, one must be armed with scientific knowledge and be able deeply to investigate the laws of historical development. But the working *class*, while it remains a working class, is unable to stand in the van of science, to advance it and investigate scientifically the laws of history; it

---

13 Lenin, *What Is To Be Done?*, p. 29.

14 K. Marx, *Manifesto*, p. 15.*

* **Original editor:** See Karl Marx and Frederick Engels, *Selected Works*, Vol. I, Moscow 1951, p. 44.

15 Lenin, *What Is To Be Done?*, p. 28.

lacks both the time and the means for that. Scientific socialism "can arise only on the basis of profound scientific knowledge. . ." — says K. Kautsky. ". . . The vehicle of science is not the proletariat, but the *bourgeois intelligentsia* (*K. Kautsky's italics*). It was in the minds of individual members of that stratum that modern socialism originated, and it was they who communicated it to the more intellectually developed proletarians. . . ."[16]

Accordingly, Lenin says: All those who worship the spontaneous working-class movement and look on with folded arms, those who continuously belittle the importance of Social-Democracy and leave the field to the Struves and Zubatovs—all imagine that this movement itself works out scientific socialism. "But that is a profound mistake."[17] Some people believe that the St. Petersburg workers who went on strike in the nineties possessed Social-Democratic consciousness, but that, too, is a mistake. There was no such consciousness among them and "there could not be. It (Social-Democratic consciousness) could be brought to them only from without. The history of all countries shows that the working class, exclusively by its own efforts, is able to develop only trade-unionist consciousness, i.e., the conviction that it is necessary to combine in unions, fight the employers and strive to compel the government to pass necessary labour legislation, etc. The theory of socialism, however, grew out of the philosophic, historical and economic theories that were elaborated by the educated representatives of the propertied classes, the intellectuals. According to their social status, the founders of modern scientific socialism, Marx and Engels, themselves belonged to the bourgeois intelligentsia."[18] That does not mean, of course, continues Lenin, "that the workers have no part in creating such an ideology. But they take part not as workers, but as socialist theoreticians, as Proudhons and Weitlings (both were working men); in other words, they take part only when, and to the extent

---

16 Lenin, *What Is To Be Done?*, p. 11, where these lines are quoted from Kautsky's well-known article in *Neue Zeit*,* 1901-01, No. 3, p. 79.

* **Original editor:** *Die Neue Zeit* (*New Times*)—a magazine issued by the German Social-Democrats, published in Stuttgart from 1883 to 1923.

17 *Ibid.*, p. 26.

18 Lenin, *What Is To Be Done?*, pp. 20-21.

that they are able, more or less, to acquire the knowledge of their age and advance that knowledge."[19]

We can picture all this to ourselves approximately as follows. There is a capitalist system. There are workers and masters. Between them a struggle is raging. So far there are no signs whatever of scientific socialism. Scientific socialism was not even thought of anywhere when the workers were already waging their struggle. . . . Yes, the workers are fighting. But they are fighting separately against their masters; they come into collision with their local authorities; here they go out on strike, there they hold meetings and demonstrations; here they demand rights from the government, there they proclaim a boycott; some talk about the political struggle, others about the economic struggle, and so forth. But that does not mean that the workers possess Social-Democratic consciousness; it does not mean that the aim of their movement is to overthrow the capitalist system, that they are as sure of the overthrow of capitalism and of the establishment of the socialist system as they are of the inevitable rising of the sun, that they regard their conquest of political power (the dictatorship of the proletariat) as an essential means for achieving the victory of socialism, etc.

Meanwhile science develops. The working-class movement gradually attracts its attention. Most scientists arrive at the opinion that the working-class movement is a revolt of troublemakers whom it would be a good thing to bring to their senses with the aid of the whip. Others believe that it is the duty of the rich to throw some crumbs to the poor, i.e., that the working-class movement is a movement of paupers whose object is to obtain alms. And out of a thousand scientists perhaps only one may prove to be a man who approaches the working-class movement scientifically, scientifically investigates the whole of social life, watches the conflict of classes, listens closely to the murmuring of the working class and, finally, proves scientifically that the capitalist system is by no means eternal, that it is just as transient as feudalism was, and that it must inevitably be superseded by its negation, the socialist system, which can be established only by the proletariat by means of a social revolution. In short, scientific socialism is elaborated.

19 *Ibid.*, p. 27.

It goes without saying that if there were no capitalism and the class struggle there would he no scientific socialism. But it is also true that these few, for example Marx and Engels, would not have worked out scientific socialism had they not possessed scientific knowledge.

What is scientific socialism *without the working-class movement?*—A compass which, if left unused, will only grow rusty and then will have to be thrown overboard.

What is the working-class movement *without socialism?*—A ship without a compass which will reach the other shore in any case, but would reach it much sooner and with less danger if it had a compass.

Combine the two and you will get a splendid vessel, which will speed straight towards the other shore and reach its haven unharmed.

Combine the working-class movement with socialism and you will get a Social-Democratic movement which will speed straight towards the "promised land."

And so, it is the duty of Social-Democracy (and not only of Social-Democratic intellectuals) to combine socialism with the working-class movement, to imbue the movement with socialist consciousness and thereby lend the spontaneous working-class movement a Social-Democratic character.

That is what Lenin says.

Some people assert that in the opinion of Lenin and the "majority," the working-class movement will perish, will fail to achieve the social revolution if it is not combined with socialist ideology. That is an invention, the invention of idle minds, which could have entered the heads only of pseudo-Marxists like An (see "What Is a Party?", *Mogzauri*[20] No. 6).

Lenin says definitely that "The working class spontaneously gravitates towards socialism,"[21] and if he does not dwell on this at great

---

20 **Original editor:** *Mogzauri (The Traveller)*—a magazine dealing with history, archeology, geography and ethnography, published in Tiflis from 1901 to November 1905. In January 1905 it became the weekly literary and political publication of the Georgian Social-Democrats, edited by F. Makharadze. It published articles by Bolshevik authors and also articles by Mensheviks.

21 Lenin, *What Is To Be Done?*, p. 29.

length, it is only because he thinks it unnecessary to prove what has already been proved. Moreover, Lenin did not set out to investigate the *spontaneous* movement; he merely wanted to show those engaged in practical Party work what they ought to do *consciously*.

Here is what Lenin says in another passage in his controversy with Martov:

"'Our Party is the conscious exponent of an unconscious process.' Exactly. And for this very reason it is wrong to want 'every striker' to have the right to call himself a Party member, for if 'every strike' were not only a spontaneous expression of a powerful *class instinct and of the class struggle, which is inevitably leading to the social revolution, but a conscious expression* of that process . . . then our Party . . . would at once put an end to the entire bourgeois society."[22]

As you see, in Lenin's opinion, even the class struggle and the class conflicts which cannot be called Social-Democratic, nevertheless inevitably lead the working class to the social revolution.

If you are interested to hear the opinion of other representatives of the "majority," here is what one of them, Comrade Gorin, said at the Second Party Congress:

"What would the situation be if the proletariat were left to itself? It would be similar to what it was on theeve of the bourgeois revolution. The bourgeois revolutionaries had no scientific ideology. The bourgeois system came into being nevertheless. Even without ideologists the proletariat would, of course, in the long run, work towards the social revolution, but it would do so instinctively. . . . Instinctively the proletariat would practise socialism, but it would lack socialist theory. Only, the process would be slow and more painful."[23]

Further explanation is superfluous.

Thus, the *spontaneous* working-class movement, the working-class movement *without socialism*, inevitably becomes petty and assumes a trade-unionist character—it submits to bourgeois ideology. Can we draw the conclusion from this that socialism is everything and the

22 Lenin, *One Step Forward, Two Steps Back*, p. 53.

23 *Minutes of the Second Party Congress*, p. 129.

working-class movement nothing? Of course not! Only idealists say that. Some day, in the far distant future, economic development will inevitably bring the working class to the social revolution, and, consequently, compel it to break off all connection with bourgeois ideology. The only point is that this path is a very long and painful one.

On the other hand, socialism *without the working-class movement*, no matter on what scientific basis it may have arisen, nevertheless remains an empty phrase and loses its significance. Can we draw the conclusion from this that the movement is everything and socialism—nothing? Of course not! Only pseudo-Marxists, who attach no importance to consciousness because it is engendered by social life itself, argue that way. Socialism can be combined with the working-class movement and thereby be transformed from an empty phrase into a sharp weapon.

The conclusion?

The conclusion is that the working-class movement must be combined with socialism; practical activities and theoretical thought must merge into one and thereby lend the spontaneous working-class movement a Social-Democratic character, for "Social-Democracy is a combination of the working-class movement with socialism."[24] Then, socialism, combined with the working-class movement, will, in the hands of the workers, be transformed from an empty phrase into a tremendous force. Then, the spontaneous movement, transformed into a Social-Democratic movement, will march rapidly along the true road to the socialist system.

What, then, is the mission of Russian Social-Democracy? What must we do?

Our duty, the duty of Social-Democracy, is to deflect the spontaneous working-class movement from the path of narrow trade unionism to the Social-Democratic path. Our duty is to introduce socialist consciousness[25] into this movement and unite the advanced forces of the working class in one centralised party. Our task is always to be at the head of the movement and combat tirelessly all those—whether

---

24 *The Erfurt Programme*, published by the Central Committee, p. 94

25 ...which Marx and Engels elaborated.

they be foes or "friends"—who hinder the accomplishment of this task.

Such, in general, is the position of the "majority."

Our "minority" dislikes the position taken by the "majority"; it is "un-Marxist," it says; it "fundamentally contradicts" Marxism! But is that so, most highly esteemed gentlemen? Where, when, on what planet? Read our articles, they say, and you will be convinced that we are right. Very well, let us read them.

We have before us an article entitled "What Is a Party?" (see *Mogzauri*, No. 6). Of what does the "critic" An accuse the Party "majority"? "It (the "majority") . . . proclaims itself the head of the Party . . . and demands submission from others . . . and to justify its conduct it often even invents new theories, such as, for example, that the working people cannot by their own efforts *assimilate* (*my italics*) 'lofty ideals,'etc."[26]

The question now is: Does the "majority" advance, or has it ever advanced, such "theories"? Never! Nowhere! On the contrary, Comrade Lenin, the ideological representative of the "majority," very definitely says that the working class very easily *assimilates* "lofty ideals," that it very easily *assimilates* socialism. Listen:

"It is often said: the working class *spontaneously* gravitates towards socialism. This is perfectly true in the sense that socialist theory defines the causes of the misery of the working class more profoundly and more correctly than any other theory, and for that reason *the workers are able to assimilate it so easily*."[27]

As you see, in the opinion of the "majority," the workers easily assimilate the "lofty ideals" which are called socialism.

So what is An getting at? Where did he dig up his queer "find"? The point is, reader, that "critic" An had something entirely different in mind. He had in mind that passage in *What Is To Be Done?* where Lenin speaks of the *elaboration* of the theory of socialism, where he says that the working class *cannot elaborate* scientific socialism by its own

---

26 *Mogzauri*, No. 6, p. 71.

27 Lenin, What Is To Be Done?, p. 29.

efforts.[28] But how is that?—you will ask. To *elaborate* the theory of socialism is one thing —to *assimilate* it is another. Why did An forget those words of Lenin's in which he so clearly speaks of the *assimilation* of "lofty ideals"? You are right, reader, but what can An do since he is so anxious to be a "critic"? Just think what a heroic deed he is performing: he invents a "theory" of his own, ascribes it to his opponent, and then bombards the fruit of his own imagination! That is criticism, if you like! At all events it is beyond doubt that An "could not by his own efforts assimilate" Lenin's book *What Is To Be Done?*

Let us now open the so-called *Social-Democrat*. What does the author of the article "Majority or Minority?" (see *Social-Democrat*, No. 1) say?

Plucking up courage, he vociferously attacks Lenin for expressing the opinion that the "natural (it ought to be "spontaneous") development of the working-class movement leads not to socialism, but to bourgeois ideology."[29] The author evidently fails to understand that the *spontaneous* working-class movement is a movement without socialism (let the author prove that this is not so), and that *such* a movement inevitably submits to bourgeois trade-unionist ideology, gravitates towards it; for in our times there can be only two ideologies, socialist and bourgeois, and where the former is absent the latter inevitably appears and occupies its place (prove the opposite!). Yes, this is exactly what Lenin says. But at the same time he does not forget about another gravitation that is characteristic of the working-class movement— gravitation towards socialism, which is only temporarily eclipsed by the gravitation towards bourgeois ideology. Lenin says definitely that "the working class spontaneously gravitates towards socialism,"[30] and he rightly observes that it is the duty of Social-Democracy to accelerate the victory of *this* gravitation by, among other things, combating the "Economists." Why, then, esteemed "critic," did you not quote these words of Lenin in your article? Were they not uttered by the very same Lenin? Because it was not to your advantage. Isn't that so?

---

28 Lenin, *What Is To Be Done?*, pp. 20-21.

29 *Social-Democrat*, No. 1, p. 14.

30 Lenin, *What Is To Be Done?*, p. 29.

"In Lenin's opinion . . . the worker, owing to his *position* (*my italics*), is a bourgeois rather than a Socialist . . ."[31]—continues the author. Well! I didn't expect anything so stupid even from such an author! Does Lenin talk about the worker's *position*? Does he say that owing to his *position* the worker is a bourgeois? Who but an idiot can say that owing to his *position* the worker is a bourgeois — the worker who owns no means of production and lives by selling his labour power? No! Lenin says something entirely different. The point is that owing to my *position* I can be a proletarian and not a bourgeois, but at the same time I can be unconscious of my *position* and, as a consequence, submit to bourgeois ideology. This is exactly how the matter stands in this case with the working class. And it means something entirely different.

In general, the author is fond of hurling empty phrases about—he shoots them off without thinking! Thus, for example, the author obstinately reiterates that "Leninism fundamentally contradicts Marxism"[32]; he reiterates this and fails to see where this "idea" leads him. Let us believe for a moment his statement that Leninism does "fundamentally contradict Marxism." But what follows? What comes of this? The following. "Leninism carried with it" *Iskra* (the old *Iskra*)—this the author does not deny—consequently *Iskra*, too, "fundamentally contradicts Marxism." The Second Party Congress—the majority, numbering 35 votes—recognised *Iskra* as the central organ of the Party and highly praised its services[33]; consequently, that congress, its programme and its tactics, also "fundamentally contradict Marxism." . . . Funny, isn't it, reader?

The author, nevertheless, continues: "In Lenin's opinion the spontaneous working-class movement is moving towards combination with the bourgeoisie. . . ." Yes, indeed, the author is undoubtedly moving towards combination with idiocy, and it would be a good thing if he digressed from that path.

But let us leave the "critic." Let us turn to Marxism.

---

31 Social-Democrat , No. 1, p. 14.

32 Social-Democrat , No. 1, p. 15.

33 See *Minutes of the Second Party Congress*, p. 141. *Ibid.*, Resolution, where *Iskra* is described as a true advocate of the principles of Social-Democratism.

Our esteemed "critic" obstinately reiterates that the stand taken by the "majority" and by its representative, Lenin, fundamentally contradicts Marxism, because, he says, Kautsky, Marx and Engels say the opposite of what Lenin advocates! Is that the case? Let us see!

"K. Kautsky," the author informs us, "writes in his *Erfurt Programme*: 'The interests of the proletariat and the bourgeoisie are so antagonistic that the strivings of these two classes cannot be combined for any more or less prolonged period. In every country where the capitalist mode of production prevails the participation of the working class in politics *sooner or later* leads to the working class separating from the bourgeois parties and forming an independent *workers' party*.'"

But what follows from this? Only that the interests of the bourgeoisie and the proletariat are antagonistic, that "sooner or later" the proletariat separates from the bourgeoisie to form an independent *workers' party* (remember: a *workers' party*, but not a *Social-Democratic workers' party*). The author assumes that here Kautsky disagrees with Lenin. But Lenin says that *sooner or later* the proletariat will not only separate from the bourgeoisie, but will bring about the social revolution, i.e., will overthrow the bourgeoisie.[34] The task of Social-Democracy—he adds—is to try to make this come about as *quickly* as possible, and to come about *consciously*. Yes, *consciously* and not spontaneously, for it is about this consciousness that Lenin writes.

". . . Where things have reached the stage of the formation of an independent workers' party," continues the "critic," citing Kautsky's book, "the party must sooner or later, of natural necessity, *assimilate* socialist tendencies if it was not inspired by them from the very outset; it must in the long run become a *socialist* workers' party, i.e., *Social-Democracy*."[35]

What does that mean? Only that the workers' party will *assimilate* socialist trends. But does Lenin deny this? Not in the least! Lenin plainly says that not only the workers' party, but the entire working

---

34 See Lenin, *One Step Forward, Two Steps Back*, p. 53.

35 *Social-Democrat*, No. 1, p. 15.

class assimilates socialism.[36] What, then, is the nonsense we hear from *Social-Democrat* and its prevaricating hero? What is the use of all this balderdash? As the saying goes: He heard the sound of a bell, but where it came from he could not tell. That's exactly what happened to our muddle-headed author.

As you see, Kautsky does not differ one iota from Lenin on that point. But all this reveals the author's thoughtlessness with exceptional clarity.

Does Kautsky say anything in support of the stand taken by the "majority"? Here is what he writes in one of his splendid articles, in which he analyses the draft programme of Austrian Social-Democracy:

"Many of our revisionist critics (the followers of Bernstein) believe that Marx asserted that economic development and the class struggle create not only the conditions for socialist production, but also, and directly, engender the *consciousness* (*K. Kautsky's italics*) of its necessity. And these critics at once object that Britain, the country most highly developed capi-talistically, is more remote than any other from this consciousness. Judging from the (Austrian) draft, one might assume that this . . . view . . . was shared by the committee that drafted the Austrian programme. In the draft programme it is stated: 'The more capitalist development increases the numbers of the proletariat, the more the proletariat is compelled and becomes fit to fight against capitalism. The proletariat *becomes conscious*' of the possibility of and of the necessity for socialism. In this connection socialist consciousness appears to be a necessary and direct result of the proletarian class struggle. But that is absolutely *untrue*. . . . Modern socialist consciousness can arise *only on the basis of profound scientific knowledge.* . . . The vehicle of science is not the proletariat, but the *bourgeois intelligentsia* (*K. Kautsky's italics*) . It was in the minds of individual members of that stratum that modern socialism originated, and it was they who communicated it (scientific socialism) to the more intellectually developed proletarians who, in their turn, introduce it into the proletarian class struggle. . . . Thus, socialist consciousness is something *introduced* into

36 Lenin, *What Is To Be Done?*, p. 19.

the proletarian class struggle *from without* and not something that *arose within it* spontaneously. Accordingly, the old Hainfeld programme[37] *quite rightly* stated that the task of Social-Democracy is to *imbue the proletariat with the consciousness* of its position and the consciousness of its task . . ."[38]

Do you not recall, reader, analogous thoughts expressed by Lenin on this question; do you not recall the well-known stand taken by the "majority"? Why did the "Tiflis Committee" and its *Social-Democrat* conceal the truth? Why, in speaking of Kautsky, did our esteemed "critic" fail to quote these words of Kautsky's in his article? Whom are these most highly esteemed gentlemen trying to deceive? Why are they so "contemptuous" towards their readers? Is it not because . . . they fear the truth, hide from the truth, and think that the truth also can be hidden? They behave like the bird which hides its head in the sand and imagines that nobody can see it! But they delude themselves as that bird does.

If socialist consciousness has been worked out on a scientific basis, and if this consciousness is introduced into the working-class movement from without by the efforts of Social-Democracy[39]—it is clear that all this happens because the working class, so long as it remains a working class, cannot lead science and work out scientific socialism by its own efforts: it lacks both the time and the means for this.

Here is what K. Kautsky says in his *Erfurt Programme*:

". . . The proletarian can at best assimilate part of the knowledge worked out by bourgeois learning and adapt it to his objects and needs, but so long as he remains a proletarian he lacks the leisure and means independently to carry science beyond the limits reached by bourgeois

---

37 **Original editor:** The Hainfeld programme was adopted at the inaugural congress of the Austrian Social-Democratic Party held in Hainfeld in 1888. In its statement of principles the programme contained a number of points that correctly explained the course of social development and the tasks of the proletariat and of the proletarian party. Later, at the Vienna Congress held in 1901, the Hainfeld programme was dropped and another, based on revisionist views, was adopted in its place.

38 *Neue Zeit*, 1901-01, XX, No. 3, p. 19. Lenin quotes this passage from Kautsky's splendid article in *What Is To Be Done?*, p. 11.

39 And not only by Social-Democratic intellectuals.

thinkers. Hence, spontaneous workers' socialism must bear all the essential marks of utopianism"[40] (utopianism is a false, unscientific theory).

Utopian socialism of this kind often assumes an anarchistic character, continues Kautsky, but ". . . As is well known, wherever the anarchist movement (meaning by that proletarian utopianism—*K. Kautsky*) really permeated the masses and became a class movement it always, sooner or later, despite its seeming radicalism, ended by being transformed into *a purely trade-unionist movement* of the narrowest kind."[41]

In other words, if the working-class movement is not combined with scientific socialism it inevitably becomes petty, assumes a "narrow trade-unionist" character and, consequently, submits to trade-unionist ideology.

"But that means belittling the workers and extolling the intelligentsia!"—howl our "critic" and his *Social-Democrat*. . . . Poor "critic"! Miserable *Social-Democrat!* They take the proletariat for a capricious young lady who must not be told the truth, who must always be paid compliments so that she will not run away! No, most highly esteemed gentlemen! We believe that the proletariat will display more staunchness than you think. We believe that it will not fear the truth! As for you. . . . What can one say to you? Even now you have shown that you fear the truth and, in your article, did not tell your readers what Kautsky's real views are. . . .

Thus, scientific socialism *without the working-class movement* is an empty phrase that can always be easily thrown to the winds.

On the other hand, the working-class movement *without socialism* is aimless trade-unionist wandering, which some time or other will, of course, lead to the social revolution, but at the cost of long pain and suffering.

The conclusion?

"The working-class movement must combine with socialism": "Social-Democracy is a combination of the working-class movement

---

40 *The Erfurt Programme*, published by the Central Committee, p. 93.

41 *Ibid.*, p. 94.

with socialism."[42]

That is what Kautsky, the Marxist theoretician, says.

We have seen that *Iskra* (the old *Iskra*) and the "majority" say the same.

We have seen that Comrade Lenin takes the same stand.

Thus, the "majority" takes a firm Marxist stand.

Clearly, "contempt for the workers," "extolling the intelligentsia," the "un-Marxist stand of the majority," and similar gems which the Menshevik "critics" scatter so profusely, are nothing more than catchwords, figments of the imagination of the Tiflis "Men-sheviks."

On the other hand, we shall see that actually it is the Tiflis "minority," the "Tiflis Committee" and its *Social-Democrat* that "fundamentally contradict Marxism." But of this anon. Meanwhile, we draw attention to the following:

In support of his utterances, the author of the article "Majority or Minority?" quotes the words of Marx (?): "The theoretician of any given class comes theoretically to the conclusion *to which the class itself has already arrived practically.*"[43]

One of two things. Either the author does not know the Georgian language, or else there is a printer's error. No literate person would say "*to which* it has already *arrived.*" It would be correct to say: "*at which* it has already *arrived,*" or "*to which* it is already *coming.*" If the author had in mind the latter (*to which* it is already *coming*), then I must observe that he is misquoting Marx; Marx did not say anything of the kind. If the author had the first formula in mind, then the sentence he quoted should have run as follows: "The theoretician of any given class arrives theoretically at the conclusion *at which* the class itself *has already arrived practically.*" In other words, since Marx and Engels arrived theoretically at the conclusion that the collapse of capitalism and the building of socialism are inevitable—it implies that the proletariat *has already* rejected capitalism *practically*, has already crushed capitalism and has built

---

42 *The Erfurt Programme*, p. 94.

43 *Social-Democrat*, No 1, p. 15.

up the socialist way of life in its place!

Poor Marx! Who knows how many more absurdities our pseudo-Marxists will ascribe to him?

But did Marx really say that? Here is what he actually said: The theoreticians who represent the petty bourgeoisie "*are . . . driven, theoretically, to the same problems and solutions to which* material interest and social position *drive the latter practically.* This is, in general, the relationship between the political and literary representatives of a class and the class they represent."[44]

As you see, Marx does not say "*already arrived to.*" These "philosophical" words were invented by our esteemed "critic."

Consequently Marx's own words possess an entirely different meaning.

What idea does Marx propound in the above-quoted proposition? Only that the theoretician of a given class *cannot create* an ideal, the elements of which do not exist in life; that he can *only indicate* the elements of the future and on that basis theoretically *create* an ideal which the given class reaches practically. The difference is that the theoretician runs ahead of the class and indicates the embryo of the future before the class does. That is what is meant by "arriving at something theoretically."

Here is what Marx and Engels say in their *Manifesto*:

"The Communists (i.e., Social-Democrats), therefore, are on the one hand, practically, the most advanced and resolute section of the working-class parties of every country, that section which *pushes forward* all others; on the other hand, theoretically, they have over the great mass of the proletariat the advantage of *clearly understanding* the line of march, the conditions, and the ultimate *general* results of the proletarian movement."

Yes, the ideologists "*push forward,*" they see much farther than the

---

44 *If The Eighteenth Brumaire** is not available, see *Minutes of the Second Party Congress*, p. 111, where these words of Marx are quoted.

* **Original editor:** See Karl Marx and Frederick Engels, *Selected Works*, Vol. I, Moscow 1951, p. 250.

"great mass of the proletariat," and this is the whole point. The ideologists push forward, and it is precisely for this reason that the idea, socialist consciousness, is of such great importance for the movement.

Is that why you attack the "majority," esteemed "critic"? If it is, then say good-bye to Marxism, and know that the "majority" is proud of its Marxist stand.

The situation of the "majority" in this case in many ways recalls that of Engels in the nineties.

The idea is the source of social life, asserted the idealists. In their opinion, social consciousness is the foundation upon which the life of society is built. That is why they were called idealists.

It had to be proved that ideas do not drop from the skies, but are engendered by life itself.

Marx and Engels entered the historical arena and magnificently accomplished this task. They proved that social life is the source of ideas and, therefore, that the life of society is the foundation on which social consciousness is built. Thereby, they dug the grave of idealism and cleared the road for materialism.

Certain semi-Marxists interpreted this as meaning that consciousness, ideas, are of very little importance in life.

The great importance of ideas had to be proved.

And so Engels came forward and, in his letters (1891-94), emphasised that while it is true that ideas do not drop from the skies but are engendered by life itself, yet once born, ideas acquire great importance, for they unite men, organise them, and put their impress upon the social life which has engendered them—ideas are of great importance in historical progress.

"This is not Marxism but the betrayal of Marxism," shouted Bernstein and his ilk. The Marxists only laughed.

There were semi-Marxists in Russia—the "Economists." They asserted that, since ideas are engendered by social life, socialist consciousness is of little importance for the working-class movement.

It had to be proved that socialist consciousness is of great importance for the working-class movement, that without it the movement would be aimless trade-unionist wandering, and nobody could say when the proletariat would rid itself of it and reach the social revolution.

And *Iskra* appeared and magnificently accomplished this task. The book *What Is To Be Done?* appeared, in which Lenin emphasised the great importance of socialist consciousness. The Party "majority" was formed and firmly took this path.

But here the little Bernsteins come out and begin to shout: This "fundamentally contradicts Marxism"!

But do you, little "Economists," know what Marxism is?

*   *   *

Surprising!—the reader will say. What's the matter?—he will ask. Why did Plekhanov write his article criticising Lenin (see the new *Iskra*, Nos. 10, 11)? What is he censuring the "majority" for? Are not the pseudo-Marxists of Tiflis and their *Social-Democrat* repeating the ideas expressed by Plekhanov? Yes, they are repeating them, but in such a clumsy way that it becomes disgusting. Yes, Plekhanov did criticise. But do you know what the point is? Plekhanov does not disagree with the "majority" and with Lenin. And not only Plekhanov. Neither Martov, nor Zasulich, nor Axelrod disagree with them. Actually, on the question we have been discussing, the leaders of the "minority" do not disagree with the old *Iskra*. And the old *Iskra* is the banner of the "majority." Don't be surprised! Here are the facts:

We are familiar with the old *Iskra's* programmatic article (see above). We know that that article fully expresses the stand taken by the "majority." Whose article is it? The article of the editorial board of *Iskra* of that time. Who were the members of that editorial board? Lenin, Plekhanov, Axelrod, Martov, Zasulich and Starover. Of these only Lenin now belongs to the "majority"; the other five are the leaders of the "minority"; but the fact remains that they were the editors of *Iskra's* programmatic article, consequently, they ought not to repudiate their own words; presumably they believed what they wrote.

But we shall leave *Iskra* if you like.

Here is what Martov writes:

"Thus, the idea of socialism first arose not among the masses of the workers, but in the studies of scholars from the ranks of the bourgeoisie."[45]

And here is what Vera Zasulich writes:

"Even the idea of the class solidarity of the entire proletariat . . . is not so simple that it could arise independently in the mind of every worker. . . . And socialism . . . most certainly does not spring up in the minds of the workers 'automatically.' . . . The ground for the theory of socialism was prepared by the entire development of both life and knowledge . . . and created by the mind of a genius who was armed with that knowledge. Similarly, the dissemination of the ideas of socialism among the workers was initiated, almost over the entire continent of Europe, by Socialists who had received their training in educational establishments for the upper classes."[46]

Let us now hear Plekhanov, who so pompously and solemnly criticises Lenin in the new *Iskra* (Nos. 10, 11). The scene is the Second Party Congress. Plekhanov is arguing against Martynov and defending Lenin. He censures Martynov, who had seized on a single sentence of Lenin's and had overlooked the book *What Is To Be Done?* as a whole, and goes on to say:

"Comrade Martynov's trick reminds me of a censor who said: 'Permit me to tear a sentence from the Lord's Prayer from its context and I will prove to you that its author deserves to be hanged.' But all the reproaches hurled at this unfortunate sentence (Lenin's) not only by Comrade Martynov but also by many, many others, are based on a misunderstanding. Comrade Martynov quotes the words of Engels:

---

45 Martov, *The Red Flag,* p. 3.

46 *Zarya,** No. 4, pp. 79-80.

* *Zarya (The Dawn)*—a Russian Social-Democratic theoretical journal founded by V. I. Lenin and published in Stuttgart. It was a contemporary of *Iskra* and had the same editors. It existed from April 1901 to August 1902.

'Modern socialism is the theoretical expression of the modern work-ing-class movement.' Comrade Lenin also agrees with Engels. . . . But Engels's words are a general proposition. The question is, who first formulates this theoretical expression? Lenin did not write a treatise on the philosophy of history but a polemical article against the 'Econ-omists,' who said: we must wait and see what the working class arrives at by its own efforts without the aid of the 'revolutionary bacillus' (i.e., without Social-Democracy). The latter was prohibited from telling the workers anything, precisely because it is a 'revolutionary bacillus,' i.e., because it possesses theoretical consciousness. But if you eliminate the 'bacillus,' all that remains is the unconscious mass, into which con-sciousness must be introduced from outside. Had you wanted to be fair to Lenin, and had you carefully read his whole book, you would have seen that that is precisely what he says."[47]

That is what Plekhanov said at the Second Party Congress.

And now, several months later, the same Plekhanov, instigated by the same Martov, Axelrod, Zasulich, Starover and others, speaks again, and seizing on the very same sentence of Lenin's that he *defended* at the congress, says: Lenin and the "majority" are not Marxists. He knows that even if a sentence from the Lord's Prayer is torn from its context and interpreted separately, the author of the Prayer might find himself on the gallows for heresy. He knows that this would be unfair, that an unbiassed critic would not do such a thing; nevertheless, he tears this sentence from Lenin's book; nevertheless he acts unfairly, and public-ly besmirches himself. And Martov, Zasulich, Axelrod and Starover pander to him and publish his article under their editorship in the new *Iskra* (Nos. 70, 71), and thereby disgrace themselves once again.

Why did they exhibit such spinelessness? Why did these leaders of the "minority" besmirch themselves? Why did they repudiate the pro-grammatic article in *Iskra* to which they themselves had subscribed? Why did they repudiate their own words? Has such falsity ever before been heard of in the Social-Democratic Party?

What happened during the few months that elapsed between the Second Congress and the appearance of Plekhanov's article?

---

47 *Minutes of the Second Party Congress*, p. 123.

What happened was this: Of the six editors, the Second Congress elected only three to be editors of *Iskra*: Plekhanov, Lenin and Martov. As for Axelrod, Starover and Zasulich—the congress appointed them to other posts. It goes without saying that the congress had a right to do this, and it was the duty of everyone to submit to it; the congress expresses the will of the Party, it is the supreme organ of the Party, and whoever acts contrary to its decisions tramples upon the will of the Party.

But these obstinate editors did not submit to the will of the Party, to Party discipline (Party discipline is the same as the will of the Party). It would appear that Party discipline was invented only for simple Party workers like us! They were angry with the congress for not electing them as editors; they stepped to the side, took Martov with them, and formed an opposition. They proclaimed a boycott against the Party, refused to carry on any Party activities and began to threaten the Party. Elect us, they said, to the editorial board, to the Central Committee and to the Party Council, otherwise we shall cause a split. And a split ensued. Thus they trampled upon the will of the Party once again.

Here are the demands of the striker-editors:

"The old editorial board of *Iskra* to be restored (i.e., give us *three seats* on the editorial board).

"A definite number of members of the opposition (i.e., of the "minority") to be installed in the Central Committee.

"*Two seats* in the Party Council to be allocated to members of the opposition, etc. . . .

"We present these *terms* as the only ones that will *enable* the Party to avoid a conflict which will threaten its very existence" (i.e., satisfy our demands, otherwise we shall cause a big split in the Party).[48]

What did the Party say to them in reply?

The Party's representative, the Central Committee, and other comrades said to them: We cannot go against the decisions of the Party congress; elections are a matter for the congress; nevertheless, we shall endeavour to restore peace and harmony, although, to tell the truth, it

---

48 *Commentary on the Minutes of the League*, p. 26.

is disgraceful to fight *for seats*; you want to split the Party *for the sake of seats*, etc.

The striker-editors took offence; they were embarrassed—indeed, it did look as though they had started the fight for the sake of seats; they pulled Plekhanov over to their side[49] and launched their heroic cause. They were obliged to seek some *"stronger" "disagreement"* between the "majority" and "minority" in order to show that they were not fighting for the sake of seats. They searched and searched until they found a passage in Lenin's book which, if torn from the context and interpreted separately, could indeed be cavilled at. A happy idea—thought the leaders of the "minority"—Lenin is the leader of the "majority," let us discredit Lenin and thereby swing the Party to our side. And so Plekhanov began to trumpet to the world that "Lenin and his followers are not Marxists." True, only yesterday they defended the very idea in Lenin's book which they are attacking today, but that cannot be helped; an opportunist is called an opportunist precisely because he has no respect for principle.

---

49 Perhaps the reader will ask how it was possible for Plekhanov to go over to the "minority," that same Plekhanov who had been an ardent supporter of the "majority." The fact is that disagreement arose between him and Lenin. When the "minority" flew into a rage and proclaimed the boycott, Plekhanov took the stand that it was necessary to yield to them entirely. Lenin did not agree with him. Plekhanov gradually began to 'incline towards the "minority." Disagreements between the two grew until they reached such a pitch that one fine day Plekhanov became an opponent of Lenin and the "majority." Here is what Lenin writes about this :

". . . Several days later I, with a member of the Council, did indeed go and see Plekhanov and our conversation with Plekhanov took the following course:

"'You know,' said Plekhanov, 'some wives (i.e., the "minority") are such shrews that you have to yield to them to avoid hysterics and a big public scandal.'

"'Perhaps,' I answered, 'but we must yield in such a way as to remain strong enough to prevent a still bigger "scandal"'" (see *Commentary on the Minutes of the League*, p. 31, where Lenin's letter is quoted).*

Lenin and Plekhanov failed to reach agreement. From that moment Plekhanov began moving over to the "minority."

We have learned from reliable sources that Plekhanov is now deserting the "minority" and has already founded his own organ, *Dnevnik Sotsial-Demokrata.***

* **Original editor:** See V. I. Lenin, *Works*, 4th Russ. ed., Vol. 7, p. 177.

** **Original editor:** *Dnevnik Sotsial-Demokrata (The Social-Democrat's Diary)*—a magazine published in Geneva at irregular intervals by G. V. Plekhanov from March 1905 to April 1912. Sixteen issues appeared. One more issue appeared in 1916.

That is why they besmirch themselves; that is the cause of their falsity.

But that is not all.

Some time passed. They saw that nobody was paying attention to their agitation against the "majority" and Lenin, apart from a few naive persons. They saw that their "affairs" were in a bad way and decided to change their colours again. On March 10, 1905, the same Plekhanov, and the same Martov and Axelrod, in the name of the Party Council, passed a resolution in which, among other things, they said:

"Comrades! (addressing themselves to the "majority"). . . . Both sides (i.e., the "majority" and the "minority") have repeatedly expressed the conviction that the existing disagreements on tactics and organisation are not of such a character as to render impossible activities within a single Party organisation"[50]; therefore, they said, let us convene a comrades' court (consisting of Bebel and others) to settle our slight disagreement.

In short, the disagreements in the Party are merely a squabble, which a comrades' court will investigate, but we are a united whole.

But how can that be? We "non-Marxists" are invited into the Party organisations, we are a united whole, and so on and so forth. . . . What does it mean? Why, you leaders of the "minority" are betraying the Party! Can "non-Marxists" be put at the head of the Party? Is there room for "non-Marxists" in the ranks of the Social-Democratic Party? Or, perhaps, you, too, have betrayed the cause of Marxism and have, therefore, changed front?

But it would be naive to expect a reply. The point is that these wonderful leaders have several "principles" in their pockets, and whenever they want a particular one they take it out. As the saying goes: They have a different opinion for every day in the week! . . .

Such are the leaders of the so-called "minority."

It is easy to picture to oneself what the tail of this leadership— the so-called Tiflis "minority"—is like. . . . The trouble also is that at times the tail pays no heed to the head and refuses to obey. For ex-

---

50 *Iskra*, No. 91, p. 3.

ample, while the leaders of the "minority" consider that conciliation is possible and call for harmony among the Party workers, the Tiflis "minority" and its *Social-Democrat* continue to rave and shout: between the "majority" and "minority" there is "a life-and-death struggle"[51]; we must exterminate each other! They are all at sixes and sevens.

The "minority" complain that we call them opportunist (unprincipled). But what else can we call them if they repudiate their own words, if they swing from side to side, if they are eternally wavering and hesitating? Can a genuine Social-Democrat change his opinions every now and again? The "minority" change theirs more often than one changes pocket handkerchiefs.

Our pseudo-Marxists obstinately reiterate that the "minority" is truly proletarian in character. Is that so? Let us see.

Kautsky says that "it is easier for the proletarian to become imbued with Party principles, he inclines towards a principled policy that is independent of the mood of the moment and of personal or local interests."[52]

But what about the "minority"? Is it inclined towards a policy that is independent of the mood of the moment, etc.? On the contrary: it is always hesitating, eternally wavering; it detests a firm principled policy, it prefers unprincipledness; it follows the mood of the moment. We are already familiar with the facts.

Kautsky says that the proletarian likes Party discipline: "The proletarian is a nonentity so long as he remains an isolated individual. His strength, his progress, his hopes and expectations are entirely derived from *organisation*. . . . " That is why he is not distracted by personal advantage or personal glory; he "performs his duty in any post he is assigned to with a voluntary discipline which pervades all his feelings and thoughts."[53]

But what about the "minority"? Is it, too, imbued with a sense of

---

51 See *Social-Democrat*, No. 1.

52 *The Erfurt Programme*, published by the Central Committee, p. 88.

53 See Lenin, *One Step Forward, Two Steps Back*, p. 93, where these words of Kautsky's are quoted.

discipline? On the contrary, it despises Party discipline and ridicules it.[54] The first to set an example in violating Party discipline were the leaders of the "minority." Recall Axelrod, Zasulich, Starover, Martov and others, who refused to submit to the decision of the Second Congress.

"Quite different is the case of the intellectual," continues Kautsky. He finds it extremely difficult to submit to Party discipline and does so by compulsion, not of his own free will. "He recognises the need of discipline only for the mass, not for the chosen few. And of course, he counts himself among these few. . . . An ideal example of an intellectual who had become thoroughly imbued with the sentiments of the proletariat, and who . . . worked in any post he was assigned to, subordinated himself whole-heartedly to our great cause, and despised the spineless whining . . . which the intellectual . . . is all too prone to indulge in when he happens to be in the minority—an ideal example of such an intellectual . . . was Liebknecht. We may also mention Marx, who never forced himself to the forefront and whose Party discipline in the International, where he often found himself in the minority, was exemplary."[55]

But what about the "minority"? Does it display anything of the "sentiments of the proletariat"? Is its conduct anything like that of Liebknecht and Marx? On the contrary, we have seen that the leaders of the "minority" have not subordinated their "ego" to our sacred cause; we have seen that it was these leaders who indulged in "spineless whining when they found themselves in the minority" at the Second Congress; we have seen that it was they who, after the congress, wailed for "front seats," and that it was they who started a Party split for the sake of these seats. . . .

Is this your "proletarian character," esteemed Mensheviks?

Then why are the workers on our side in some towns? the Mensheviks ask us.

Yes, it is true, in some towns the workers are on the side of the

54 See *Minutes of the League.*

55 See Lenin, *One Step Forward, Two Steps Back,* p. 93, where these lines of Kautsky's are quoted.

"minority," but that proves nothing. Workers even follow the revision-ists (the opportunists in Germany) in some towns, but that does not prove that their stand is a proletarian one; it does not prove that they are not opportunists. One day a crow found a rose, but that did not prove that a crow is a nightingale. It is not for nothing that the saying goes:

When a crow picks up a rose
"I'm a nightingale," it crows.

* * *

It is now clear *on what grounds* the disagreements in the Party arose. As is evident, two trends have appeared in our Party: the trend of *proletarian firmness*, and the trend of *intellectual wavering*. And this intellectual wavering is expressed by the present "minority." The Tiflis "Committee" and its *Social-Democrat* are the obedient slaves of this "minority"!

That is the whole point.

True, our pseudo-Marxists often shout that they are opposed to the "mentality of the intellectual," and they accuse the "majority" of "intellectual wavering"; but this reminds us of the case of the thief who stole some money and began to shout: "Stop thief!"

Moreover, it is well known that the tongue ever turns to the aching tooth.

Reproduced from the pamphlet
Published by the Caucasian Union
Committee of the R.S.D.L.P., May 1905
Translated from the Georgian

ARMED INSURRECTION AND OUR TACTICS

The revolutionary movement "has already brought about the necessity for an armed uprising"—this idea, expressed by the Third Congress of our Party, finds increasing confirmation day after day. The flames of revolution are flaring up with ever-increasing intensity, now here and now there calling forth local uprisings. The three days' barricade and street fighting in Lodz, the strike of many tens of thousands of workers in Ivanovo-Voznesensk with the inevitable bloody collisions with the troops, the uprising in Odessa, the "mutiny" in the Black Sea Fleet and in the Libau naval depot, and the "week" in Tiflis—are all harbingers of the approaching storm. It is approaching, approaching irresistibly, it will break over Russia any day and, in a mighty, cleansing flood, sweep away all that is antiquated and rotten; it will wipe out the disgrace called the autocracy, under which the Russian people have suffered for ages. The last convulsive efforts of tsarism—the intensification of repression of every kind, the proclamation of martial law over half the country and the multiplication of gallows, all accompanied by alluring speeches addressed to the liberals and by false promises of reform—these things will not save-it from the fate history has in store for it. The days of the autocracy are numbered; the storm is inevitable. A new social order is already being born, welcomed by the entire people, who are expecting renovation and regeneration from it.

What new questions is this approaching storm raising before our Party? How must we adjust our organisation and tactics to the new requirements of life so that we may take a more active and organised part in the uprising, which is the only necessary beginning of the revolution? To guide the uprising, should we—the advanced detachment of the class which is not only the vanguard, but also the main driving force of the revolution—set up special bodies, or is the existing Party machinery enough?

These questions have been confronting the Party and demanding immediate solution for several months already. For those who worship "spontaneity," who degrade the Party's objects to the level of simply following in the wake of life, who drag at the tail and do not march at the head as the advanced class-conscious detachment should do, such questions do not exist. Insurrection is spontaneous, they say, it is impossible to organise and prepare it, every prearranged plan of action is a utopia (they are opposed to any sort of "plan"—why, that is "consciousness" and not a "spontaneous phenomenon"!), a waste of effort—social life follows its own, unknown paths and will shatter all our projects. Hence, they say, we must confine ourselves to conducting propaganda and agitation in favour of the idea of insurrection, the idea of the "self-arming" of the masses; we must only exercise "political guidance"; as regards "technical" guidance of the insurgent people, let anybody who likes undertake that.

But we have always exercised such guidance up to now!—the opponents of the "khvostist policy" reply. Wide agitation and propaganda, political guidance of the proletariat, are absolutely essential. That goes without saying. But to confine ourselves to such general tasks means either evading an answer to the question which life bluntly puts to us, or revealing utter inability to adjust our tactics to the requirements of the rapidly growing revolutionary struggle. We must, of course, now intensify political agitation tenfold, we must try to establish our influence not only over the proletariat, but also over those numerous strata of the "people" who are gradually joining the revolution; we must try to popularise among all classes of the population the idea that an uprising is necessary. But we cannot confine ourselves solely to this! To enable the proletariat to utilise the impending revolution for the purposes of its own class struggle, to enable it to establish a democratic system that will provide the greatest guarantees for the subsequent struggle for socialism—it, the proletariat, around which the opposition is rallying, must not only be in the centre of the struggle, but become the leader and guide of the uprising. It is *the technical guidance and organisational preparation of the all-Russian uprising* that constitute the new tasks with which life has confronted the proletariat. And if our Party wishes to be the real political leader of the working class it cannot and must not repudiate these new tasks.

And so, what must we do to achieve this object? What must our first steps be?

Many of our organisations have already answered this question in a practical way by directing part of their forces and resources to the purpose of arming the proletariat. Our struggle against the autocracy has entered the stage when the necessity of arming is universally admitted. But mere realisation of the necessity of arming is not enough —*the practical task must be bluntly and clearly put before the Party*. Hence, our committees must at once, forthwith, proceed to arm the people locally, to set up special groups to arrange this matter, to organise district groups for the purpose of procuring arms, to organise workshops for the manufacture of different kinds of explosives, to draw up plans for seizing state and private stores of arms and arsenals. We must not only arm the people "with a burning desire to arm themselves," as the new *Iskra* advises us, but also "take the most energetic measures to arm the proletariat" in actual fact, as the Third Party Congress made it incumbent upon us to do. It is easier on this issue than on any other to reach agreement with the section that has split off from the Party (if it is really in earnest about arming and is not merely talking about "a burning desire to arm themselves"), as well as with the national Social-Democratic organisations, such as, for example, the Armenian Federalists and others who have set themselves the same object. Such an attempt has already been made in Baku, where after the February massacre our committee, the Balakhany-Bibi-Eibat group and the Gnchak Committee[1] set up among themselves an organising committee for procuring arms. It is absolutely essential that this difficult and responsible undertaking be organised by joint efforts, and we believe that factional interests should least of all hinder the amalgamation of all the Social-Democratic forces on this ground.

In addition to increasing stocks of arms and organising their pro-

---

1 **Original editor:** Gnchak Committee—a committee of the Armenian petty-bourgeois party called Gnchak which was formed in Geneva in 1887 on the initiative of Armenian students. In Transcaucasia the party assumed the title of Armenian Social-Democratic Party and conducted a splitting policy in the labour movement. After the revolution of 1905-07 the party degenerated into a reactionary nationalist group.

curement and manufacture, it is necessary to devote most serious attention to the task of organising fighting squads of every kind for the purpose of utilising the arms that are being procured. Under no circumstances should actions such as distributing arms directly to the masses be resorted to. In view of the fact that our resources are limited and that it is extremely difficult to conceal weapons from the vigilant eyes of the police, we shall be unable to arm any considerable section of the population, and all our efforts will be wasted. It will be quite different when we set up a special fighting organisation. Our fighting squads will learn to handle their weapons, and during the uprising —irrespective of whether it breaks out spontaneously or is prepared beforehand—they will come out as the chief and leading units around which the insurgent people will rally, and under whose leadership they will march into battle. Thanks to their experience and organisation, and also to the fact that they will be well armed, it will be possible to utilise all the forces of the insurgent people and thereby achieve the immediate object—the arming of the entire people and the execution of the prearranged plan of action. They will quickly capture various stores of arms, government and public offices, the post office, the telephone exchange, and so forth, which will be necessary for the further development of the revolution.

But these fighting squads will be needed not only when the revolutionary uprising has already spread over the whole town; their role will be no less important on the eve of the uprising. During the past six months it has become convincingly clear to us that the autocracy, which has discredited itself in the eyes of all classes of the population, has concentrated all its energy on mobilising the dark forces of the country—professional hooligans, or the ignorant and fanatical elements among the Tatars—for the purpose of fighting the revolutionaries. Armed and protected by the police, they are terrorising the population and creating a tense atmosphere for the liberation movement. Our fighting organisations must always be ready to offer due resistance to all the attempts made by these dark forces, and must try to convert the anger and the resistance called forth by their actions into an anti-government movement. The armed fighting squads, ready to go out into the streets and take their place at the head of the masses of the people at any moment, can easily achieve the object set by the Third Congress—"to organise armed resistance to the actions of the Black Hundreds, and generally, of all reactionary elements led by the government" ("Resolution on Attitude Towards the Government's Tactics on the Eve of the Revolution"—see "Announcement").[240]

One of the main tasks of our fighting squads, and of military-technical organisation in general, should be to draw up the plan of the uprising for their particular districts and co-ordinate it with the plan drawn up by the Party centre for the whole of Russia. Ascertain the enemy's weakest spots, choose the points from which the attack against him is to be launched, distribute all the forces over the district and thoroughly study the topography of the town—all this must be done beforehand, so that we shall not be taken by surprise under any circumstances. It is totally inappropriate here to go into a detailed analysis of this aspect of our organisations' activity. Strict secrecy in drawing up the plan of action must be accompanied by the widest possible dissemination among the proletariat of military-technical knowledge which is absolutely necessary for conducting street fighting. For this purpose we must utilise the services of the military men in the organisation. For this purpose also we must utilise the services of a number of other comrades who will be extremely useful in this matter because of their natural talent and inclinations.

Only such thorough preparation for insurrection can ensure for Social-Democracy the leading role in the forthcoming battles between the people and the autocracy.

Only complete fighting preparedness will enable the proletariat to transform the isolated clashes with the police and the troops into a nation-wide uprising with the object of setting up a provisional revolutionary government in place of the tsarist government.

The supporters of the "khvostist policy" notwithstanding, the organised proletariat will exert all its efforts to concentrate both the technical and political leadership of the uprising in its own hands. This leadership is the essential condition which will enable us to utilise the

---

2 See *Resolutions and Decisions of C.P.S.U.(B.) Congresses, Conferences and Central Committee Plenums*, Part I, 6th Russ. ed., 1940, p. 45.

impending revolution in the interests of our class struggle.

Proletariatis Brdzola
(*The Proletarian Struggle*), No. 10,
July 15, 1905
Unsigned
Translated from the Georgian

THE PROVISIONAL REVOLUTIONARY GOVERNMENT AND SOCIAL-DEMOCRACY[1]

I

The people's revolution is gaining impetus. The proletariat is arming and raising the banner of revolt. The peasantry are straightening their backs and rallying around the proletariat. The time is not far distant when the general uprising will break out, and the hated throne of the hated tsar will be "swept from the face of the earth." The tsarist government will be overthrown. On its ruins will be set up the government of the revolution—the provisional revolutionary government, which will disarm the dark forces, arm the people and immediately proceed to convoke a Constituent Assembly. Thus, the rule of the tsar will give way to the rule of the people. That is the path which the people's revolution is now taking.

What must the provisional government do?

It must disarm the dark forces, curb the enemies of the revolution so that they shall not be able to restore the tsarist autocracy. It must arm the people and help to carry the revolution through to the end. It must introduce freedom of speech, of the press, of assembly, and so forth. It must abolish indirect taxes and introduce a progressive profits tax and progressive death duties. It must organise peasant committees which will settle the land question in the countryside. It must also dis-

---

1 **Original editor:** Only the first part of J. V. Stalin's article "The Provisional Revolutionary Government and Social-Democracy" was published in No. 11 of *Proletariatis Brdzola*. Judging from the manuscript notes of the plan for Nos. 12, 13 and 14 of *Proletariatis Brdzola*, drawn up by J. V. Stalin and preserved in the archives, it was intended to publish the second part of this article in No. 13 of that newspaper. Owing to the fact that *Proletariatis Brdzola* ceased publication with No. 12, the second part of the article was not published. Only the manuscript of the Russian translation of this part of the article was preserved in the files of the gendarmerie. The Georgian text of the manuscript has not been found.

establish the church and secularise education. . . .

In addition to these general demands, the provisional government must also satisfy the class demands of the workers: freedom to strike and freedom of association, the eight-hour day, state insurance for workers, hygienic conditions of labour, establishment of "labour exchanges," and so forth.

In short, the provisional government must fully carry out our minimum programme[2] and immediately proceed to convene a popular Constituent Assembly which will give "perpetual" legal force to the changes that will have taken place in social life.

Who should constitute the provisional government?

The revolution will be brought about by the people, and the people are the proletariat and the peasantry. Clearly, it is they who should undertake the task of carrying the revolution through to the end, of curbing the reaction, of arming the people, and so forth. To achieve all this the proletariat and the peasantry must have champions of their interests in the provisional government. The proletariat and the peasantry will dominate in the streets, they will shed their blood—clearly therefore, they should dominate in the provisional government too.

All this is true, we are told; but what is there in common between the proletariat and the peasantry?

Common between them is their hatred of the survivals of serfdom, the life-and-death struggle they are waging against the tsarist government, their desire for a democratic republic.

This, however, cannot make us forget the truth that the differences between them are much greater.

What are these differences?

That the proletariat is the enemy of private property, it hates the bourgeois system, and it needs a democratic republic only in order to muster its forces for the purpose of overthrowing the bourgeois regime, whereas the peasantry are tied to private property, are bound to the bourgeois system, and need, a democratic republic in order to

---

2 For the minimum programme see "Announcement About the Second Congress of the R.S.D.L.P."

strengthen the foundations of the bourgeois regime.

Needless to say the peasantry[3] will go against the proletariat only in so far as the proletariat will want to abolish private property. On the other hand, it is also clear that the peasantry will support the proletariat only in so far as the proletariat will want to overthrow the autocracy. The present revolution is a bourgeois revolution, i.e., it does not affect private property, hence, at present the peasantry have no reason for turning their weapons against the proletariat. But the present revolution totally rejects tsarist rule, hence, it is in the peasants' interests resolutely to join the proletariat, the leading force of the revolution. Clearly, also, it is in the proletariat's interests to support the peasantry and jointly with them attack the common enemy—the tsarist government. It is not for nothing that the great Engels says that before the victory of the democratic revolution the proletariat must attack the existing system side by side with the petty bourgeoisie.[4] And if our victory cannot be called a victory until the enemies of the revolution are completely curbed, if it is the duty of the provisional government to curb the enemy and arm the people, if the provisional government must undertake the task of consummating the victory—then it is self-evident that, in addition to those who champion the interests of the petty bourgeoisie, the provisional government must include representatives of the proletariat to champion its interests. It would be sheer lunacy if the proletariat, acting as the leader of the revolution left it entirely to the petty bourgeoisie to carry the revolution to its end: this would be self-betrayal. It must not be forgotten, however, that the proletariat, as the enemy of private property, must have its own party, and must not turn aside from its path for a single moment.

In other words, the proletariat and the peasantry must by their combined efforts put an end to the tsarist government; by their combined efforts they must curb the enemies of the revolution, and precisely for this reason not only the peasantry, but the proletariat also must have champions of its interests—Social-Democrats—in the provisional government.

---

3 i.e., the petty bourgeoisie.

4 See *Iskra*, No. 96. This passage is reproduced in *Social-Democrat*, No. 5. See "Democracy and Social-Democracy."

This is so clear and obvious that one would think it would be unnecessary to talk about it.

But out steps the "minority" and, having doubts about this, obstinately reiterates: it is unbecoming for Social-Democracy to be represented in the provisional government, it is contrary to principles.

Let us examine this question. What are the arguments of the "minority"? First of all, they refer to the Amsterdam Congress.[5] This congress, in opposition to Jauresism, passed a resolution to the effect that Socialists must not seek representation in bourgeois governments; and as the provisional government will be a bourgeois government, it will be improper for us to be represented in it. That is how the "minority" argues, failing to realise that if the decision of the congress is to be interpreted in this schoolboy fashion we should take no part in the revolution either. It works out like this: we are enemies of the bourgeoisie; the present revolution is a bourgeois revolution—hence, we should take no part in this revolution! This is the path to which the logic of the "minority" is pushing us. Social-Democracy says, however, that we proletarians should not only take part in the present revolution, but also be at the head of it, guide it, and carry it through to the end. But it will be impossible to carry the revolution through to the end unless we are represented in the provisional government. Obviously, the logic of the "minority" has not a leg to stand on. One of two things: either we, copying the liberals, must reject the idea that the proletariat is the leader of the revolution—and in that case the question of our going into the provisional government automatically falls away; or we must openly recognise this Social-Democratic idea and thereby recognise the necessity of our going into the provisional government. The "minority," however, do not wish to break with either side; they wish to be both liberal and Social-Democratic! How pitilessly they are outraging innocent logic. . . .

The Amsterdam Congress, however, had in mind the permanent government of France and not a provisional revolutionary government. The government of France is a reactionary, conservative government; it protects the old and fights the new—it goes without saying

5 The Amsterdam Congress of the Second International was held in August 1904.

that no true Social-Democrat will join such a government; but a pro-visional government is revolutionary and progressive; it fights the old and clears the road for the new, it serves the interests of the revolu-tion—and it goes without saying that the true Social-Democrat will go into such a government and take an active part in consummating the cause of the revolution. As you see— these are different things. Con-sequently, it is useless for the "minority" to clutch at the Amsterdam Congress: that will not save it.

Evidently, the "minority" realises this itself and, therefore, comes out with another argument: it appeals to the shades of Marx and En-gels. Thus, for example, *Social-Democrat* obstinately reiterates that Marx and Engels "emphatically repudiated" the idea of entering a provi-sional government. But where and when did they repudiate this? What does Marx say, for example? It appears that Marx says that ". . . the democratic petty bourgeois . . . preach to the proletariat . . . the estab-lishment of a large opposition party which will embrace all shades of opinion in the democratic party . . ." that "such a union would turn out solely to their (the petty bourgeois) advantage and altogether to the disadvantage of the proletariat,"[6] etc.[7] In short, the proletariat must have a separate class party. But who is opposed to this, "learned critic"? Why are you tilling at windmills?

Nevertheless, the "critic" goes on quoting Marx. "In the case of a struggle against a common adversary no special union is required. As soon as such an adversary has to be fought directly, the interests of both parties, for the moment, coincide, and . . . this association, cal-culated to last only for the moment, will arise of itself. . . . During the struggle and after the struggle, the workers must, at every opportunity, put forward their own needs (it ought to be: demands) alongside of the needs (demands) of the bourgeois democrats. . . . In a word, from the first moment of victory, mistrust must be directed . . . against the workers' previous allies, against the party that wishes to exploit the

---

6 See *Social-Democrat*, No. 5.

7 **Original editor**: Karl Marx and Frederick Engels, "Address of the Central Committee to the Communist League" (see Karl Marx and Frederick Engels, *Selected Works*, Vol. I, Moscow 1951, p. 102).

common victory for itself alone."[8] In other words, the proletariat must pursue its own road and support the petty bourgeoisie only in so far as this does not run counter to its own interests. But who is opposed to this, astonishing "critic"? And why did you have to refer to the words of Marx? Does Marx say anything about a provisional revolutionary government? Not a word! Does Marx say that entering a provisional government during the democratic revolution is opposed to our principles? Not a word! Why then does our author go into such childish raptures? Where did he dig up this "contradiction in principle" between us and Marx? Poor "critic"! He puffs and strains in the effort to find such a contradiction, but to his chagrin nothing comes of it.

What does Engels say according to the Mensheviks? It appears that in a letter to Turati he says that the impending revolution in Italy will be a petty bourgeois and not a socialist revolution; that before its victory the proletariat must come out against the existing regime jointly with the petty bourgeoisie, but must, without fail, have its own party; that it would be extremely dangerous for the Socialists to enter the new government after the victory of the revolution. If they did that they would repeat the blunder made by Louis Blanc and other French Socialists in 1848, etc.[9] In other words, in so far as the Italian revolution will be a democratic and not a socialist revolution it would be a great mistake to dream of the rule of the proletariat and remain in the government *after the victory*; only *before the victory* can the proletariat come out jointly with the petty bourgeoisie against the common enemy. But who is arguing against this? Who says that we must confuse the democratic revolution with the socialist revolution? What was the purpose of referring to Turati, a follower of Bernstein? Or why was it necessary to recall Louis Blanc? Louis Blanc was a petty-bourgeois "Socialist"; we are discussing Social-Democrats. There was no Social-Democratic Party in Louis Blanc's time, but here we are discussing precisely such a party. The French Socialists had in view the conquest of political power; what interests us here is the question of entering a

---

8 See *Social-Democrat*, No. 5.

9 See *Social-Democrat*, No. 5. *Social-Democrat* gives these words in quotation marks. One would think that these words of Engels are quoted literally, but this is not the case. The author merely gives in his own words the gist of Engels's letter.

REVOLUTIONARY GOVERNMENT   113

provisional government. . . . Did Engels say that entering a provisional government during a democratic revolution is opposed to our principles? He said nothing of the kind! Then what is all this talk about, Mr. Menshevik? How is it you fail to understand that to confuse questions is not to solve them? And why did you have to trouble the shades of Marx and Engels for nothing?

Evidently, the "minority" realises that the names of Marx and Engels will not save it, and so now it clutches at a third "argument." You want to put a double curb on the enemies of the revolution, the "minority" tells us. You want the "pressure of the proletariat upon the revolution to come not only from 'below,' not only from the streets, but also from above, from the chambers of the provisional government."[10] But this is opposed to principle, the "minority" tells us reproachfully.

Thus, the "minority" asserts that we must influence the course of the revolution "only from below." The "majority," however, is of the opinion that we must supplement action from "below" with action from "above" in order that the pressure should come from all sides.

Who, then, is opposing the principle of Social-Democracy, the "majority" or the "minority"?

Let us turn to Engels. In the seventies an uprising broke out in Spain. The question of a provisional revolutionary government came up. At that time the Bakuninists (Anarchists) were active there. They repudiated all action from above, and this gave rise to a controversy between them and Engels. The Bakuninists preached the very thing that the "minority" are saying today. "The Bakuninists," says Engels, "for years had been propagating the idea that all revolutionary action from above downward was pernicious, and that everything must be organised and carried out from below upward."[11] In their opinion, "every organisation of a political, so-called provisional or revolution-

10 See *Iskra*, No. 93.

11 See *Proletary*, No. 3, in which these words of Engels are quoted.*

* This refers to V. I. Lenin's work "On a Provisional Revolutionary Government" in which he quotes from F. Engels's article "The Bakuninists at Work" (see V. I. Lenin, *Works*, 4th Russ. ed., Vol. 8, pp. 443, 444 and 446).

ary power, could only be a new fraud and would be as dangerous to the proletariat as all now existing governments."[12] Engels ridicules this view and says that life has ruthlessly refuted this doctrine of the Bakuninists. The Bakuninists were obliged to yield to the demands of life and they . . . "wholly against their anarchist principles, had to form a revolutionary government."[13] Thus, they "trampled upon the dogma which they had only just proclaimed: that the establishment of the revolutionary government was only a deception and a new betrayal of the working class."[14]

This is what Engels says.

It turns out, therefore, that the principle of the "minority" — action only from "below" — is an anarchist principle, which does, indeed, fundamentally contradict Social-Democratic tactics. The view of the "minority" that participation in a provisional government in any way would be fatal to the workers is an anarchist phrase, which Engels ridiculed in his day. It also turns out that life will refute the views of the "minority" and will easily smash them as it did in the case of the Bakuninists.

The "minority," however, persists in its obstinacy — we shall not go against our principles, it says. These people have a queer idea of what Social-Democratic principles are. Let us take, for example, their principles as regards the provisional revolutionary government and the State Duma. The "minority" is against entering a provisional government brought into being in the interests of the revolution—this is opposed to principles, it says. But it is in favour of entering the State Duma, which was brought into being in the interests of the autocracy—that, it appears, is not opposed to principles! The "minority" is against entering a provisional government which the revolutionary people will set up, and to which the people will give legal sanction— that is opposed to principles, it says. But it is in favour of entering the State Duma which is convoked by the autocratic tsar and to which the

---

12 *Ibid.*

13 *Ibid.*

14 *Ibid.*

tsar gives legal sanction—that, it appears, is not opposed to principles! The "minority" is against entering a provisional government whose mission it will be to bury the autocracy—that is opposed to principles. But it is in favour of entering the State Duma, whose mission it is to bolster up the autocracy—that, it appears, is not opposed to principles. . . . What principles are you talking about, most esteemed gentlemen? The principles of the liberals or of the Social-Democrats? You would do very well if you gave a straight answer to this question. We have our doubts.

But let us leave these questions.

The point is that in its quest for principles the "minority" has slipped onto the path of the Anarchists.

That has now become clear.

II

Our Mensheviks did not like the resolutions that were adopted by the Third Party Congress. Their genuinely revolutionary meaning stirred up the Menshevik "marsh" and stimulated in it an appetite for "criticism." Evidently, it was the resolution on the provisional revolutionary government that mainly disturbed their opportunist minds, and they set out to "destroy" it. But as they were unable to find anything in it to clutch at and criticise, they resorted to their customary and, it must be said, cheap weapon—demagogy! This resolution was drawn up as a bait for the workers, to deceive and dazzle them—write these "critics." And, evidently, they are very pleased with the fuss they are making. They imagine that they have struck their opponent dead, that they are victor-critics, and they exclaim: "And they (the authors of the resolution) want to lead the proletariat!" You look at these "critics" and before your eyes rises the hero in Gogol's story who, in a state of mental aberration, imagined that he was the King of Spain. Such is the fate of all megalomaniacs!

Let us examine the actual "criticism" which we find in *Social-Democrat*, No. 5. As you know already, our Mensheviks cannot think of the bloody spectre of a provisional revolutionary government without fear and trembling, and so they call upon their saints, the Marty-novs and Akimovs, to rid them of this monster and to replace it by the Zemsky Sobor—now by the State Duma. With this object they laud the "Zemsky Sobor" to the skies and try to palm off this rotten off-spring of rotten tsarism as good coin of the realm: "We know that the Great French Revolution established a *republic* without having a provi-sional government," they write. Is that all? Don't you know any more than that, "esteemed gentlemen"? It is very little! You really ought to know a little more! You ought to know, for example, that the Great French Revolution triumphed as a bourgeois revolutionary movement, whereas the Russian "revolutionary movement will triumph as the movement of the workers or will not triumph at all," as G. Plekhanov quite rightly says. In France, the bourgeoisie was at the head of the revolution; in Russia, it is the proletariat. *There*, the former guided the destiny of the revolution; *here* it is the latter. And is it not clear that with such a realignment of the leading revolutionary forces the results cannot be identical for the respective classes? If, in France, the bour-geoisie, being at the head of the revolution, reaped its fruits, must it also reap them in Russia, notwithstanding the fact that the proletariat stands at the head of the revolution? Yes, say our Mensheviks; what took place *there*, in France, must also take place *here*, in Russia. These gentlemen, like undertakers, take the measure of one long dead and apply it to the living. Moreover, in doing so they resorted to a rather big fraud: they cut off the head of the subject that interests us and shifted the point of the controversy to its tail. We, like all revolutionary Social-Democrats, are talking about establishing a democratic repub-lic. They, however, hid the word "democratic" and began to talk large about a "republic." "We know that the Great French Revolution estab-lished a republic," they preach. Yes, it established a republic, but what kind of republic—a truly democratic one? The kind that the Russian Social-Democratic Labour Party is demanding? Did that republic grant the people the right of universal suffrage? Were the elections at that time really direct? Was a progressive income tax introduced? Was any-thing said there about improving conditions of labour, shortening the working day, higher wages and so forth? . . . No. There was nothing of the kind there, nor could there have been, for at that time the workers lacked Social-Democratic education. That is why their interests were forgotten and ignored by the bourgeoisie in the French republic of that time. And is it before such a republic that you bow your "highly respected" heads, gentlemen? Is this your ideal? You are welcome to it! But remember, esteemed gentlemen, that worshipping such a republic has nothing in common with Social-Democracy and its programme— it is democratism of the worst sort. And you are smuggling all this in under the label of Social-Democracy.

Furthermore, the Mensheviks ought to know that the Russian bourgeoisie with their Zemsky Sobor will not even grant us a republic such as was introduced in France—it has no intention whatever of abolishing the monarchy. Knowing how "insolent" the workers are where there is no monarchy, it is striving to keep this fortress intact and to convert it into its own weapon against its uncompromising foe —the proletariat. This is its object in negotiating in the name of the "people" with the butcher-tsar and advising him to convoke a Zemsky Sobor in the interests of the "country" and the throne, and in order to avert "anarchy." Are you Mensheviks really unaware of all this?

We need a republic not like the one introduced by the French bourgeoisie in the eighteenth century, but like the one the Russian Social-Democratic Labour Party is demanding in the twentieth century. And such a republic can be created only by a victorious popular uprising, headed by the proletariat, and by the provisional revolutionary government which it sets up. Only such a provisional government can *provisionally* carry out our minimum programme and submit changes of this nature for endorsement to the Constituent Assembly which it convokes.

Our "critics" do not believe that a Constituent Assembly convoked in conformity with our programme could express the will of the people (and how can they imagine this when they go no further than the Great French Revolution which occurred 115 or 116 years ago). "Rich and influential persons," continue the "critics," "possess so many means of wangling the elections in their favour that all talk about the actual will of the people is absolutely beside the point. To prevent poor voters from becoming instruments for expressing the will of the rich a tremendous struggle must be waged and a long period of Party discipline" (which the Mensheviks do not recognise?) "is needed." "All this has not been achieved even in Europe (?) in spite of its long period of political training. And yet our Bolsheviks think that this talisman lies in the hands of a provisional government!"

This is khvostism indeed! Here you have a life-size picture of "their late majesties" the "tactics-process" and the "organisation-process." It is impossible to demand in Russia what has not yet been achieved in Europe, the "critics" tell us for our edification! But we know that our minimum programme has not been fully achieved in "Europe," or even in America; consequently, in the opinion of the Mensheviks, whoever accepts it and fights for its achievement in Russia after the fall of the autocracy is an incorrigible dreamer, a miserable Don Quixote! In short, our minimum programme is false and utopian, and has nothing in common with real "life"! Isn't that so, Messieurs "Critics"? That is what it appears to be according to you. But in that case, show more courage and say so openly, without equivocation! We shall then know whom we are dealing with, and you will rid yourselves of the programme formalities which you so heartily detest! As it is, you talk so timidly and furtively about the programme being of little importance that many people, except, of course, the Bolsheviks, still think that you recognise the Russian Social-Democratic programme that was adopted at the Second Party Congress. What's the use of this hypocritical conduct?

This brings us right down to the roots of our disagreements. You do not believe in our programme and you challenge its correctness; we, however, always take it is our starting point and co-ordinate all our activities with it!

We believe that "rich and influential persons" will not be able to bribe and fool all the people if there is freedom for election propaganda; for we shall counter their influence and their gold with the words of Social-Democratic truth (and we, unlike you, do not doubt this truth in the least) and thereby we shall reduce the effect of the fraudulent tricks of the bourgeoisie. You, however, do not believe this, and are, therefore, trying to pull the revolution in the direction of reformism.

"In 1848," continue the "critics," "the provisional government in France (again France!) in which there were also workers, convoked a

Constituent Assembly to which not a single representative of the Paris proletariat was elected." This is another example of utter failure to understand Social-Democratic theory and of the stereotyped conception of history! What is the use of flinging phrases about? Although there were workers in the provisional government in France, nothing came of it; therefore, Social-Democracy in Russia must refrain from entering a provisional government because here, too, nothing will come of it, argue the "critics." But is it a matter of workers entering the provisional government? Do we say that any kind of workers, no matter of what trend, should go into the provisional revolutionary government? No. So far we have not become your followers and do not supply every worker with a Social-Democratic certificate. It never entered our heads to call the workers who were in the French provisional government members of the Social-Democratic Party! What is the use of this misplaced analogy? What comparison can there be between the political consciousness of the French proletariat in 1848 and the political consciousness of the Russian proletariat at the present time? Did the French proletariat of that time come out even once in a political demonstration against the existing system? Did it ever celebrate the First of May under the slogan of fighting against the bourgeois system? Was it organised in a Social-Democratic Labour Party? Did it have the programme of Social-Democracy? We know that it did not. The French proletariat had not even an inkling of all this. The question is, therefore, could the French proletariat at that time reap the fruits of the revolution to the same extent that the Russian proletariat can, a proletariat that has long been organised in a Social-Democratic Party, has a very definite Social-Democratic programme, and is consciously laying the road towards its goal? Anyone who is in the least capable of understanding realities will answer this question in the negative. Only those who are capable of learning historical facts by rote, but are incapable of explaining their causes in conformity with place and time can identify these two different magnitudes.

"We need," the "critics" preach to us again and again, "violence on the part of the people, uninterrupted revolution, and we must not be satisfied with elections and then disperse to our homes." Again slander! Who told you, esteemed gentlemen, that we shall be satisfied with elections and then disperse to our homes? Mention his name!

Our "critics" are also upset by our demand that the provisional revolutionary government should carry out our minimum programme, and they exclaim: "This reveals complete ignorance of the subject; the point is that the political and economic demands in our programme can be achieved only by means of legislation, but a provisional government is not a legislative body." Reading this prosecutor's speech against "infringement of the law" one begins to wonder whether this article was not contributed to the *Social-Democrat* by some liberal bourgeois who stands in awe before the law.[15] How else can one explain the bourgeois sophistry it expresses to the effect that a provisional revolutionary government has no right to abolish old and introduce new laws? Does not this argument smack of vulgar liberalism? And is it not strange to hear it coming from the mouth of a revolutionary? It reminds us of the man who was condemned to be beheaded and who begged that care should be taken not to touch the pimple on his neck. However, everything can be forgiven the "critics" who cannot distinguish between a provisional revolutionary government and an ordinary cabinet (and besides, they are not to blame, their teachers, the Martynovs and Akimovs, reduced them to this state). What is a cabinet? The result of the *existence* of a permanent government. What is a provisional revolutionary government? The result of the *destruction* of a permanent government. The former puts *existing* laws into operation with the aid of a standing army. The latter abolishes the existing laws and in place of them gives legal sanction to the will of the revolution with the assistance of the insurgent people. What is there in common between the two?

Let us assume that the revolution has triumphed and that the victorious people have set up a provisional revolutionary government. The question arises: What is this government to do if it has no right to abolish and introduce laws? Wait for the Constituent Assembly? But the convocation of this Assembly also demands the introduction of

---

15 This idea seems to be all the more justified for the reason that of all the bourgeoisie of Tiflis, the Mensheviks, in No. 5 of *Social-Democrat*, proclaimed only about a dozen merchants as traitors to the "common cause." Evidently, all the rest are their supporters and have a "common cause" with the Mensheviks. It would not be surprising if one of these supporters of the "common cause" sent to the organ of his colleagues a "critical" article against the uncompromising "majority."

new laws such as: universal, direct, etc., suffrage, freedom of speech, of the press, of assembly, and so forth. And all this is contained in our minimum programme. If the provisional revolutionary government is unable to put it into practice, what will it be guided by in convening the Constituent Assembly? Not by a programme drawn up by Bulygin[16] and sanctioned by Nicholas II, surely?

Let us assume also that, after suffering heavy losses owing to lack of arms, the victorious people calls upon the provisional revolutionary government to abolish the standing army and to arm the people in order to combat counter-revolution. At that moment the Mensheviks come out and say: it is not the function of this department (the provisional revolutionary government) but of another—the Constituent Assembly—to abolish the standing army and to arm the people. Appeal to that other department. Don't demand action that infringes the law, etc. Fine counsellors, indeed!

Let us now see on what grounds the Mensheviks deprive the provisional revolutionary government of "legal capacity." Firstly, on the ground that it is not a legislative body, and secondly, that if it passes laws, the Constituent Assembly will have nothing to do. Such is the disgraceful result of the arguments of these political infants! It appears that they do not even know that, pending the setting up of a permanent government, the triumphant revolution, and the provisional revolutionary government which expresses its will, are the masters of the situation and, consequently, can abolish old and introduce new laws! If this were not the case, if the provisional revolutionary government lacked these powers, there would be no reason for its existence, and the insurgent people would not set up such a body. Strange that the Mensheviks have forgotten the ABC of revolution.

The Mensheviks ask: What will the Constituent Assembly do if our minimum programme is carried out by the provisional revolutionary government? Are you afraid that it will suffer from unemployment,

---

16 This refers to a bill to set up a State Duma with only advisory powers and to regulations governing the elections to the Duma drawn up by a commission under the chairmanship of the Minister of the Interior, Bulygin. The bill and the regulations were published together with the tsar's manifesto on August 6 (19), 1905. The Bolsheviks proclaimed an active boycott of the Bulygin Duma. That Duma was swept away by the force of the revolution before it could assemble.

esteemed gentlemen? Don't be afraid. It will have plenty of work to do. It will sanction the changes brought about by the provisional revolutionary government with the assistance of the insurgent people and will draft a constitution for the country, and our minimum programme will be only a part of it. That is what we shall demand from the Constituent Assembly!

"They (the Bolsheviks) cannot conceive of a split between the petty bourgeoisie and the workers, a split that will also affect the elections, and, consequently, the provisional government will want to oppress the working-class voters for the benefit of *its own* class," write the "critics." Who can understand this wisdom? What is the meaning of: "the provisional government will want to oppress the working-class voters for the benefit of its own class"!!? What provisional government are they talking about? What windmills are these Don Quixotes tilting at? Has anybody said that if the petty bourgeoisie is in sole control of the provisional revolutionary government it will protect the interests of the workers? Why ascribe one's own nonsense to others? We say that under certain circumstances it is permissible for our Social-Democratic delegates to enter a provisional revolutionary government together with the representatives of the democracy. That being the case, if we are discussing a provisional revolutionary government which includes Social-Democrats, how is it possible to call it petty-bourgeois in composition? We base our arguments in favour of entering a provisional revolutionary government on the fact that, in the main, the carrying out of our minimum programme does not run counter tothe interests of the democracy—the peasantry and the urban petty bourgeoisie (whom you Mensheviks invite into your party)—and, therefore, we deem it possible to carry it out in conjunction with the democracy. If, however, the democracy hinders the carrying out of some of its points, our delegates, backed by their voters, the proletariat, in the street, will try to carry this programme out by force, if that force is available (if it is not, we shall not enter the provisional government, in fact we shall not be elected). As you see, Social-Democracy must enter the provisional revolutionary government precisely in order to champion Social-Democratic views in it, i.e., to prevent the other classes from encroaching upon the interests of the proletariat.

The representatives of the Russian Social-Democratic Labour Party in the provisional revolutionary government will proclaim war not upon the proletariat, as the Mensheviks imagine in their folly, but, jointly with the proletariat, upon the enemies of the proletariat. But what do you, Mensheviks, care about all this? What do you care about the revolution and its provisional government? Your place is in the "State Duma"....[17]

Part I of this article was
published in *Proletariatis Brdzola*
(*The Proletarian Struggle*), No. 11,
August 15, 1905
Part II is published for the first time
Unsigned
Translated from the Georgian

---

17 *Here the manuscript breaks off.—Ed.*

A REPLY TO SOCIAL-DEMOCRAT[1]

First of all I must apologise to the reader for being late with this reply. It could not be helped; circumstances obliged me to work in another field, and I was compelled to put off my answer for a time; you yourselves know that we cannot dispose of ourselves as we please.

I must also say the following: many people think that the author of the pamphlet *Briefly About the Disagreements in the Party* was the Union

---

1 **Original editor:** J. V. Stalin's article "A Reply to *Social-Democrat*," published in No. 11 of *Proletariatis Brdzola*, met with a lively response in the Bolshevik centre abroad. Briefly summing up the gist of the article, V. I. Lenin wrote in *Proletary*: "We note in the article 'A Reply to *Social-Democrat*' an excellent presentation of the celebrated question of the 'introduction of consciousness from without.' The author divides this question into four independent parts:

"1) The philosophical question of the relation between consciousness and being. Being determines consciousness. Corresponding to the existence of two classes, two forms of consciousness are worked out, the bourgeois and the socialist. Socialist consciousness corresponds to the position of the proletariat.

"2) 'Who can, and who does, work out this socialist consciousness (scientific socialism)?'

"'Modern socialist consciousness can arise only on the basis of profound scientific knowledge' (Kautsky), i.e., 'it is worked out by a few Social-Democratic intellectuals who possess the necessary means and leisure.'

"3) How does this consciousness permeate the minds of the proletariat? 'It is here that Social-Democracy (and not only Social-Democratic intellectuals) comes in and introduces socialist consciousness into the working-class movement.'

"4) What does Social-Democracy meet with among the proletariat when it goes among them to preach socialism? An instinctive striving towards socialism. 'Together with the proletariat there arises of natural necessity a socialist tendency among the proletarians themselves as well as among those who adopt the proletarian standpoint. This explains the rise of socialist strivings.' (Kautsky.)

"From this the Mensheviks draw the following ridiculous conclusion: 'Hence it is obvious that socialism is not introduced among the proletariat from without, but, on the contrary, emanates from the proletariat and enters the heads of those who adopt the views of the proletariat'!" (See V. I. Lenin, *Works*, 4th Russ. ed., Vol. 9, p. 357.)

Committee and not one individual. I must state that I am the author of that pamphlet. The Union Committee acted only as editor.

And now to the point.

My opponent accuses me of being "unable to see the subject of the controversy," of "obscuring the issue,"[2] and he says that "the controversy centres around organisational and not programmatic questions" (p. 2).

Only a little observation is needed to reveal that the author's assertion is false. The fact is that my pamphlet was an answer to the *first* number of the *Social-Democrat*— the pamphlet had already been sent to the press when the second number of the *Social-Democrat* appeared. What does the author say in the first number? Only that the "majority" has taken the stand of idealism, and that this stand "fundamentally contradicts" Marxism. Here there is *not even a hint* of organisational questions. What was I to say in reply? Only what I did say, namely: that the stand of the "majority" is that of genuine Marxism, and if the "minority" has failed to understand this, it shows that it has itself retreated from genuine Marxism. That is what anybody who understands anything about polemics would have answered. But the author persists in asking: Why don't you deal with organisational questions? I do not deal with those questions, my dear philosopher, because you yourself did not then say a word about them. One cannot answer questions that have not yet been raised. Clearly, "obscuring the issue," "hushing up the subject of the controversy," and so forth, are the author's inventions. On the other hand, I have grounds for suspecting that the author himself is hushing up certain questions. He says that "the controversy centres around organisational questions," but there are also disagreements between us on *tactical* questions, which are far more important than disagreements on organisational questions. Our "critic," however, does not say a word about these disagreements in his pamphlet. Now this is exactly what is called "obscuring the issue."

---

2 See "A Reply to the Union Committee,"* p. 4.

* **Original editor:** "A Reply to the Union Committee" was published as a supplement to No. 3 of the *Social-Democrat* of June 1, 1905. It was written by N. Jordania, the leader of the Georgian Mensheviks, whose views had been subjected to scathing criticism by J. V. Stalin in his pamphlet *Briefly About the Disagreements in the Party* and in other works.

What do I say in my pamphlet?

Modern social life is built on capitalist lines. There exist two large classes, the bourgeoisie and the proletariat, and between them a life-and-death struggle is going on. The conditions of life of the bourgeoisie compel it to strengthen the capitalist system. But the conditions of life of the proletariat compel it to undermine the capitalist system, to destroy it. Corresponding to these two classes, two kinds of consciousness are worked out: the bourgeois and the socialist. Socialist consciousness corresponds to the position of the proletariat. Hence, the proletariat accepts this consciousness, assimilates it, and fights the capitalist system with redoubled vigour. Needless to say, if there were no capitalism and no class struggle, there would be no socialist consciousness. But the question now is: who works out, who is able to work out this socialist consciousness (i.e., scientific socialism)? Kautsky says, and I repeat his idea, that the masses of proletarians, as long as they remain proletarians, have neither the time nor the opportunity to work out socialist consciousness. "Modern socialist consciousness can arise only on the basis of profound scientific knowledge,"[3] says Kautsky. The vehicles of science are the intellectuals, including, for example, Marx, Engels and others, who have both the time and opportunity to put themselves in the van of science and work out socialist consciousness. Clearly, socialist consciousness is worked out by a few Social-Democratic intellectuals who possess the time and opportunity to do so.

But what importance can socialist consciousness have in itself if it is not disseminated among the proletariat? It can remain only an empty phrase! Things will take an altogether different turn when that consciousness is disseminated among the proletariat: the proletariat will become conscious of its position and will *more rapidly* move towards the socialist way of life. It is here that Social-Democracy (and not only Social-Democratic intellectuals) comes in and introduces socialist consciousness into the working-class movement. This is what Kautsky has in mind when he says "socialist consciousness is something introduced

---

3 See K. Kautsky's article quoted in *What Is To Be Done?*, p. 27.

into the proletarian class struggle from without."[4]

Thus, socialist consciousness is worked out by a few Social-Democratic intellectuals. But this consciousness is introduced into the working-class movement by the entire Social-Democracy, which lends the spontaneous proletarian struggle a conscious character.

That is what I discuss in my pamphlet.

Such is the stand taken by Marxism and, with it, by the "majority."

What does my opponent advance in opposition to this?

Properly speaking, nothing of importance. He devotes himself more to hurling abuse than to elucidating the question. Evidently, he is very angry! He does not dare to raise questions openly, he gives no straight answer to them, but cravenly evades the issue, hypocritically obscures clearly formulated questions, and at the same time assures everybody: I have explained all the questions at one stroke. Thus, for example, the author does not even raise the question *of the elaboration* of socialist consciousness, and does not dare to say openly whose side he takes on this question: Kautsky's or the "Economists'." True, in the first number of the *Social-Democrat* our "critic" made rather bold statements; at that time he openly spoke in the language of the "Economists." But what can one do? Then he was in one mood, now he is in a "different mood," and instead of criticising, he evades this issue, perhaps because he realises that he is wrong, but he does not dare openly to admit his mistake. In general, our author has found himself between two fires. He is at a loss as to which side to take. If he takes the side of the "Economists" he must break with Kautsky and Marxism, which is not to his advantage; if, however, he breaks with "Economism" and takes Kautsky's side, he must subscribe to what the "majority" says — but he lacks the courage to do this. And so he remains between two fires. What could our "critic" do? He decided that the best thing is to say nothing, and, indeed, he cravenly evades the issue that was raised above.

What does the author say about *introducing consciousness*?

Here, too, he betrays the same vacillation and cowardice. He shuf-

---

4 *Ibid.*

fles the question and declares with great aplomb: Kautsky does not say that "intellectuals introduce socialism into the working class from without" (p. 7).

Excellent, but neither do we Bolsheviks say that, Mr. "Critic." Why did you have to tilt at windmills? How is it you cannot understand that in our opinion, the opinion of the Bolsheviks, socialist consciousness is introduced into the working-class movement by Social-Democracy,[5]* and not only by Social-Democratic intellectuals? Why do you think that the Social-Democratic Party consists exclusively of intellectuals? Do you not know that there are many more advanced workers than intellectuals in the ranks of Social-Democracy? Cannot Social-Democratic workers introduce socialist consciousness into the working-class movement?

Evidently, the author himself realises that his "proof" is unconvincing and so he passes on to other "proof."

Our "critic" continues as follows: "Kautsky writes: 'Together with the proletariat there arises of natural necessity a socialist *tendency* among the proletarians themselves as well as among those who adopt the prole tarian standpoint; this explains the rise of socialist *strivings.*' Hence, it is obvious"—comments our "critic"—"that *socialism* is not introduced among the proletariat from without, but, on the contrary, emanates from the proletariat and enters the heads of those who adopt the views of the proletariat" ("A Reply to the Union Committee," p. 8).

Thus writes our "critic," and he imagines that he has explained the matter! What do Kautsky's words mean? Only that socialist *strivings* automatically arise among the proletariat. And this is true, of course. But we are not discussing socialist strivings, but socialist *consciousness*! What is there in common between the two? Are strivings and consciousness the same thing? Cannot the author distinguish between "socialist tendencies" and "socialist consciousness"? And is it not a sign of paucity of ideas when, from what Kautsky says, he deduces that "socialism is not introduced from without"? What is there in common between the "rise of socialist tendencies" and the introducing of socialist con-

---

5 See *Briefly About the Disagreements in the Party*, p. 18. (See present volume, p. 104. — Ed.)

sciousness? Did not this same Kautsky say that "socialist consciousness is something introduced into the proletarian class struggle *from
without*" (see *What Is To Be Done?*, p. 27)?

Evidently, the author realises that he is in a false position and in
conclusion he is obliged to add: "It does indeed follow from the quotation from Kautsky that socialist consciousness is introduced into the
class struggle from without" (see "A Reply to the Union Committee,"
p. 7). Nevertheless, he does not dare openly and boldly to admit this
scientific truth. Here, too, our Menshevik betrays the same vacillation
and cowardice in the face of logic as he did before.

Such is the ambiguous "reply" Mr. "Critic" gives to the two major
questions.

What can be said about the other, minor questions that automatically emerge from these big questions? It will be better if the reader
himself compares my pamphlet with our author's pamphlet. But one
other question must be dealt with. If we are to believe the author, our
opinion is that "the split took place because the congress . . . did not
elect Axelrod, Zasulich and Starover as editors . . ." ("A Reply," p. 13)
and, consequently, that we "deny the split, conceal how deeply it af-
fects principle, and present the entire opposition as if it were a case of
three 'rebellious' editors" (*ibid.*, p. 16).

Here the author is again confusing the issue. As a matter of fact
two questions are raised here: the *cause* of the split, and the *form* in
which the disagreements manifested themselves.

To the first question I give the following straight answer: "It is
now clear *on what grounds* the disagreements in the Party arose. As is
evident, two trends have appeared in our Party: the trend of *proletarian
firmness*, and the trend of *intellectual wavering*. And this intellectual wavering is expressed by the present 'minority'." (see *Briefly*, p. 46).[6] As
you see, here I *attribute* the disagreements to the existence of an intellectual and a proletarian trend in our Party and not to the conduct of
Martov-Axelrod. The conduct of Martov and the others is merely an
expression of intellectual wavering. But evidently, our Menshevik failed
to understand this passage in my pamphlet.

---

6 See present volume, p. 132.— *Ed.*

As regards the second question, I did, indeed, say, and always shall say, that the leaders of the "minority" shed tears over "front seats" and lent the struggle within the Party precisely such a *form*. Our author refuses to admit this. It is, nevertheless, a fact that the leaders of the "minority" proclaimed a boycott of the Party, openly demanded seats on the Central Committee, on the Central Organ and on the Party Council and, in addition, declared: "We present these terms as the only ones that will enable the Party to avoid a conflict which will threaten its very existence" (see *Commentary*, p. 26). What does this mean if not that the leaders of the "minority" inscribed on their banner, not an ideological struggle, but "a struggle for seats"? It is common knowledge that nobody prevented them from conducting a struggle around ideas and principles. Did not the Bolsheviks say to them: Establish your own organ and defend your views, the Party can provide you with such an organ (see *Commentary*)? Why did they not agree to this if they were really interested in principles and not in "front seats"?

We call all this the political spinelessness of the Menshevik leaders. Do not be offended, gentlemen, when we call a spade a spade.

Formerly, the leaders of the "minority" did not disagree with Marxism and Lenin on the point that socialist consciousness is introduced into the working-class movement from without (see the programmatic article in *Iskra*, No. 1). But later they began to waver and launched a struggle against Lenin, burning what they had worshipped the day before. I called that swinging from one side to another. Do not be offended at this either, Messieurs Mensheviks.

Yesterday you worshipped the centres and hurled thunderbolts at us because, as you said, we expressed lack of confidence in the Central Committee. But today you are undermining not only the centres, but centralism (see "The First All-Russian Conference"). I call this lack of principle, and I hope you will not be angry with me for this either, Messieurs Mensheviks.

If we combine such features as political spinelessness, fighting for seats, vacillation, lack of principle and others of the same kind, we shall get a certain general feature known as *intellectual wavering*, and it is primarily intellectuals who suffer from this. Clearly, intellectual wavering is the ground (the basis) on which "fighting for seats," "lack of principle," and so forth, arise. The vacillation of the intellectuals, however, springs from their social position. That is how we explain the Party split. Do you understand at last, dear author, what difference there is between the cause of the split and the forms it assumes? I have my doubts.

Such is the absurd and ambiguous stand taken by the *Social-Demo-crat* and its queer "critic." On the other hand, this "critic" displays great daring in another field. In his pamphlet of eight pages, he manages to tell eight lies about the Bolsheviks, and such lies that they make you laugh. You do not believe it? Here are the facts.

First lie. In the author's opinion, "Lenin wants to restrict the Party, to convert it into a narrow organisation of professionals" (p. 2). But Lenin says: "It should not be thought that Party organisations must consist solely of professional revolutionaries. We need the most di-versified organisations of every type, rank and shade, from extremely narrow and secret organisations to very broad and free ones" (*Minutes*, p. 240).

Second lie. According to the author, Lenin wants to "bring into the Party only committee members" (p. 2). But Lenin says: "All *groups, cir-cles, sub-committees, etc.*, must enjoy the status of committee institutions, or of branches of committees. Some of them will openly express a wish to join the Russian Social-Democratic Labour Party and, provid-ed that this is endorsed by the committee, *will join it*" (see "A Letter to a Comrade," p. 17).[7] [8]

Third lie. In the author's opinion, "Lenin is demanding the estab-lishment of the domination of intellectuals in the Party" (p. 5). But Lenin says: "The committees should contain . . . as far as possible, all the principal *leaders* of the working-class movement from among the workers themselves" (see "A Letter to a Comrade," pp. 7-8), i.e., the voices of the advanced workers must predominate not only in all other organisations, but also in the committees.

---

7 **Original editor:** See V. I. Lenin, *Works*, 4th Russ. ed., Vol. 6, p. 219.

8 As you see, in Lenin's opinion, organisations may be accepted into the Party not only by the Central Committee, but also by local committees.

Fourth lie. The author says that the passage quoted on page 12 of my pamphlet: "the working class spontaneously gravitates towards socialism," etc. — is "entirely a fabrication" (p. 6). As a matter of fact, I simply took and translated this passage from *What Is To Be Done?* This is what we read in that book, on page 29: "The working class spontaneously gravitates towards socialism, but the more widespread (and continuously revived in the most diverse forms) bourgeois ideology nevertheless spontaneously imposes itself upon the working class still more." This is the passage that is translated on page 12 of my pamphlet. This is what our "critic" called a fabrication! I do not know whether to ascribe this to the author's absent-mindedness or chicanery.

Fifth lie. In the author's opinion, "Lenin does not say anywhere that the workers strive towards socialism of 'natural necessity'" (p. 7). But Lenin says that the "working class spontaneously gravitates towards socialism" (*What Is To Be Done?*, p. 29).

Sixth lie. The author ascribes to me the idea that "socialism is introduced into the working class from without by the intelligentsia" (p. 7), whereas I say that Social-Democracy (and not only Social-Democratic intellectuals) introduces socialist consciousness into the movement (p. 18).

Seventh lie. In the author's opinion, Lenin says that socialist ideology arose "quite independently of the working-class movement" (p. 9). But such an idea certainly never entered Lenin's head. He says that socialist ideology arose "quite independently of the *spontaneous growth* of the working-class movement" (What Is To Be Done?, p. 21).

Eighth lie. The author says that my statement: "Plekhanov is *quitting* the 'minority,' is tittle-tattle." As a matter of fact, what I said has been confirmed. Plekhanov has *already* quit the "minority." . . .[9]

I shall not deal with the petty lies with which the author has so plentifully spiced his pamphlet.

It must be admitted, however, that the author did say one thing that was true. He tells us that "when any organisation begins to engage in tittle-tattle—its days are numbered" (p. 15). This is the downright

---

9 And yet the author has the audacity to accuse us, in No. 5 of the *Social-Democrat*, of having distorted the facts concerning the Third Congress!

truth, of course. The only question is: Who is engaging in tittle-tat-tle—the *Social-Democrat* and its queer knight, or the Union Committee? We leave that to the reader to decide.

One more question and we have finished. The author says with an air of great importance: "The Union Committee reproaches us for re-peating Plekhanov's ideas. We regard it as a virtue to repeat the ideas of Plekhanov, Kautsky and other equally well-known Marxists"(p. 15). So you regard it as a virtue to repeat the ideas of Plekhanov and Kautsky? Splendid, gentlemen! Well, then, listen:

Kautsky says that "socialist consciousness is something *introduced* into the proletarian class struggle *from without and not something that arose out of it spontaneously*" (see passage quoted from Kautsky in *What Is To Be Done?*, p. 27). The same Kautsky says that "the task of Social-De-mocracy is to imbue the proletariat with the consciousness of its position and the consciousness of its task" (*ibid.*). We hope that you, Mr. Menshevik, will repeat these words of Kautsky's and dispel our doubts. Let us pass to Plekhanov. Plekhanov says: ". . . Nor do I under-stand why it is thought that Lenin's draft,[10] if adopted, would close the doors of our Party to numerous workers. Workers who wish to join the Party will not be afraid to join an organisation. They are not afraid of discipline. But many intellectuals, thoroughly imbued with bourgeois individualism, will be afraid to join. Now that is exactly the good side about it. These bourgeois individualists are, usually, also representa-tives of opportunism of every sort. We must keep them at a distance. Lenin's draft may serve as a barrier against their invasion of the Party, and for that reason alone all opponents of opportunism should vote for it" (see *Minutes*, p. 246).

We hope that you, Mr. "Critic," will throw off your mask and with proletarian straightforwardness repeat these words of Plekhanov's.

If you fail to do this, it will show that your statements in the press are thoughtless and irresponsible.

---

10 Plekhanov is discussing Lenin's and Martov's formulations of §1 of the *Rules of the Party*.

Proletariatis Brdzola
The Proletarian Struggle), No. 11,
August 15, 1905
Unsigned
Translated from the Georgian

REACTION IS GROWING

Dark clouds are gathering over us. The decrepit autocracy is raising its head and arming itself with "fire and sword." Reaction is on the march! Let no one talk to us about the tsar's "reforms," the object of which is to strengthen the despicable autocracy: the "reforms" are a screen for the bullets and whips to which the brutal tsarist government is so generously treating us.

There was a time when the government refrained from shedding blood within the country. At that time it was waging war against the "external enemy," and it needed "internal tranquillity." That is why it showed a certain amount of "leniency" towards the "internal enemy" and turned a "blind eye" on the movement that was flaring up

Now times are different. Frightened by the spectre of revolution, the tsarist government hastened to conclude peace with the "external enemy," with Japan, in order to muster its forces and "thoroughly" settle accounts with the "internal enemy." And so reaction set in. The government had already revealed its "plans" before that, in *Moskovskiye Vedomosti*.[1] It . . . "was obliged to wage two parallel wars . . ." wrote that reactionary newspaper—"an external war and an internal war. If it waged neither of them with sufficient energy . . . it may be explained partly by the fact that one war hindered the other. . . . If the war in the Far East now terminates . . ." the government ". . . will, at last, have its hands free victoriously to terminate the internal war too . . . without any negotiations to crush" . . . "the internal enemies.". . . "With the termination of the war, Russia (read: the government) will concentrate all her attention on her internal life and, mainly, on quelling sedition"

---

1 *Moskovskiye Vedomosti* (*Moscow Gazette*)—a newspaper, began publication in 1756 and expressed the interests of the most reactionary circles of the feudal nobility and clergy. In 1905 it became the organ of the Black Hundreds. It was closed down after the October Revolution in 1917.

(see *Moskovskiye Vedomosti*, August 18).

Such were the "plans" of the tsarist government in concluding peace with Japan.

Then, when peace was concluded, it announced these "plans" once again through the mouth of its minister: "We shall drown the extremist parties in Russia in blood," said the minister. Through its viceroys and governor-generals it is already putting the above-mentioned "plans" into execution: it is not for nothing that it has transformed Russia into a military camp, it is not for nothing that it has inundated the centres of the movement with Cossacks and troops and has turned machine guns against the proletariat one would think that the government is setting out to conquer boundless Russia a second time!

As you see, the government is proclaiming war on the revolution and is directing its first blows against its advanced detachment—the proletariat. That is how its threats against the "extremist parties" are to be interpreted. It will not, of course, "neglect" the peasantry and will generously treat it to whips and bullets if it proves to be "unwise enough" to demand a human existence; but meanwhile the government is trying to deceive it: it is promising it land and inviting it into the Duma, painting pictures of "all sorts of liberties" in the future.

As regards the "gentry," the government will, of course, treat it "more delicately," and will try to enter into an alliance with it: that is exactly what the State Duma exists for. Needless to say, Messieurs the liberal bourgeoisie will not reject an "agreement." As far back as August 5 they stated through the mouth of their leader that they were enthusiastic over the tsar's reforms: ". . . All efforts must be exerted to prevent Russia . . . from following the revolutionary path pursued by France" (see *Russkiye Vedomosti*[2] of August 5, article by Vinogradov). Needless to say, the sly liberals would rather betray the revolution than Nicholas II. This was sufficiently proved by their last congress. . . .

In short, the tsarist government is exerting all efforts to crush the people's revolution.

---

2 **Original editor:** *Russkiye Vedomosti (Russian Gazette)*—a newspaper founded in Moscow in 1863 by the liberal professors at the Moscow University and by leading Zemstvo people. It expressed the interests of the liberal landlords and bourgeoisie. In 1905 became the organ of the Right-wing Cadets.

Bullets for the proletariat, false promises for the peasantry and "rights" for the big bourgeoisie—such are the weapons with which the reaction is arming.

Either the defeat of the revolution or death — such is the autocracy's slogan today.

On the other hand, the forces of the revolution are on the alert too, and are continuing their great work. The crisis which has been intensified by the war together with the political strikes which are breaking out with growing frequency, have stirred up the proletariat of the whole of Russia and have brought it face to face with the tsarist autocracy. Martial law, far from intimidating the proletariat, has, on the contrary, merely poured oil on the flames, and has still further worsened the situation. No one who hears the countless cries of proletarians: "Down with the tsarist government, down with the tsarist Duma!", no one who has felt the pulse of the working class, can doubt that the revolutionary spirit of the proletariat, the leader of the revolution, will rise higher and higher. As regards the peasantry—the war mobilisation which wrecked their homes by depriving their families of their best bread-winners, roused them against the present regime. If we also bear in mind that to this has been added the famine which has afflicted twenty-six gubernias, it will not be difficult to guess what path the long-suffering peasantry must take. And lastly, the troops, too, are beginning to murmur and this murmur is daily becoming more menacing for the autocracy. The Cossacks—the prop of the autocracy—are beginning to evoke the hatred of the troops: recently the troops in Novaya Alexandria wiped out three hundred Cossacks.[3] The number of facts like these is steadily growing. . . .

In short, life is preparing another revolutionary wave, which is gradually rising and sweeping against the reaction. The recent events

---

3 See *Proletary,** No. 15 where Martov's "plan" is published.

* **Original editor:** *Proletary (The Proletarian)*—an illegal Bolshevik weekly newspaper, the Central Organ of the Russian Social-Democratic Labour Party, founded by the decision of the Third Congress of the Party. It was published in Geneva from May 14 (27) to November 12 (25), 1905. In all, twenty-six numbers were published. V. I. Lenin was chief editor. *Proletary* continued the policy of the old, Leninist *Iskra*, and was the successor to the Bolshevik newspaper *Vperyod.* It ceased publication on V. I. Lenin's return to St. Petersburg.

in Moscow and St. Petersburg are harbingers of this wave.

What should be our attitude towards all these events? What should we Social-Democrats do?

To listen to the Menshevik Martov, we ought to elect this very day a Constituent Assembly to uproot the foundations of the tsarist autocracy forever. In his opinion, illegal elections ought to be held simultaneously with the legal elections to the Duma. Electoral committees should be set up to call upon "the people to elect their representatives by means of universal suffrage. At a certain moment these representatives should gather in a certain town and proclaim themselves a Constituent Assembly. . . ." This is how "the liquidation of the autocracy should take place."[4] In other words, we can conduct a general election all over Russia in spite of the fact that the autocracy still lives! "Illegal" representatives of the people can proclaim themselves a Constituent Assembly and establish a democratic republic in spite of the fact that the autocracy is running riot! It appears that neither arms, nor an uprising, nor a provisional government is needed—the democratic republic will come of its own accord; all that is needed is that the "illegal" representatives should call themselves a Constituent Assembly! Good Martov has forgotten only one thing, that one fine day his fairyland "Constituent Assembly" will find itself in the Fortress of Peter and Paul! Martov in Geneva fails to understand that the practical workers in Russia have no time to play at bourgeois spillikins.

No, we want to do something else.

Dark reaction is mustering sinister forces and is doing its utmost to unite them—our task is to unite the Social-Democratic forces and to weld them more closely.

Dark reaction is convening the Duma; it wants to gain new allies and to enlarge the army of the counter-revolution—our task is to proclaim an active boycott of the Duma, to expose its counter-revolutionary face to the whole world and to multiply the ranks of the supporters of the revolution.

Dark reaction has launched a deadly attack against the revolution;

---

4 See *Proletary*, No. 15 where Martov's "plan" is published.

it wants to cause confusion in our ranks and to dig the grave of the people's revolution—our task is to close our ranks, to launch a country-wide *simultaneous* attack against the tsarist autocracy and wipe out the memory of it forever.

Not Martov's house of cards, but a general uprising—that is what we need.

The salvation of the people lies in the victorious uprising of the people themselves.

Either the victory of the revolution or death—such should be our revolutionary slogan today.

Proletariatis Brdzola
(*The Proletarian Struggle*), No. 12,
October 15, 1905
Unsigned
Translated from the Georgian

THE BOURGEOISIE IS LAYING A TRAP

In the middle of September a congress of "persons active in rural and urban affairs" was held. At this congress a new "party"[1] was formed, headed by a Central Committee and with local bodies in different towns. The congress adopted a "programme," defined its "tactics," and drew up a special appeal which this newly-hatched "party" is to issue to the people. In short, the "persons active in rural and urban affairs" formed their own "party."

Who are these "persons"? What are they called?

The bourgeois liberals.

Who are the bourgeois liberals?

The class-conscious representatives of the wealthy bourgeoisie.

The wealthy bourgeoisie are our uncompromising enemies, their wealth is based upon our poverty, their joy is based upon our sorrow. Clearly, their class-conscious representatives will be our sworn enemies who will *consciously* try to smash us.

Thus, a "party" of the enemies of the people has been formed, and it intends to issue an appeal to the people.

What do these gentlemen want? What do they advocate in their appeal?

They are not Socialists, they detest the socialist movement. That

---

1 **Original editor:** *The Constitutional-Democratic Party* (Cadet Party)—the principal party of the liberal-monarchist bourgeoisie. Was formed in October 1905. Under the cloak of a spurious democratism and calling themselves the party of "Popular Freedom," the Cadets tried to win the peasantry to their side. They strove to preserve tsarism in the form of a constitutional monarchy. Subsequently, the Cadets became the party of the imperialist bourgeoisie. After the victory of the October Socialist Revolution the Cadets organised counter-revolutionary conspiracies and revolts against the Soviet Republic.

means that they are out to strengthen the bourgeois system and are waging a life-and-death struggle against the proletariat. That is why they enjoy great sympathy in bourgeois circles.

Nor are they Democrats, they detest the democratic republic. That means that they are out to strengthen the tsar's throne and are also fighting zealously against the long-suffering peasantry. That is why Nicholas II "graciously" permitted them to hold meetings and to convene a "party" congress.

All they want is slightly to curtail the powers of the tsar, and then only on the condition that these powers are transferred to the bourgeoisie. As regards tsarism itself, it must, in their opinion, certainly remain as a reliable bulwark of the wealthy bourgeoisie, which will use it against the proletariat. That is why they say in their "draft constitution" that "the throne of the Romanovs must remain inviolable," i.e., they want a curtailed constitution with a limited monarchy.

Messieurs the bourgeois liberals "have no objection" to the people being granted the franchise, provided, however, that the chamber of the people's representatives is dominated by a chamber representing the rich, which will certainly exert all efforts to modify and annul the decisions of the chamber of the people's representatives. That is why they say in their programme: "We need two chambers."

Messieurs the bourgeois liberals will be "very glad" if freedom of speech, of the press and of association is granted, provided, however, that freedom to strike is restricted. That is why they talk such a lot about the "rights of man and the citizen" but say nothing intelligible about freedom to strike, except for hypocritical prattle about nebulous "economic reforms."

Nor do these queer gentlemen withhold their charity from the peasantry—they "have no objection" to the land of the landlords being transferred to the peasants, provided, however, the peasants buy this land from the landlords and do not "receive it gratis." You see how benevolent these sorry "personages" are!

If they live to see all these wishes carried out, the result will be that the powers of the tsar will pass into the hands of the bourgeoisie, and the tsarist autocracy will gradually be transformed into the autocracy of the bourgeoisie. That is what the "persons active in rural and urban affairs" are driving at. That is why they are haunted by the people's revolution even in their sleep and talk so much about "pacifying Russia."

It is not surprising, after this, that these luckless "personages" placed such great hopes on the so-called State Duma. As we know, the tsarist Duma is the negation of the people's revolution, and this is very much to the advantage of our liberal bourgeoisie. As we know, the tsarist Duma provides "some slight" field of activity for the wealthy bourgeoisie, and this is exactly what our bourgeois liberals need so much. That is why they base their entire "programme" and the conduct of all their activities on the assumption that the Duma will exist—the bankruptcy of the Duma would inevitably lead to the collapse of all their "plans." That is why they are so frightened by the boycott of the Duma; that is why they advise us to go into the Duma. "It will be a great mistake if we do not go into the tsarist Duma," they say through the mouth of their leader Yakushkin, It will indeed be "a great mistake," but for whom, the people, or the people's enemies?—that is the question.

What is the function of the tsarist Duma? What do the "persons active in rural and urban affairs" have to say about this?

". . . The *first and main* task of the Duma is to reform the Duma itself," they say in their appeal.. "The voters must make the electors pledge themselves to elect candidates who, *primarily*, will want to reform the Duma," they say in the same appeal.

What is to be the nature of this "reform"? That the Duma should have "the decisive voice in framing laws . . . and in the discussion of state revenue and expenditure . . . and the right to control the activities of the ministers." In other words, the electors must *primarily* demand an extension of the powers of the Duma. So that is what the "reform" of the Duma turns out to be! Who will get into the Duma? Mainly the big bourgeoisie. Clearly, the extension of the powers of the Duma will mean strengthening the big bourgeoisie politically. And so, the "persons active in rural and urban affairs" advise the people to elect bourgeois liberals to the Duma and to instruct them *primarily* to help to strengthen the big bourgeoisie! First of all, and most of all, it appears, we must take care to strengthen our enemies, and with our own hands—that is what Messieurs the liberal bourgeoisie are advising us to do today. Very "friendly" advice, we must say! But what about the rights of the people? Who is to take care of that? Oh, Messieurs the liberal bourgeoisie will not forget the people, we can be quite sure about that! They assure us that *when* they get into the Duma, and *when* they entrench themselves in it, they will demand rights for the people too. And with the aid of hypocritical utterances of this kind the "persons active in rural and urban affairs" hope to achieve their aim. . . . So that is why they are advising us *primarily* to extend the powers of the Duma. . . .

Bebel said: Whatever the enemy advises us to do is harmful for us. The enemy advises us to go into the Duma—clearly, going into the Duma will be harmful for us. The enemy advises that the powers of the Duma should be extended—clearly, the extension of the powers of the Duma will be harmful for us. What we must do is to undermine confidence in the Duma and discredit it in the eyes of the people. What we need is not the extension of the powers of the Duma, but the extension of the rights of the people. And if the enemy talks sweetly to us and promises us indefinite "rights," it shows that he is laying a trap for us and wants us, with our own hands, to build a fortress for him. We can expect nothing better from the bourgeois liberals.

But what will you say about certain "Social-Democrats" who are preaching to us the tactics of the bourgeois liberals? What will you say about the Caucasian "minority" which repeats, word for word, the insidious advice of our enemies? This, for example, is what the Caucasian "minority" says: "We deem it necessary to go into the State Duma" (see *The Second Conference*, p. 7). This is exactly what Messieurs the bourgeois liberals "deem necessary."

The same "minority" advises us: "If the Bulygin Commission . . . grants the right to elect deputies *only to the propertied classes*, we must intervene in these elections and, by revolutionary means, compel the electors to elect progressive candidates and, in the Zemsky Sobor, demand a Constituent Assembly. Lastly, by every possible means . . . compel the Zemsky Sobor either to convoke a Constituent Assembly or *proclaim itself such*" (see the *Social-Democrat*, No. 1). In other words, even if the propertied classes alone enjoy the franchise, even if only representatives of the propertied classes gather in the Duma — we must still demand that this assembly of representatives of the propertied classes be granted the powers of a Constituent Assembly! Even if the rights of the people are curtailed, we must still try to extend the powers of the Duma as much as possible! Needless to say, if the franchise is granted only to the propertied classes, the election of "progressive candidates" will remain an empty phrase.

As you saw above, the bourgeois liberals preach the same thing.

One of two things: either the bourgeois liberals have become Menshevised, or the Caucasian "minority" have become liberalised.

Be that as it may, there can be no doubt that the newly-hatched "party" of the bourgeois liberals is skilfully setting a trap. . . .

What we must do now is—smash this trap, expose it for all to see, and wage a ruthless struggle against the liberal enemies of the people.

Proletariatis Brdzola
(*The Proletarian Struggle*), No. 12
October 15, 1905
Unsigned
Translated from the Georgian

CITIZENS!

The mighty giant—the proletariat of all Russia—is stirring again. . . . Russia is in the throes of a broad, country-wide strike movement. All over the boundless expanse of Russia life has come to a standstill as if by the wave of a magic wand. In St. Petersburg alone and on its railways, over a million workers have gone on strike. Moscow—the old, tranquil, sluggish capital, faithful to the Romanovs—is completely enveloped in a revolutionary conflagration. Kharkov, Kiev, Yekaterinoslav and other cultural and industrial centres, the whole of central and south Russia, the whole of Poland and, lastly, the whole of the Caucasus, have come to a standstill and are threateningly looking the autocracy straight-in the face.

What is going to happen? The whole of Russia is waiting with bated breath for an answer to this question. The proletariat is hurling a challenge at the accursed two-headed monster. Will this challenge be followed by a real clash, will the strike develop into an open, armed uprising, or will it, like previous strikes, end "peacefully" and "subside"?

Citizens! Whatever the answer to this question may be, in whichever way the present strike ends, one thing must be clear and beyond doubt to all: we are on the eve of an all-Russian, nation-wide uprising—and I he hour of this uprising is near. The general political strike now raging—of dimensions unprecedented and unexampled not only in the history of Russia but in the history of the whole world—may, perhaps, end today without developing into a nation-wide uprising, but tomorrow it will shake the country again with even greater force and develop into that mighty armed uprising which must settle the age-long contest between the Russian people and the tsarist autocracy and smash the head of this despicable monster.

A nation-wide armed uprising—that is the fateful climax to which

all the events that have recently taken place in the political and social life of our country are leading with historical inevitability! A nation-wide armed uprising—such is the great task that today confronts
the proletariat of Russia and is imperatively demanding execution!

Citizens! It is in the interests of all of you, except the handful
of financial and landed aristocrats, to join in the rallying cry of the
proletariat and to strive jointly with it to bring about this all-saving,
nation-wide uprising.

The criminal tsarist autocracy has brought our country to the
brink of doom. The ruination of a hundred million Russian peasants,
the downtrodden and distressed condition of the working class, the
excessive national debt and burdensome taxes, the lack of rights of
the entire population, the endless tyranny and violence that reign in all
spheres of life, and lastly, the utter insecurity of the lives and property
of the citizens—such is the frightful picture that Russia presents today.
This cannot go on much longer! The autocracy, which has caused all
these grim horrors, must be destroyed! And it will be destroyed! The
autocracy realises this, and the more it realises it the more grim these
horrors become, the more frightful becomes the hellish dance which
it is whipping up around itself. In addition to the hundreds and thousands of peaceful citizens—workers whom it has killed in the streets
of towns, in addition to the tens of thousands of workers and intellectuals, the best sons of the people, whom it has sent to languish in
prison and in exile, in addition to the incessant murders and violence
perpetrated by the tsar's bashi-bazouks in the countryside, among the
peasantry all over Russia—and finally, the autocracy has invented new
horrors. It has begun to sow enmity and hatred among the people
themselves and to incite different strata of the population and whole
nationalities against each other. It has armed and unleashed Russian
hooligans against the Russian workers and intellectuals, the unenlightened and starving masses of Russians and Moldavians in Bessarabia
against the Jews, and lastly, the ignorant and fanatical Tatar masses
against the Armenians. With the assistance of Tatars it has demolished
one of the revolutionary centres of Russia and the most revolutionary
centre of the Cau-casus—Baku—and has frightened the whole of the
Armenian province away from the revolution. It has converted the

entire Caucasus with its numerous tribes into a military camp where the population anticipates attack at any moment not only by the autocracy, but also by neighbouring tribes, the unfortunate victims of the autocracy. This cannot go on any longer! And only revolution can put a stop to it!

It would be strange and ridiculous to expect the autocracy, which created all these hellish horrors, to be willing, or able, to stop them. No reform, no patching of the autocracy—such as a State Duma, Zemstvos, and so forth, to which the liberal party wishes to limit itself—can put a stop to these horrors. On the contrary, every attempt in this direction, and every resistance to the revolutionary impulses of the proletariat, will only serve to intensify these horrors.

Citizens! The proletariat, the most revolutionary class in our society, the class which has up to now borne the brunt of the struggle against the autocracy, and which will remain to the end its most determined and unrelenting enemy, is preparing for open, armed action. And it calls upon you, all classes of society, for assistance and support. Arm yourselves and help it to arm, and prepare for the decisive battle.

Citizens! The hour of the uprising is near! We must meet it fully armed! Only if we do that, only by means of a general, country-wide and simultaneous armed uprising will we be able to vanquish our despicable foe—the accursed tsarist autocracy—and on its ruins erect the free democratic republic that we need.

Down With the Autocracy!

Long Live the General Armed Uprising!

Long Live the Democratic Republic!

Long Live the Fighting Proletariat of Russia!

Reproduced from the manifesto printed in October 1905 in the printing plant of the Tiflis Committee of the R.S.D.L.P. Signed: *Tiflis Committee*

TO ALL THE WORKERS

The thunder of revolution is roaring! The revolutionary people of Russia have risen and have surrounded the tsarist government in order to storm it! Red flags are flying, barricades are being erected, the people are taking to arms and are storming government offices. Again the call of the brave is heard; life, which had subsided, is seething again. The ship of the revolution has hoisted sail and is speeding towards freedom. That ship is being steered by the Russian proletariat.

What do the proletarians of Russia want? Whither are they steering?

Let us overthrow the tsarist Duma and set up a popular Constituent Assembly—this is what the proletarians of Russia are saying today. The proletariat will not demand petty concessions from the government, it will not call for the repeal of "martial law" and "floggings" in some towns and villages. The proletariat will not stoop to such trifles. Whoever demands concessions from the government does not believe that the government will perish—but the proletariat confidently believes that it will. Whoever expects "favours" from the government has no confidence in the might of the revolution —but the proletariat is inspired with this confidence.

No! The proletariat will not dissipate its energy in making senseless demands. It presents only one demand to the tsarist autocracy: Down with it! Death to it! And so, over the vast expanse of Russia the revolutionary cry of the workers rings out more and more boldly: Down with the State Duma! Long live a popular Constituent Assembly! This is the goal towards which the proletariat of Russia is striving today.

The tsar will not grant a popular Constituent Assembly, the tsar will not abolish his own autocracy—that he will not do! The curtailed "constitution" which he is "granting" is a temporary concession, the tsar's hypocritical promise and nothing more! It goes without saying that we shall take advantage of this concession, we shall not refuse to wrest from the crow a nut with which to smash its head. But the fact remains that the people can place no trust in the tsar's promises—they must trust only themselves; they must rely only on their own strength: the liberation of the people must be brought about by the people themselves. Only on the bones of the oppressors can the people's freedom be erected, only with the blood of the oppressors can the soil be fertilised for the sovereignty of the people! Only when the armed people come out headed by the proletariat and raise the banner of a general uprising can the tsarist government, which rests on bayonets, be overthrown. Not empty phrases, not senseless "self-arming," but real arming and an armed uprising— that is what the proletarians of the whole of Russia are steering towards today.

A victorious uprising will lead to the defeat of the government. But vanquished governments have often risen to their feet again. It may rise to its feet again in our country. On the morrow of the uprising, the dark forces which lay low during the uprising will creep out of their lairs and try to put the government on its feet again. That is how vanquished governments rise from the dead. The people must curb these dark forces without fail, they must make them bite the dust. But to do this the victorious people must, on the very morrow of the uprising, arm to a man, young and old, form themselves into a revolutionary army, and be ever ready to protect their hard-won rights by force of arms.

Only when the victorious people have formed themselves into a revolutionary army will they be able finally to crush the dark forces which go into hiding. Only a revolutionary army can lend force to the actions of a provisional government, only a provisional government can convoke a popular Constituent Assembly which must establish a democratic republic. A revolutionary army and a revolutionary provisional government—this is the goal towards which the proletarians of Russia are striving today.

Such is the path that the Russian revolution has taken. This path leads to the sovereignty of the people, and the proletariat calls upon all the friends of the people to march along this path.

The tsarist autocracy is barring the road of the people's revolution, it wants with the aid of the manifesto it issued yesterday to check this great movement—clearly, the waves of the revolution will engulf the tsarist autocracy and sweep it away. . . .

Contempt and hatred for all those who fail to take the path of the proletariat — they are despicably betraying the revolution! Shame upon those who, having taken this path in fact, say something else in words— they cravenly fear the truth!

We do not fear the truth, we do not fear revolution! Let the thunder roar still louder, let the storm rage more fiercely! The hour of victory is near!

Let us then enthusiastically proclaim the slogans of the proletariat of Russia:

Down With the State Duma!

Long Live the Armed Uprising!

Long Live the Revolutionary Army!

Long Live the Provisional Revolutionary Government!

Long Live the Popular Constituent Assembly!

Long Live the Democratic Republic!

Long Live the Proletariat!

Reproduced from the manifesto printed
on October 19, 1905 at the underground
(Avlabar) printing plant of the Caucasian
Union of the R.S.D.L.P.
Signed: *Tiflis Committee*
Translated from the Georgian

TIFLIS, NOVEMBER 20, 1905

The Great Russian Revolution has started! We have already passed through the first stormy act of this revolution, an act whose formal close was the Manifesto of October 17. The autocratic tsar "by the grace of God" bowed his "crowned head" to the revolutionary people and promised them "the unshakable foundations of civil liberty." . . .

But this was only the first act. It was only the beginning of the end. We are on the threshold of great events that will be worthy of the Great Russian Revolution. These events are advancing upon us with the inexorable rigour of history, with iron necessity. The tsar and the people, the autocracy of the tsar and the sovereignty of the people— are two antagonistic, diametrically opposed principles. The defeat of one and the victory of the other can come about only as the result of a decisive clash between the two, as the result of a desperate, life-and-death struggle. This struggle has not yet taken place. It still lies ahead. And the mighty Titan of the Russian revolution—the all-Russian proletariat—is preparing for it with might and main.

The liberal bourgeoisie is trying to avert this fateful clash. It is of the opinion that the time has come to put a stop to "anarchy" and to start peaceful, "constructive" work, the work of "state building." It is right, This bourgeoisie is satisfied with what the proletariat has already torn from tsarism by its first revolutionary action. It can now confidently conclude an alliance—on advantageous terms—with the tsarist government and by combined efforts attack the common enemy, attack its "gravedigger"—the revolutionary proletariat. Bourgeois freedom, freedom to exploit, is already ensured, and the bourgeoisie is quite satisfied. Never having been revolutionary, the Russian bourgeoisie is already openly going over to the side of reaction. A good riddance! We shall not grieve very much over this. The fate of the revolution was never in the hands of liberalism. The course and the outcome of the Russian revolution will be determined entirely by the conduct of the revolutionary proletariat and the revolutionary peasantry.

Led by Social-Democracy, the revolutionary urban proletariat and the revolutionary peasantry which is following it, will, in spite of all the machinations of the liberals, staunchly continue their struggle until they achieve the complete overthrow of the autocracy and erect a free democratic republic on its ruins.

Such is the immediate political task of the socialist proletariat, such is its aim in the present revolution; and, backed by the peasantry, it will achieve its aim at all costs.

It has also clearly and definitely mapped the road which must lead it to a democratic republic.

1) The decisive, desperate clash to which we referred above, 2) a revolutionary army organised in the course of this "clash," 3) the democratic dictatorship of the proletariat and peasantry in the shape of a provisional revolutionary government, which will spring up as a result of the victorious "clash," 4) a Constituent Assembly convened by that government on the basis of universal, direct, equal and secret suffrage—such are the stages through which the Great Russian Revolution must pass before it arrives at the desired goal.

No threats on the part of the government, no high-sounding tsarist manifestoes, no provisional governments of the type of the Witte government which the autocracy set up to save itself, no State Duma convened by the tsarist government, even if on the basis of universal, etc., suffrage—can turn the proletariat from the only true revolutionary path which must lead it to the democratic republic.

Will the proletariat have strength enough to reach the end of this path, will it have strength enough to emerge with honour from the gigantic, bloody struggle which awaits it on this path?

Yes, it will!

That is what the proletariat itself thinks, and it is boldly and resolutely preparing for battle.

Kavkazsky Rabochy Listok
(*Caucasian Workers' Newssheet*),[1] No. 1,
November 20, 1905
Unsigned

---

1 *Kavkazsky Rabochy Listok* (*Caucasian Workers' Newssheet*)—the first legal daily Bolshevik newspaper in the Caucasus, published in Tiflis in Russian from November 20 to December 14, 1905. It was directed by J. V. Stalin and S. G. Shaumyan. At the Fourth Conference of the Caucasian Union of the R.S.D.L.P it was recognised as the official organ of the Caucasian Union. In all, seventeen numbers were published. The last two numbers appeared under the title of *Yelizavetpolsky Vestnik* (*Yelizavetpol Herald*).

TWO CLASHES

(CONCERNING JANUARY 9)

You probably remember January 9 of last year. . . . That was the day on which the St. Petersburg proletariat came face to face with the tsarist government and, without wishing to do so, clashed with it. Yes, without wishing to do so, for the proletariat went peacefully to the tsar for "bread and justice," but was met as an enemy, with a hail of bullets. It had placed its hopes in portraits of the tsar and in church banners, but both portraits and banners were torn into shreds and thrown into its face, thus providing glaring proof that arms must be countered only by arms. And it took to arms wherever they were available—it took to arms in order to meet the enemy as an enemy and to wreak vengeance on him. But, leaving thousands of victims on the battle-field and sustaining heavy losses, the proletariat retreated, with anger burning in its breast. . . .

This is what January 9 of last year reminds us of.

Today, when the proletariat of Russia is commemorating January 9, it is not out of place to ask: Why did the St. Petersburg proletariat retreat after the clash last year, and in what way does that clash differ from the general clash that took place in December?

First of all it retreated because then it lacked that minimum of revolutionary consciousness that is absolutely essential if an uprising is to be victorious. Can the proletariat that goes with prayer and hope to a bloody tsar who has based his entire existence on the oppression of the people, can the proletariat which trustfully goes to its sworn enemy to beg "a crumb of charity"—can such people really gain the upper hand in street fighting? . . .

True, later on, after a little time had passed, rifle volleys opened the eyes of the deceived proletariat and revealed the vile features of the autocracy; true, after that the proletariat began to exclaim angrily: "The tsar gave it to us—we'll now give it to him!" But what is the use of that when you are unarmed? What can you do with bare hands in street fighting, even if you are enlightened? For does not an enemy bullet pierce an enlightened head as easily as an unenlightened one?

Yes, lack of arms—that was the second reason for the retreat of the St. Petersburg proletariat.

But what could St. Petersburg have done alone even if it had possessed arms? When blood was flowing in St. Petersburg and barricades were being erected, nobody raised a finger in other towns—that is why the government was able to bring in troops from other places and flood the streets with blood. It was only afterwards, when the St. Petersburg proletariat had buried its fallen comrades and had returned to its everyday occupations—only then was the cry of workers on strike heard in different towns: "Greetings to the St. Petersburg heroes!" But of what use were these belated greetings to anybody? That is why the government did not take these sporadic and unorganised actions seriously; the proletariat was split up in separate groups, so the government was able to scatter it without much effort.

Hence, the third reason for the retreat of the St. Petersburg proletariat was the absence of an organised general uprising, the unorganised action of the proletariat.

But who was there to organise a general uprising? The people as a whole could not undertake this task, and the vanguard of the proletariat—the proletarian party—was itself unorganised, for it was torn by internal disagreements. The internal war, the split in the party, weakened it more and more every day. It is not surprising that the young party, split into two parts, was unable to undertake the task of organising a general uprising.

Hence, the fourth reason for the proletariat's retreat was the absence of a single and united party.

And lastly, if the peasantry and the troops failed to join the uprising and infuse fresh strength into it, it was because they could not see any exceptional strength in the feeble and short-lived uprising, and, as is common knowledge, nobody joins the feeble.

That is why the heroic proletariat of St. Petersburg retreated in January last year.

* * *

Time passed. Roused by the crisis and lack of rights, the proletariat prepared for another clash. Those who thought that the losses sustained on January 9 would crush the fighting spirit of the proletariat were mis-taken—on the contrary, it prepared for the "last" clash with greater ardour and devotion, it fought the troops and Cossacks with greater courage and determination, The revolt of the sailors in the Black Sea and Baltic Sea, the revolt of the workers in Odessa, Lodz and other towns, and the continuous clashes between the peasants and the police clearly revealed how unquenchable was the revolutionary fire burning in the breasts of the people.

The proletariat has recently been acquiring with amazing rapidity the revolutionary consciousness it lacked on January 9. It is said that ten years of propaganda could not have brought about such an increase in the proletariat's class consciousness as these days of uprising have done. That is so, nor could it be otherwise, for the process of class conflicts is a great school in which the revolutionary consciousness of the people grows hour by hour.

A general armed uprising, which at first was preached only by a small group of the proletariat, an armed uprising, about which some comrades were even doubtful, gradually won the sympathy of the proletariat—and it feverishly organised Red detachments, procured arms, etc. The October general strike clearly demonstrated the feasibility of simultaneous action by the proletariat. This, in its turn, proved the feasibility of an organised uprising—and the proletariat resolutely took this path.

All that was needed was a united party, a single and indivisible Social-Democratic Party to direct the organisation of the general uprising, to co-ordinate the preparations for the revolution that were going on separately in different towns, and to take the initiative in the assault. That was all the more necessary because life itself was preparing the ground or a new upsurge—day by day, the crisis in the towns, starvation in the countryside, and other factors of a similar nature were making another revolutionary upheaval inevitable. The trouble was that such a party was then only in the process of formation; enfeebled by the split, the party was only just recovering and beginning to unite its ranks.

It was precisely at that moment that the proletariat of Russia entered into the second clash, the glorious December clash.

Let us now discuss this clash.

In discussing the January clash we said that it lacked revolutionary consciousness; as regards the December clash we must say that this consciousness existed. Eleven months of revolutionary storm had sufficiently opened the eyes of the militant proletariat of Russia, and the slogans: Down with the autocracy! Long live the democratic republic! became the slogans of the day, the slogans of the masses. This time you saw no church banners, no icons, no portraits of the tsar—instead, red flags fluttered and portraits of Marx and Engels were carried. This time you heard no singing of psalms or of "God Save the Tsar"—instead, the strains of the *Marseillaise* and the *Varshavyanka* deafened the tyrants.

Thus, in respect to revolutionary consciousness, the December clash differed radically from the January clash.

In the January clash there was a lack of arms, the people went into battle unarmed. The December clash marked a step forward, all the fighters now rushed for arms, with revolvers, rifles, bombs and in some places even machine guns in their hands. Procure arms by force of arms—this became the slogan of the day. Everybody sought arms, everybody felt the need for arms, the only sad thing about it was that very few arms were procurable, and only an inconsiderable number of proletarians could come out armed.

The January uprising was utterly sporadic and unorganised; in it everybody acted haphazard. In this respect, too, the December uprising marked a step forward. The St. Petersburg and Moscow Soviets of Workers' Deputies, and the "majority" and "minority" centres "took measures" as far as possible to make the revolutionary action simultaneous. They called upon the proletariat of Russia to launch a simultaneous offensive. Nothing of the kind was done during the January uprising. But that call had not been preceded by prolonged and persevering Party activity in preparation for the uprising, and so the call remained a call, and the action turned out to be sporadic and unorganised. There existed only the desire for a simultaneous and organised uprising.

The January uprising was "led" mainly by the Gapons. In this respect the December uprising had the advantage in that the Social-Democrats were at the head of it. The sad thing, however, was that the latter were split into separate groups, that they did not constitute a single united party, and, therefore, could not coordinate their activities. Once again the uprising found the Russian Social-Democratic Labour Party unprepared and divided. . . .

The January clash had no plan, it was not guided by any definite policy, the question whether to take the offensive or defensive did not confront it. The December clash merely had the advantage that it clearly raised this question, but it did so only in the course of the struggle, not at the very beginning. As regards the answer to this question, the December uprising revealed the same weakness as the January one. Had the Moscow revolutionaries adhered to the policy of offensive from the very beginning, had they at the very beginning attacked, say, the Nikolayevsky Railway Station and captured it, the uprising would, of course, have lasted longer and would have taken a more desirable turn. Or had the Lettish revolutionaries, for example, resolutely pursued a policy of offensive and had not wavered, then they undoubtedly would first of all have captured batteries of artillery, thereby depriving the authorities of all support; for the authorities had at first allowed the revolutionaries to capture towns, but later they passed to the offensive and with the aid of artillery recaptured the places they had lost.[1]

---

1 In December 1905, the Latvian towns of Tukums, Talsen, Rujen, Friedrichstadt, and others, were captured by armed detachments of insurgent workers, agricultural labourers and peasants, and guerilla warfare began against the tsarist troops. In January 1906 the uprising in Latvia was crushed by punitive expeditions under the command of generals Orlov, Sologub, and others.

The same must be said about other towns. Marx was right when he said: In an uprising only audacity conquers, and only those who adhere to the policy of offensive can be audacious to the end.

This was the cause of the proletariat's retreat in the middle of December.

If the overwhelming mass of the peasantry and troops failed to join in the December clash, if that clash even roused dissatisfaction among certain "democratic" circles—it was because it lacked that strength and durability which are so necessary for the uprising to spread and be victorious.

From what has been said it is clear what we, the Russian Social-Democrats, must do today.

Firstly, our task is to complete what we have begun—to form a single and indivisible party. The all-Russian conferences of the "majority" and the "minority" have already drawn up the organisational principles of unification. Lenin's formula defining membership of the Party, and democratic centralism, have been accepted. The respective centres that direct ideological and practical activities have already merged, and the merging of the local organisations is already almost completed. All that is needed is a Unity Congress that will officially endorse the unification that has actually taken place and thereby give us a single and indivisible Russian Social-Democratic Labour Party. Our task is to facilitate the execution of this task, which is so precious to us, and to make careful preparations for the Unity Congress, which, as is known, should open in the very near future.

Secondly, our task is to help the Party to organise the armed uprising, actively to intervene in this sacred cause and to work tirelessly for it. Our task is to multiply the Red detachments, to train and weld them together; our task is to procure arms by force of arms, to reconnoitre the disposition of government institutions, calculate the enemy's forces, study his strong and weak sides, and draw up a plan for the uprising accordingly. Our task is to conduct systematic agitation in favour of an uprising in the army and in the villages, especially in those villages that are situated close to towns, to arm the reliable elements in them, etc., etc. . . .

Thirdly, our task is to cast away all hesitation, to condemn all indefiniteness, and resolutely to pursue a policy of offensive. . . .

In short, *a united party, an uprising organised by the Party, and a policy of offensive*—this is what we need today to achieve the victory of the uprising.

And the more famine in the countryside and the industrial crisis in the towns become intensified and grow, the more acute and imperative does this task become.

Some people, it appears, are beset with doubts about the correctness of this elementary truth, and they ask in a spirit of despair: What can the Party, even if it is united, do if it fails to rally the proletariat around itself? The proletariat, they say, is routed, it has lost hope and is not in the mood to take the initiative; we must, they say, now expect salvation to come from the countryside; the initiative must come from there, etc. One cannot help saying that the comrades who argue in this way are profoundly mistaken. The proletariat is by no means routed, for the rout of the proletariat means its death; on the contrary, it is as much alive as it was before and is gaining strength every day. It has merely retreated in order, after mustering its forces, to enter the final clash with the tsarist government.

When, on December 15, the Soviet of Workers' Deputies of Moscow—the very Moscow which in fact led the December uprising—publicly announced: We are temporarily suspending the struggle in order to make serious preparations to raise the banner of an uprising again—it expressed the cherished thoughts of the entire Russian proletariat.

And if some comrades nevertheless deny facts, if they no longer place their hopes in the proletariat and now clutch at the rural bourgeoisie—the question is: With whom are we dealing, with Socialist-Revolutionaries or Social-Democrats? For no Social-Democrat will doubt the truth that the actual (and not only ideological) leader of the rural population is the urban proletariat.

At one time we were assured that the autocracy was crushed after October 17, but we did not believe it, because the rout of the autocracy means its death; but far from being dead, it mustered fresh forces for another attack. We said that the autocracy had only retreated. It turned out that we were right. . . .

No, comrades! The proletariat of Russia is not defeated, it has only retreated and is now preparing for fresh glorious battles. The proletariat of Russia will not lower its blood-stained banner; it will yield the leadership of the uprising to no one; it will be the only worthy leader of the Russian revolution.

January 7, 1906
Reproduced from the pamphlet
published by the Caucasian
Union Committee of the R.S.D.L.P.
Translated from the Georgian

THE STATE DUMA AND THE TACTICS
OF SOCIAL-DEMOCRACY[1]

You have no doubt heard of the emancipation of the peasants. That was the time when the government received a double blow: one from outside—defeat in the Crimea, and one inside—the peasant movement. That is why the government, harassed on two sides, was compelled to yield and talk about emancipating the peasants: "We must emancipate the peasants ourselves from above, otherwise the people will rise in revolt and secure their emancipation themselves from below." We know what that "emancipation from above" was. . . . The fact that the people at that time allowed themselves to be deceived, that the government's hypocritical plans succeeded, that it strengthened its position by means of these reforms and thereby postponed the victory of the people, shows, among other things, that the people were still unenlightened and could easily be deceived.

The same thing is being repeated in the life of Russia today. As is well known, today, too, the government is receiving a double blow: from outside—defeat in Manchuria, and inside—the people's revolu-

---

1 J. V. Stalin's article "The State Duma and the Tactics of Social-Democracy" was published on March 8, 1906, in the newspaper *Gantiadi* (*The Dawn*), the daily organ of the united Tiflis Committee of the R.S.D.L.P., which came out from March 5 to 10, 1906. The article was an official expression of the Bolsheviks' stand on the question of the tactics to be adopted towards the Duma. The preceding number of *Gantiadi* had contained an article entitled "The State Duma Elections and Our Tactics," signed H., which expressed the Menshevik stand on this question. J. V. Stalin's article was accompanied by the following editorial comment: "In yesterday's issue we published an article expressing the views of one section of our comrades on the question of whether to go into the State Duma or not. Today, as we promised, we are publishing another article expressing the principles adhered to on this question by another section of our comrades. As the readers will see, there is a fundamental difference between these two articles: the author of the first article is in favour of taking part in the Duma elections; the author of the second article is opposed to this. Neither of the two authors is expressing merely his own point of view. Both express the line of tactics of the two trends that exist in the Party. This is the case not only here, but all over Russia."

tion. And the government, harassed on two sides, has been compelled to yield again and, as it did then, it is again talking about "reforms from above": "We must give the people a State Duma from above, otherwise the people will rise in revolt and convoke a Constituent Assembly themselves from below." Thus, by convening the Duma, they want to subdue the people's revolution in the same way as, once upon a time, they subdued the great peasant movement by "emancipating the peasants."

Hence, our task is—to frustrate with all determination the plans of the reaction, to sweep away the State Duma, and thereby clear the road for the people's revolution.

But what will the Duma be? What will be its composition?

The Duma will be a mongrel parliament. Nominally, it will enjoy powers to decide; but actually, it will have only advisory powers, because the Upper Chamber, and a government armed to the teeth, will stand over it in the capacity of censors. The Manifesto definitely states that no decision of the Duma can be put into force unless it is approved by the Upper Chamber and the tsar.

The Duma will not be a people's parliament, it will be a parliament of the enemies of the people, because voting in the election of the Duma will be neither universal, equal, direct nor secret. The paltry electoral rights that are granted to the workers exist only on paper. Of the 98 electors who are to elect the Duma deputies for the Tiflis Gubernia, only two can be workers; the other 96 electors must belong to other classes—that is what the Manifesto says. Of the 32 electors who are to elect the Duma deputies for the Batum and Sukhum areas, only one can be a representative of the workers; the other 31 electors must come from other classes—that is what the Manifesto says. The same thing applies to the other gubernias. Needless to say, only representatives of the other classes will be elected to the Duma. *Not one deputy from the workers, not one vote for the workers—this is the basis upon which the Duma is being built.* If to all this we add martial law, if we bear in mind the suppression of freedom of speech, press, assembly and association, then it will be self-evident what kind of people will gather in the tsar's Duma. . . .

Needless to say, this makes it more than ever necessary resolutely to strive to sweep away this Duma and to raise the banner of revolution.

How can we sweep away the Duma—by participating in the elections or by boycotting them?—that is the question now.

Some say: We must certainly participate in the elections in order to entangle the reaction in its own snare and, thereby, utterly wreck the State Duma.

Others say in answer to this: By participating in the elections you will involuntarily help the reaction to set up the Duma and you will fall right into the trap laid by the reaction. And that means: first, you will create a tsarist Duma in conjunction with the reaction, and then life will compel you to try to wreck the Duma which you yourselves have created. This line is incompatible with the principles of our policy. One of two things: either keep out of the elections and proceed to wreck the Duma, or abandon the idea of wrecking the Duma and proceed with the elections so that you shall not have to destroy what you yourselves have created.

Clearly, the only correct path is active boycott, by means of which we shall isolate the reaction from the people, organise the wrecking of the Duma, and thereby cut the ground completely from under the feet of this mongrel parliament.

That is how the advocates of a boycott argue.

Which of the two sides is right?

To pursue genuinely Social-Democratic tactics two conditions are necessary: first, that those tactics should not run counter to the course of social life; and second, that they should raise the revolutionary spirit of the masses higher and higher.

The tactics of participating in the elections run counter to the course of social life, for life is sapping the foundations of the Duma, whereas participation in the elections will strengthen those foundations; consequently, participation runs counter to life.

The boycott tactics, however, spring automatically from the course of the revolution, for, jointly with the revolution, they discredit and sap the foundations of the police Duma from the very outset.

The tactics of participating in the elections weaken the revolutionary spirit of the people, for the advocates of participation call upon the people to take part in police-controlled elections and not to resort to revolutionary action; they see salvation in ballot papers and not in action by the people. But the police-controlled elections will give the people a false idea of what the State Duma is; they will rouse false hopes and the people will involuntarily think: evidently the Duma is not so bad, otherwise the Social-Democrats would not advise us to take part in electing it; perhaps fortune will smile on us and the Duma will benefit us.

The boycott tactics, however, do not sow any false hopes about the Duma, but openly and unambiguously say that salvation lies only in the victorious action of the people, that the emancipation of the people can be achieved only by the people themselves; and as the Duma is an obstacle to this, we must set to work at once to remove it. In this case, the people rely only upon themselves and from the very outset take a hostile stand against the Duma as the citadel of reaction; and that will raise the revolutionary spirit of the people higher and higher and thereby prepare the ground for general victorious action.

Revolutionary tactics must be clear, distinct and definite; the boycott tactics possess these qualities.

It is said: verbal agitation alone is not enough; the masses must be convinced by facts that the Duma is useless and this will help to wreck it. For this purpose participation in the elections and not active boycott is needed.

In answer to this we say the following. It goes without saying that agitation with facts is far more important than verbal explanation. The very reason for our going to *people's* election meetings is to demonstrate to the people, *in conflict* with other parties, *in collisions* with them, the perfidy of the reaction and the bourgeoisie, and in this way "agitate" the electors "with facts." If this does not satisfy the comrades, if to all this they add participation in the election, then we must say that, taken by themselves, elections—the dropping or not dropping of a ballot paper into a ballot box—do not add one iota either to "factual" or to "verbal" agitation. But the harm caused by this is great, because, by this "agitation with facts," the advocates of participation involuntarily sanction the setting up of the Duma, and thereby strengthen the ground beneath it. How do those comrades intend to compensate for the great harm thus done? By dropping ballot papers into the ballot box? This is not even worth discussing.

On the other hand, there must also be a limit to "agitation with facts." When Gapon marched at the head of the St. Petersburg workers with crosses and icons he also said: the people believe in the benevolence of the tsar, they are not yet convinced that the government is criminal, and we must, therefore, lead them to the tsar's palace. Gapon was mistaken, of course. His tactics were harmful tactics, as January 9 proved. That shows that we must give Gapon tactics the widest possible berth. The boycott tactics, however, are the only tactics that utterly refute Gapon's sophistry.

It is said: the boycott will separate the masses from their vanguard, because, with the boycott, only the vanguard will follow you; the masses, however, will remain with the reactionaries and liberals, who will pull them over to their side.

To that we reply that where this takes place the masses evidently sympathise with the other parties and will not anyhow elect Social-Democrats as their delegates, however much we may participate in the elections. Elections by themselves cannot possibly revolutionise the masses! As regards agitation in connection with the elections, it is being conducted by both sides, with the difference, however, that the advocates of the boycott are conducting more uncompromising and determined agitation against the Duma than the advocates of participation in the elections, because sharp criticism of the Duma may induce the masses to abstain from voting, and this does not enter into the plans of the advocates of participation in the elections. If this agitation proves effective, the people will rally around the Social-Democrats; and when the Social-Democrats call for a boycott of the Duma, then the people will at once follow them and the reactionaries will be left only with their infamous hooligans. If, however, the agitation "has no effect," then the elections will result in nothing but harm, because by employing the tactics of going into the Duma we would endorse the activities of the reactionaries. As you see, the boycott is the best means of rallying the people around Social-Democracy, in those places, of course, where it is possible to rally them; but where it is not, the elections can result in nothing but harm.

Moreover, the tactics of going into the Duma dim the revolutionary consciousness of the people. The point is that all the reactionary and liberal parties are participating in the elections. What difference is there between them and the revolutionaries? To this question the participation tactics fail to give the masses a straight answer. The masses might easily confuse the non-revolutionary Cadets with the revolutionary Social-Democrats. The boycott tactics, however, draw a sharp line between revolutionaries and the non-revolutionaries who want to save the foundations of the old regime with the aid of the Duma. And the drawing of this line is extremely important for the revolutionary enlightenment of the people.

And lastly, we are told that with the aid of the elections we shall create Soviets of Workers' Deputies, and thereby unite the revolutionary masses organisationally.

To this we answer that under present conditions, when even the most inoffensive meetings are suppressed, it will be absolutely impossible for Soviets of Workers' Deputies to function, and, consequently, to set this task is a piece of self-deception.

Thus, the participation tactics involuntarily serve to strengthen the tsarist Duma, weaken the revolutionary spirit of the masses, dim the revolutionary consciousness of the people, are unable to create any revolutionary organisations, run counter to the development of social life, and therefore should be rejected by Social-Democracy.

Boycott tactics—this is the direction in which the development of the revolution is now going. This is the direction in which Social-Democracy, too, should go.

Gantiadi (The Dawn), No. 3, March 8, 1906
Signed: *J. Besoshvili*
Translated from the Georgian

THE AGRARIAN QUESTION

I

The old order is breaking up, the countryside is in upheaval. The peasantry, who only yesterday were crushed and downtrodden, are today rising to their feet and straightening their backs. The peasant movement, which only yesterday was helpless, is today sweeping like a turbulent flood against the old order: get out of the way—or I'll sweep you away! "The peasants want the landlords' land," "The peasants want to abolish the remnants of serfdom"—such are the voices now heard in the rebellious villages and hamlets of Russia.

Those who count on silencing the peasants by means of bullets are mistaken: life has shown us that this only serves still further to inflame and intensify the revolutionary peasant movement.

And those who try to pacify the peasants with empty promises and "peasants' banks" are also mistaken: the peasants want land, they dream of this land, and, of course, they will not be satisfied until they have seized the landlords' land. Of what use are empty promises and "peasants' banks" to them?

The peasants want to seize the landlords' land. In this way they seek to abolish the remnants of serfdom—and those who are not betraying the peasants must strive to settle the agrarian question precisely on this basis.

But how are the peasants to gain possession of the landlords' land?

It is said that the only way is—"purchase on easy terms." The government and the landlords have plenty of spare land, these gentlemen tell us; if the peasants purchase this land, everything will settle itself, and in this way the wolves will be sated and the sheep remain whole.

But they do not ask what the peasants are to buy the land with after they have been stripped not only of their money but also of their very skins. They do not stop to think that in buying the land the peasants will have only bad land foisted upon them, while the landlords will keep the good land for themselves, as they succeeded in doing during the "emancipation of the serfs"! Besides, why should the peasants buy the land which has been theirs for ages? Have not both the government's and the landlords' lands been watered by the sweat of the peasants? Did not these lands belong to the peasants? Were not the peasants deprived of this heritage of their fathers and grandfathers? What justice is there in the demand that the peasants should buy the very land that was taken from them? And is the question of the peasant movement a question of buying and selling? Is not the aim of the peasant movement to emancipate the peasants? Who will free the peasants from the yoke of serfdom if not the peasants themselves? And yet, these gentlemen assure us that the landlords will emancipate the peasants, if only they are given a little hard cash. And, believe it or not, this "emancipation," it seems, is to be carried out under the direction of the tsarist bureaucracy, the selfsame bureaucracy which more than once has met the starving peasants with cannons and machine guns! . . .

No! Buying out the land will not save the peasant. Whoever advises them to accept "purchase on easy terms" is a traitor, because he is trying to catch the peasants in the real-estate agent's net and does not want the emancipation of the peasants to be brought about by the peasants themselves.

Since the peasants want to seize the landlords' land, since they must abolish the survivals of serfdom in this way, since "purchase on easy terms" will not save them, since the emancipation of the peasants must be brought about by the peasants themselves, then there cannot be the slightest doubt that the only way is to take the land from the landlords, that is, to confiscate these lands.

That is the way out.

The question is—how far should this confiscation go? Has it any limit, should the peasants take only part of the land, or all of it?

Some say that to take all the land would be going too far, that it is sufficient to take part of the land to satisfy the peasants. Let us assume that it is so, but what is to be done if the peasants demand more? We cannot stand in their way and say: Halt! Don't go any further! That would be reactionary! And have not events in Russia shown that the peasants are actually demanding the confiscation of all the landlords' land? Besides, what does "taking a part" mean? What part should be taken from the landlords, one half or one third? Who is to settle this question—the landlords alone, or the landlords in conjunction with the peasants? As you see, this still leaves plenty of scope for the real-estate agent, there is still scope for bargaining between the landlords and the peasants; and this is fundamentally opposed to the task of emancipating the peasants. The peasants must, once and for all, get accustomed to the idea that it is necessary not to bargain with the landlords, but to fight them. We must not mend the yoke of serfdom, but smash it, so as to abolish the remnants of serfdom forever. To "take only part" means patching up the survivals of serfdom, which is incompatible with the task of emancipating the peasants.

Clearly, the only way is to *take all the land* from the landlords. That alone will enable the peasant movement to achieve its aim, that alone can stimulate the energy of the people, that alone can sweep away the fossilised remnants of serfdom.

Thus: the present movement in the countryside is a democratic peasant movement. The aim of this movement is to abolish the remnants of serfdom. To abolish these remnants it is necessary to confiscate all landlord and government lands.

Certain gentlemen ask us accusingly: Why did not Social-Democracy demand the confiscation of all the land before? Why, until recently, did it speak only about confiscating the "otrezki"[1]?

Because, gentlemen, in 1903, when the Party talked about the "otrezki," the Russian peasantry had not yet been drawn into the movement. It was the Party's duty to carry into the countryside a slogan that would fire the peasants' hearts and rouse them against the remnants of serfdom. Confiscate the "otrezki" was precisely such a

---

1 Literally "cuts." The plots of land the landlords took from the peasants when serfdom was abolished in Russia in 1861.—Tr.

slogan, because the "otrezki" vividly reminded the Russian peasants of the injustice of the remnants of serfdom.

But times have changed. The peasant movement has grown. It is no longer necessary to call it into being—it is already in full swing. The question today is not *how to get the peasants moving*, but *what the peasants who are already moving should demand*. Clearly, here definite demands are what is needed, and so the Party tells the peasants that they ought to demand the confiscation of all landlord and government lands.

This shows that everything has its time and place, and this applies to the "otrezki" as well as to the confiscation of all the land.

II

We have seen that the present movement in the countryside is a movement for the emancipation of the peasants, we have also seen that to emancipate the peasants it is necessary to abolish the remnants of *serfdom*, and to abolish these remnants it is necessary to confiscate all landlord and government land, so as to clear the road for the new way of life, for the free development of capitalism.

Let us assume that all this has been done. How should this land be subsequently distributed? Into whose ownership should it be transferred?

Some say that the confiscated land should be granted to each village as *common* property; that the *private* ownership of land must be abolished *forthwith*, that each village should become complete owner of the land and then itself divide the land among the peasants in *equal* "allotments," and in this way socialism will be introduced in the countryside forthwith—instead of wage-labour there will be equal land tenure.

This is called "*socialisation of the land*," the Socialist-Revolutionaries tell us.

Is this solution acceptable for us? Let us examine it. Let us first deal with the point that in introducing socialism, the Socialist-Revolutionaries want to *begin* with the countryside. Is this possible? Everybody knows that the town is more developed than the countryside, that the town is the leader of the countryside, and, consequently, every activity for socialism must begin in the town. The Socialist-Revolutionaries, however, want to convert the countryside into the leader of the town and to compel the countryside to begin introducing socialism, which of course is impossible owing to the backwardness of the countryside. Hence, it is obvious that the "socialism" of the Socialist-Revolutionaries will be stillborn socialism.

Let us now pass to the point that they want to introduce socialism in the countryside *forthwith*. Introducing socialism means abolishing commodity production, abolishing the money system, razing capitalism to its foundations and socialising all the means of production. The Socialist-Revolutionaries, however, want to leave all this intact and to socialise only the land, which is absolutely impossible. If commodity production remains intact, the land, too, will become a commodity and will come on to the market any day, and the "socialism" of the Socialist-Revolutionaries will be blown sky-high. Clearly, they want to introduce socialism within the framework of capitalism, which, of course, is inconceivable. That is exactly why it is said that the "socialism" of the Socialist-Revolutionaries is bourgeois socialism.

As regards *equal land tenure*, it must be said that this is merely an empty phrase. Equal land tenure needs equality of property, but among the peasantry inequality of property prevails, and this the present democratic revolution cannot abolish. Is it conceivable that the owner of eight pair of oxen will make the same use of the land as one who owns no oxen at all? And yet the Socialist-Revolutionaries believe that "equal land tenure" will lead to the abolition of wage-labour, and that it will stop the development of capital, which, of course, is absurd. Evidently, the Socialist-Revolutionaries want to combat the *further* development of capitalism and turn back the wheel of history—in this they seek salvation. Science, however, tells us that the victory of socialism depends upon the *development* of capitalism, and whoever combats this development is combating socialism. That is why the Socialist-Revolutionaries are also called *Socialist-Reactionaries*.

We shall not dwell on the fact that the peasants want to fight to abolish feudal property not in opposition to bourgeois property, but on the basis of bourgeois property—they want to divide the confiscated land among themselves as private property and will not be satisfied with "socialisation of the land."

Hence you see that "socialisation of the land" is unacceptable.

Others say that the confiscated land should be transferred to a democratic state, and that the peasants should be only the tenants of this state.

This is called "*nationalisation of the land.*"

Is the nationalisation of the land acceptable? If we bear in mind that the future state, however democratic it may be, will nevertheless be a bourgeois state, that the transfer of the land to such a state will enhance the political strength of the bourgeoisie, which would be greatly to the disadvantage of the rural and urban proletariat; if we also bear in mind that the peasants themselves will be opposed to "nationalisation of the land" and will not be satisfied with being merely tenants— it will be self-evident that "nationalisation of the land" is not in the interest of the present-day movement.

Consequently, "nationalisation of the land" is also unacceptable.

Still others say that the land should be transferred to local government bodies, and that the peasants should be the tenants of these bodies.

This is called "*municipalisation of the land.*"

Is the municipalisation of the land acceptable? What does "municipalisation of the land" mean? It means, firstly, that the peasants will not receive as their property the land which they confiscate from the landlords and the government in the course of the struggle. How will the peasants look upon this? The peasants want to receive land as their property; the peasants want to divide the confiscated land among themselves; they dream of this land as their property, and when they are told that this land is to be transferred not to them but to the local government bodies, they will certainly disagree with the advocates of "municipalisation." We must not forget this.

Moreover, what will happen if in their revolutionary ardour the peasants take possession of all the confiscated land and leave nothing for the local government bodies? We cannot stand in their way and say: Halt! This land must be transferred to the local government bodies and not to you, it will be quite enough for you to be tenants!

Secondly, if we accept the "municipalisation" slogan we must at once raise it among the people and at once explain to the peasants that the land for which they are fighting, which they want to seize, is not to become their property, but the property of local government bodies. Of course, if the Party enjoys great influence among the peasants they may agree with it, but, needless to say, the peasants will no longer fight with their previous ardour, and this will be extremely harmful for the present revolution. If, however, the Party does not enjoy great influence among the peasants, the latter will desert the Party and turn their backs upon it, and this will cause a conflict between the peasants and the Party and greatly weaken the forces of the revolution.

We shall be told: often the wishes of the peasantry run counter to the course of development; we cannot ignore the course of history and always follow the wishes of the peasants—the Party should have its own principles. That is gospel truth! The Party must be guided by its principles. But the party which rejected all the above-mentioned strivings of the peasantry would betray its principles. If the peasants' desire to seize the landlords' lands and to divide them among themselves does not run counter to the course of history; if, on the contrary, these strivings spring entirely from the present democratic revolution, if a real struggle against feudal property can be waged only on the basis of bourgeois property, and if the strivings of the peasants express precisely this trend—then it is self-evident that the Party cannot reject these demands of the peasants, for refusal to back these demands would mean refusing to develop the revolution. On the other hand, if the Party has principles, if it does not wish to become a brake upon the revolution, it must help the peasants to achieve what they are striving for. And what they are striving for totally contradicts the "municipalisation of the land"!

As you see, "municipalisation of the land" is also unacceptable.

III

We have seen that neither "socialisation," nor "nationalisation," nor "municipalisation" can properly meet the interests of the present revolution.

How should the confiscated land be distributed? Into whose ownership should it be transferred?

Clearly, the land which the peasants confiscate *should be transferred to the peasants* to enable them to *divide* this land among themselves. This is how the question raised above should be settled. The division of the land will call forth the mobilisation of property. The poor will sell their land and take the path of proletarianisation; the wealthy will acquire additional land and proceed to improve their methods of cultivation; the rural population will split up into classes; an acute class struggle will flare up, and in this way the foundation for the further development of capitalism will be laid.

As you see, the division of the land follows logically from present-day economic development.

On the other hand, the slogan *"The land to the peasants, only to the peasants and to nobody else"* will encourage the peasantry, infuse new strength into them, and help the incipient revolutionary movement in the countryside to achieve its aim.

As you see, the course of the present revolution also points to the necessity of dividing the land.

Our opponents say to us accusingly that in that way we shall regenerate the petty bourgeoisie, and that this radically contradicts the doctrines of Marx. This is what *Revolutsionnaya Rossiya*[2] writes:

"By helping the peasantry to expropriate the landlords you are unconsciously helping to install petty-bourgeois farming on the ruins of the already more or less developed forms of capitalist farming. Is this not a 'step backwards' from the point of view of orthodox Marxism?" (See *Revolutsionnaya Rossiya*, No. 75.)

I must say that Messieurs the "Critics" have mixed up the facts. They have forgotten that landlord farming is not capitalist farming, that it is a survival of feudal farming, and, consequently, the expropri-

---

2 *Revolutsionnaya Rossiya* (*Revolutionary Russia*)—the organ of the Socialist-Revolutionaries, published from the end of 1900 to 1905. At first it was published by the League of Socialist-Revolutionaries, but in January 1902 it became the central organ of the Socialist-Revolutionary Party.

ation of the landlords will destroy the remnants of feudal farming and not capitalist farming. They have also forgotten that from the point of view of Marxism, capitalist farming has never followed directly after feudal farming, nor can it do so—between them stands petty-bourgeois farming, which supersedes feudal farming and subsequently develops into capitalist farming. Karl Marx said in Volume III of *Capital* that historically feudal farming was followed by petty-bourgeois farming and that large-scale capitalist farming developed only after that—there was no direct leap from one to the other, nor could there be. And yet these strange "critics" tell us that to take away the landlords' lands and to divide them up means retrogression from the point of view of Marxism! Soon they will say to us accusingly that "the abolition of serfdom" was also retrogression from the point of view of Marxism, because at that time too some of the land was "taken away" from the landlords and transferred to small owners—the peasants! What funny people they are! They do not understand that Marxism looks at everything from the historical point of view, that from the point of view of Marxism, petty-bourgeois farming is progressive compared with feudal farming, that, the destruction of feudal farming and the introduction of petty-bourgeois farming are essential conditions for the development of capitalism, which will subsequently eliminate petty-bourgeois farming. . . .

But let us leave these "critics" in peace.

The point is that the *transfer of the land to the peasants* and the *division of these lands* will sap the foundations of the survivals of serfdom, prepare the ground for the development of capitalist farming, give a great impetus to the revolutionary upsurge, and precisely for these reasons those measures are acceptable to the Social-Democratic Party.

Thus, to abolish the remnants of serfdom it is necessary to confiscate all the land of the landlords, and then the peasants must take this land as their property and divide it up among themselves in conformity with their interests.

That is the basis on which the Party's agrarian programme must be built.

We shall be told: All this applies to the peasants, but what do you intend to do with the rural proletarians? To this we reply that for the peasants we need a *democratic* agrarian programme, but for the rural and urban proletarians we have a *socialist* programme, which expresses their class interests. Their current interests are provided for in the sixteen points of our minimum programme dealing with the improvement of conditions of labour (see the Party's programme that was adopted at the Second Congress). Meanwhile, the Party's direct socialist activities consist in conducting socialist propaganda among the rural proletarians, in uniting them in their own socialist organisations, and merging them with the urban proletarians in a separate political party. The Party is in constant touch with this section of the peasantry and says to them: In so far as you are bringing about a democratic revolution you must maintain contact with the militant peasants and fight the landlords, but in so far as you are marching towards socialism, then resolutely unite with the urban proletarians and fight relentlessly against every bourgeois, be he peasant or landlord. Together with the peasants for a democratic republic! Together with the workers for socialism!—that is what the Party says to the rural proletarians.

The proletarian movement and its *socialist programme* fan the flames of the class struggle in order to abolish the whole *class system* forever; for their part the peasant movement and its *democratic agrarian programme* fan the flames of the *struggle between the social estates* in the countryside in order to eradicate the whole *social estate system*.

*   *   *

P.S. In concluding this article we cannot refrain from commenting on a letter we have received from a reader who writes us the following: "After all, your first article failed to satisfy me. Was not the Party opposed to the confiscation of all the land? If it was, why did it not say so?"

No, dear reader, the Party was never opposed to such confiscation. Already at the Second Congress, at the very congress which adopted the point on the "otrezki"—at that congress (in 1903) the Party, through the mouth of Plekhanov and Lenin, said that we would back the peasants if they demanded the confiscation of all the land[3] Two years later (1905) the two groups in the Party, the "Bolsheviks" at the Third Congress, and the "Mensheviks" at the First Conference, unanimously stated that they would whole-heartedly back the peasants on the question of confiscating *all* the land.[4] Then the newspapers of both Party trends, *Iskra* and *Proletary*, as well as *Novaya Zhizn*[5] and *Nachalo*,[6] repeatedly called upon the peasantry to confiscate all the land. . . . As you see, from the very outset the Party has stood for the confiscation of *all* the land and, consequently, you have no grounds for thinking that the Party has dragged at the tail of the peasant movement. The peasant movement had not really started yet, the peasants were not yet demanding even the "otrezki," but already at its Second Congress the Party was speaking about confiscating *all* the land.

If, nevertheless, you ask us why we did not, in 1903, introduce the demand for the confiscation of all the land in our programme, we shall answer by putting another question: Why did not the Socialist-Revolutionaries, in 1900, introduce in their programme the demand for a *democratic republic*? Were they opposed to this demand?[7] Why did they at that time talk only about nationalisation, and why are they now dinning socialisation into our ears? Today we say nothing in our minimum programme about a seven-hour day, but does that mean that we are opposed to this? What is the point then? Only that in 1903, when the movement had not yet taken root, the demand for the confiscation of all the land would merely have remained on paper, the still feeble movement would not have been able to cope with this demand, and that is why the demand for the "otrezki" was more suitable for that

---

3 See *Minutes of the Second Congress.*

4 See *Minutes of the Third Congress* and "The First Conference."

5 **Original editor:** *Novaya Zhizn (New Life)*—the first legal Bolshevik newspaper, published in St. Petersburg from October 27 to December 3, 1905. When V. I. Lenin arrived from abroad, *Novaya Zhizn* began to appear under his personal direction. An active part in the publication of the newspaper was taken by Maxim Gorky. On the appearance of No. 27 of *Novaya Zhizn* the paper was suppressed by the authorities. No. 28, the last number to be published, came out illegally.

6 **Original editor:** *Nachalo (The Beginning)*—a legal daily newspaper published in St. Petersburg by the Mensheviks from November 13 to December 2, 1905.

7 See *Our Tasks*, published by the League of Socialist-Revolutionaries, 1900.

period. But subsequently, when the movement grew and put forward *practical* questions, the Party had to show that the movement could not, and must not, stop at the "otrezki"; that the confiscation of all the land was necessary.

Such are the facts.

And finally, a few words about *Tsnobis Purtseli*[8] (see No. 3033). This newspaper printed a lot of nonsense about "fashions" and "principles," and asserted that at one time the Party elevated "otrezki" to a principle. From what has been said above the reader can see that this is a *lie*, that the Party *publicly* recognised the confiscation of all the land in principle from the very outset. The fact that *Tsnobis Purtseli* cannot distinguish between principles and practical questions need not worry us—it will grow up and learn to distinguish between them.[9]

Elva (The Lightning), Nos. 5, 9 and 10,
March 17, 22 and 23, 1906
Signed: *J. Besoshvili*
Translated from the Georgian

---

8 **Original editor:** *Tsnobis Purtseli (News Bulletin)*—a daily Georgian newspaper published in Tiflis from 1896 to 1906. At the end of 1900 it became the mouthpiece of the Georgian nationalists, and in 1904 became the organ of the Georgian Social-Federalists.

9 *Tsnobis Purtseli* "heard" somewhere that the "Russian Social-Democrats . . . have adopted a new agrarian programme by virtue of which . . . they support the municipalisation of the land." I must say that the Russian Social-Democrats have adopted no such programme. The adoption of a programme is the function of a congress, but no congress has been held yet. Clearly, *Tsnobis Purtseli* has been misled by somebody or something. *Tsnobis Purtseli* would do well if it stopped stuffing its readers with rumours.

CONCERNING THE AGRARIAN QUESTION

You probably remember the last article on "municipalisation" (see *Elva*,[1] No. 12). We have no wish to discuss all the questions the author touches upon—that is neither interesting nor necessary. We wish to touch upon only two main questions: Does municipalisation contradict the abolition of the remnants of serfdom? And is the division of the land reactionary? This is exactly how our comrade presents the question. Evidently, he imagines that municipalisation, division of the land and similar questions are questions of *principle*; the Party, however, puts the agrarian question on an *altogether different basis*.

The point is that Social-Democracy regards neither nationalisation, nor municipalisation, nor the division of the land as *questions of principle, and raises no objection on principle to any of them*. Read Marx's *Manifesto*, Kautsky's *The Agrarian Question, Minutes of the Second Congress*, and *The Agrarian Question in Russia*, also by Kautsky, and you will see that this is precisely the case. The Party regards all these questions from the *practical* point of view, and puts the agrarian question on a *practical basis*: what *most fully* carries out our principle — municipalisation, nationalisation or division of the land?

This is the basis on which the Party puts the question.

It goes without saying that the *principle* of the agrarian programme—the abolition of the remnants of serfdom and the free development of the class struggle—*remains unchanged*; only the means of carrying out this principle have changed.

That is how the author should have presented the question, name-

---

1 *Elva* (*The Lightning*)—a daily Georgian newspaper, organ of the united Tiflis Committee of the R.S.D.L.P., began publication after the suppression of *Gantiadi*. The first number was issued on March 12 and the last on April 15, 1906. On behalf of the Bolsheviks the leading articles were written by J. V. Stalin. In all, twenty-seven numbers were issued.

ly: *Which is the better means* of securing the abolition of the remnants of serfdom and the development of the class struggle—municipalisation, or the division of the land? He, however, quite unexpectedly steps into the sphere of principles, palms off *practical* questions as questions of *principle*, and asks us: Does so-called municipalisation "contradict the abolition of the remnants of serfdom and the development of capitalism"? Neither nationalisation nor the division of the land contradicts the abolition of the remnants of serfdom and the development of capitalism; but that does not mean that there is no difference between them, that the advocate of municipalisation should at the same time advocate nationalisation and the division of the land! Clearly, there is some *practical difference* between them. That is the whole point, and that is why the Party puts the question on a *practical* basis. The author, however, as we noted above, carried the question to an entirely different plane, confused the principle with the means of carrying out this principle, and thus, involuntarily, evaded the question that is raised by the Party.

The author further assures us that the division of the land is reactionary, i.e., he hurls at us the same reproach that we have heard more than once from the Socialist-Revolutionaries. When those metaphysicians, the Socialist-Revolutionaries, tell us that the division of the land is reactionary from the standpoint of Marxism, this reproach does not surprise us in the least, for we know perfectly well that they do not look at the question from the standpoint of dialectics; they refuse to understand that everything has its time and place, that something which may be reactionary *tomorrow* may be revolutionary *today*. But when dialectical-materialists hurl that reproach at us we cannot help asking: What, then, is the difference between dialecticians and metaphysicians? It goes without saying that the division of the land would be reactionary if it were directed *against the development of capitalism*; but if it is directed *against the remnants of serfdom*, it is self-evident that the division of the land is a revolutionary measure which Social-Democracy must support. What is the division of the land directed against today: against capitalism or against the remnants of serfdom? There can be no doubt that it is directed against the remnants of serfdom. Hence, the question settles itself.

True, after capitalism has sufficiently established itself in the countryside, division of the land will become a reactionary measure, for
it will then be directed against the development of capitalism. Then,
Social-Democracy will not support it. At the present time Social-Democracy strongly champions the demand for a democratic republic
as a revolutionary measure, but later on, when the dictatorship of the
proletariat becomes a practical question, the democratic republic will
already be reactionary, and Social-Democracy will strive to destroy it.
The same thing must be said about the division of the land. Division
of the land, and petty-bourgeois farming generally, is revolutionary
when a struggle is being waged against the remnants of serfdom; but
the same division of the land is reactionary *when* it is directed against
the development of capitalism. Such is the dialectical view of social
development. Karl Marx regards petty-bourgeois farming in the same
dialectical way when in Volume III of *Capital* he calls it progressive
compared with feudal economy.

In addition to all this, K. Kautsky says the following about the
division of the land :

"The division of the land reserve, i.e., the large estates, which the
Russian peasants are demanding and are already beginning to carry out
in practice . . . is not only inevitable and necessary, but also *highly beneficial. And Social-Democracy has every ground for supporting this process*" (see
The Agrarian Question in Russia, p. 11).

Of enormous importance for the settlement of a question is the
correct method of presenting it. Every question must be presented
dialectically, i.e., we must never forget that everything changes, that
everything has its time and place, and, consequently, we must also present questions in conformity with concrete circumstances. That is the
first condition for the settlement of the agrarian question. Secondly,
we must also not forget that today Russian Social-Democrats put the
agrarian question on a practical basis, and whoever wishes to settle that
question must stand on that basis. That is the second condition for
the settlement of the agrarian question. Our comrade, however, took
neither of these conditions into consideration.

Well then, the comrade will answer, let us assume that the division of the land is revolutionary. Clearly, we shall strive to support this revolutionary movement; but that does not mean that we ought to introduce the demands of this movement into our programme—those demands are totally out of place in the programme, etc. Evidently the author is confusing the minimum programme with the maximum programme. He knows that the *socialist* programme (i.e., the maximum programme) should contain only proletarian demands; but he forgets that the *democratic* programme (i.e., the minimum programme), and the agrarian programme in particular, is not a socialist programme, and, consequently, it will certainly contain bourgeois-democratic demands, which we *support*. Political freedom is a bourgeois demand; but despite that it occupies an honourable place in our minimum programme. But why go so far? Take Clause 2 of the agrarian programme and read: the Party demands ". . . the abolition of all laws which *restrict the peasant in the disposal of his land*"—read all that and answer: what is socialistic about this clause? Nothing, you will say, because it demands freedom for bourgeois property, and not its abolition. Nevertheless, this clause is in our minimum programme. What is the point then? Only that the maximum programme and the minimum programme are two different concepts, which must not be confused. True, the Anarchists will be displeased with that; but we cannot help it. We are not Anarchists! . . .

As regards the peasants' striving for the division of the land, we have already said that its importance is measured by the trend of economic development; and as this striving of the peasants "springs directly" from this trend, our Party must support, and not counteract it.

Elva (The Lightning), No. 14,
March 29, 1906
Signed: *J. Besoshvili*
Translated from the Georgian

CONCERNING THE REVISION

OF THE AGRARIAN PROGRAMME

(SPEECH DELIVERED AT THE SEVENTH SITTING

OF THE FOURTH CONGRESS OF THE R.S.D.L.P.[1]

APRIL 13 [26], 1906)

First of all I will speak about the mode of argument adopted by certain comrades. Comrade Plekhanov talked a lot about Comrade Lenin's "anarchistic propensities," about the fatal consequences of "Leninism," and so on, and so forth; but he said very little about the agrarian question. And yet he is down as one of the speakers on the agrarian question. I am of the opinion that this mode of argument, which creates an atmosphere of irritation, in addition to being out of harmony with the character of our congress, which is called a Unity Congress, tells us absolutely nothing about the presentation of the agrarian question. We could talk about Comrade Plekhanov's Cadet propensities, but we would not, thereby, carry the settlement of the agrarian question a single step forward.

1 **Original editor:** The Fourth ("Unity") Congress of the R.S.D.L.P. was held in Stockholm from April 10 to 25 (April 23 to May 8, New Style), 1906. Representatives were also present from the national Social-Democratic parties of Poland and Lithuania, Latvia and from the Bund. Many of the Bolshevik organisations were broken up by the government after the armed uprising in December 1905 and were therefore unable to send delegates. The Mensheviks had a majority at this congress, although a small one. The predominance of the Mensheviks at the congress determined the character of its decisions on a number of questions. J. V. Stalin attended the congress as a delegate from the Tiflis organisation of the Bolsheviks under the pseudonym of Ivanovich. He took part in the debates on the draft agrarian programme, on the current situation, and on the State Duma. In addition, he made several statements of fact, in which he exposed the opportunist tactics of the Transcaucasian Mensheviks on the question of the State Duma, on the agreement with the Bund, and other questions.

Further, John,[2] from certain data of the life of Guria, the Lettish region, etc., draws an inference in favour of municipalisation for the whole of Russia. I must say that, speaking generally, that is not the way to draw up a programme. In drawing up a programme we must take as the starting point not the specific features of certain parts of certain border regions, but the features common to the majority of localities in Russia. A programme without a dominating line is not a programme, but a mechanical combination of different propositions. That is exactly how it stands with John's draft. Moreover, John is quoting incorrect data. In his opinion the very process of development of the peasant movement speaks in favour of his draft because in Guria, for example, in the very process of this movement, a regional local government body was formed which took control of the forests, etc. But first of all, Guria is not a region, but one of the uyezds in the Kutais Gubernia; secondly, there has never been in Guria a revolutionary local government body covering the whole of Guria; there have been only small local government bodies, which are not the same thing as a regional local government body; thirdly, control is one thing—ownership is quite another. Speaking generally, lots of legends are afloat concerning Guria, and the Russian comrades are quite mistaken in taking them for the truth. . . .

As regards the essence of the subject, I must say that the following proposition should serve as the starting point for our programme: since we are concluding a temporary revolutionary alliance with the militant peasantry, and therefore, since we cannot ignore the demands of this peasantry—we must support these demands if, on the whole, they do not run counter to the trend of economic development and the course of the revolution. The peasants are demanding division; division does not run counter to the phenomena I have mentioned; hence, we must support complete confiscation and division. From this point of view both nationalisation and municipalisation are equally unacceptable. By advancing the slogan of municipalisation, or of nationalisation, we gain nothing and make the alliance between the revolutionary peasantry and the proletariat impossible. Those who say that division is reactionary confuse two stages of development: the

---

2 **Original editor:** John—the pseudonym of P. P. Maslov.

capitalist and the pre-capitalist stages. Undoubtedly, in the capitalist stage, division is reactionary; but under pre-capitalist conditions (under the conditions prevailing in the Russian countryside, for example), division, on the whole, is revolutionary. Of course, forests, waters, etc., cannot be divided, but these can be nationalised, and that does not run counter to the revolutionary demands put forward by the peasants. Furthermore, the slogan: Revolutionary Committees — which John proposes instead of Revolutionary Peasant Committees —fundamentally contradicts the spirit of the agrarian revolution. The object of the agrarian revolution is primarily and mainly to emancipate the peasants; consequently, the slogan, Peasant Committees, is the only slogan that corresponds to the spirit of the agrarian revolution. If the emancipation of the proletariat must be the act of the proletariat itself, then the emancipation of the peasants must be the act of the peasants themselves.

Minutes of the Unity Congress
of the Russian Social-Democratic
Labour Party held in Stockholm
in 1906
Moscow 1907, pp. 59-60

ON THE PRESENT SITUATION

(SPEECH DELIVERED AT THE FIFTEENTH SITTING OF THE FOURTH CONGRESS OF THE R.S.D.L.P. APRIL 17 [30], 1906)

It is no secret to anyone that two paths are now discernible in the development of the social and political life of Russia: the path of pseudo-reform and the path of revolution. It is clear also that the big factory owners and the landlords, headed by the tsarist government, are taking the first path, while the revolutionary peasantry and the petty bourgeoisie, headed by the proletariat, are taking the second. The crisis that is developing in the towns and the famine in the countryside are making another upheaval inevitable—consequently, here vacillation is impermissible. *Either* the revolution is on the upgrade—and in that case we must carry the revolution through to the end—*or* it is on the downgrade, in which case we cannot and should not set ourselves such a task. Rudenko is wrong in thinking that this method of presenting the question is not dialectical. Rudenko is looking for a middle course; he wants to say that the revolution is and is not on the upgrade, and that it should and should not be carried to the end, because, in his opinion, dialectics makes it incumbent to present the question in this way! That is not our conception of Marxian dialectics. . . .

And so we are on the eve of another upheaval; the revolution is on the upgrade and we must carry it to the end. On this we are all agreed. But under what circumstances can we, and should we, do this? Under the hegemony of the proletariat, or under the hegemony of bourgeois democracy? This is where our main disagreement begins.

Comrade Martynov has said already in his *Two Dictatorships* that the hegemony of the proletariat in the present bourgeois revolution is a harmful utopia. The same idea ran through the speech he delivered yesterday. The Comrades who applauded him evidently agree with him. If that is the case, if in the opinion of the Menshevik comrades what we need is not the hegemony of the proletariat, but the hegemony of the democratic bourgeoisie, then it is self-evident that we should take no direct active part either in the organisation of an armed uprising, or in the seizure of power. Such is the "scheme" of the Mensheviks.

On the other hand, if the class interests of the proletariat lead to its hegemony, if the proletariat must be at the head of the present revolution and not drag at its tail, it goes without saying that the proletariat cannot refrain either from taking an active part in the organisation of an armed uprising or from seizing power. Such is the "scheme" of the Bolsheviks.

Either the hegemony of the proletariat, or the hegemony of the democratic bourgeoisie—that is how the question stands in the Party, that is where we differ.

Minutes of the Unity Congress
of the Russian Social-Democratic
Labour Party held in Stockholm
in 1906
Moscow 1907, p. 187

MARX AND ENGELS ON INSURRECTION

The Menshevik N. H.[1] knows that audacity wins the day and has the audacity to accuse the Bolsheviks once again of being Blanquists (see *Simartleh*,[2] No. 7).

There is nothing surprising in this, of course. Bernstein and Vollmar, the German opportunists, have for a long time been saying that Kautsky and Bebel are Blanquists. Jaures and Millerand, the French opportunists, have been for a long time accusing Guesde and Lafargue of being Blanquists and Jacobins. Nevertheless, everyone knows that Bernstein, Millerand, Jaures and the others, are opportunists, that they are *betraying Marxism*, whereas Kautsky, Bebel, Guesde, Lafargue and the others are revolutionary Marxists. What is there surprising in the fact that the Russian opportunists, and their follower N. H., copy the European opportunists and call us Blanquists? It shows only that the Bolsheviks, like Kautsky and Guesde, are revolutionary Marxists.[3]

We could here conclude our talk with N. H., but he makes the question "more profound" and tries to prove his point. Very well, let us not offend him and hear what he has to say.

N. H. disagrees with the following opinion expressed by the Bolsheviks:

---

1 **Original editor:** N. H.—Noah Homeriki, a Menshevik.

2 **Original editor:** *Simartleh* (*Truth*)—a daily political and literary newspaper published by the Georgian Mensheviks in Tiflis in 1906.

3 K. Kautsky and J. Guesde at that time had not yet gone over to the camp of the opportunists. The Russian revolution of 1905-07, which greatly influenced the international revolutionary movement and the working class of Germany in particular, caused K. Kautsky to take the stand of revolutionary Social-Democracy on a number of questions.

"Let us suppose that[4] the people in the towns are imbued with hatred for the government[5]; they can always rise up for the struggle if the opportunity offers. That means that quantitatively we are ready. But this is *not enough*. If an uprising is to be successful, it is necessary to draw up in advance a plan of the struggle, to draw up in advance the tactics of the battle; it is necessary to have organised detachments, and so forth" (see *Akhali Tskhovreba*, No. 6)

N. H. disagrees with this. Why? Because, he says, it is Blanquism! And so, N. H. wants neither "tactics of the battle," nor "organised detachments," nor organised action—all that, it appears, is unimportant and unnecessary. The Bolsheviks say that by itself "hatred for the government is not enough," consciousness by itself "is not enough"; it is necessary to have, in addition, "detachments and tactics of the battle." N. H. rejects all that and calls it Blanquism.

Let us note this and proceed.

N. H. dislikes the following idea expressed by Lenin:

We must collect the experience of the uprisings in Moscow, the Donets Basin, Rostov-on-Don and other places, *disseminate* this *experience*, perseveringly and painstakingly *prepare* new fighting forces and *train and steel* them in a series of militant guerilla actions. The new upheaval may not yet break out in the spring, but it is approaching; in all probability it is not very far off. We must meet it armed, organised in military fashion, and be capable of taking determined offensive action" (see *Partiiniye Izvestia*).[6]

---

4 Here N. H. substituted the word "when" for the words "let us suppose that," which slightly alters the meaning.

5 Here N. H. omitted the words "for the government" (see *Akhali Tskhovreba,*[*] No. 6).

[*] **Original editor**: *Akhali Tskhovreba (New Life)*—a daily Bolshevik newspaper published in Tiflis from June 20 to July 14, 1906, under the direction of J. V. Stalin. M. Davitashvili, G. Telia, G. Kikodze and others were permanent members of the staff. In all, twenty numbers were issued.

6 **Original editor**: This passage is quoted from an article by V. I. Lenin entitled "The Present Situation in Russia and the Tactics of the Workers' Party" (see *Works*, 4th Russ. ed., Vol. 10, pp. 98-99), published in *Partiiniye Izvestia (Party News)*, the organ of the united Central Committee of the R.S.D.L.P. *Partiiniye Izvestia* was published illegally in St. Petersburg just prior to the Fourth ("Unity") Congress of the Party. Two numbers were issued: No. 1 on February 7 and No. 2 on March 20, 1906.

N. H. disagrees with this idea of Lenin's. Why? Because, he says, it is Blanquism!

And so, in N. H.'s opinion, we must *not* "collect the experience of the December uprising" and must *not* "disseminate it." True, an upheaval is approaching, but in N. H.'s opinion we must *not* "meet it armed," we must *not* prepare "for determined offensive action." Why? Probably because we are more likely to be victorious if we are unarmed and unprepared! The Bolsheviks say that we can expect an upheaval and, therefore, our duty is to prepare for it both in respect to consciousness and in respect to arms. N. H. knows that an upheaval is to be expected, but he refuses to recognise anything more than verbal agitation and therefore doubts whether it is necessary to arm, and thinks it superfluous. The Bolsheviks say that consciousness and organisation must be introduced into the sporadic insurrection which has broken out spontaneously. But N. H. refuses to recognise this—it is Blanquism, he says. The Bolsheviks say that at a definite moment "determined offensive action" must be taken. But N. H. dislikes both *determination* and *offensive action*—all this is Blanquism, he says.

Let us note the foregoing and see what attitude Marx and Engels took towards armed insurrection.

Here is what Marx wrote in the fifties:

". . . The insurrectionary career once entered upon, act with the greatest determination, and *on the offensive*. The defensive is the death of every armed rising. . . . Surprise your antagonists while their forces are scattering, prepare new successes, however small, but daily keep up the moral ascendant which the first successful rising has given to you; rally thus those vacillating elements to your side which always follow the strongest impulse and which always look out for the safer side; force your enemies to a retreat before they can collect their strength against you; in the words of Danton, the greatest master of revolutionary policy yet known : *de l'audace, de l'audace, encore de l'audace!*" (See Karl Marx, *Historical Sketches*, p. 95.)[7]

This is what Karl Marx, the greatest of Marxists, says.

---

7 Karl Marx and Frederick Engels, *Revolution and Counter-revolution in Germany* (see Karl Marx, Selected Works, Vol. II, Moscow 1936, p. 135).

As you see, in Marx's opinion, whoever wants insurrection to triumph must take the path of the *offensive*. But we know that whoever takes the path of the offensive must have arms, military knowledge and trained detachments. Without these an offensive is impossible. Bold offensive action, in Marx's opinion, is the flesh and blood of every uprising. N. H., however, ridicules everything: bold offensive action, the policy of offensive, organised detachments and the dissemination of military knowledge. All that is Blanquism, he says! It appears, then, that N. H. is a Marxist, but Marx is a Blanquist! Poor Marx! If only he could rise from his grave and hear N. H.'s prattle.

And what does Engels say about insurrection? In a passage in one of his pamphlets he refers to the Spanish uprising, and answering the Anarchists, he goes on to say :

"Nevertheless, the uprising, even if begun in a brainless way, would have had a good chance to succeed, if it had only been conducted with some intelligence, say in the manner of Spanish military revolts, in which the garrison of one town rises, marches on to the next, sweeps along with it that town's garrison that had been influenced beforehand and, growing into an avalanche, presses on to the capital, until a fortunate engagement or the coming over to their side of the troops sent against them decides the victory. This method was particularly practicable on that occasion. The insurgents *had long before been organised* everywhere into volunteer battalions (do you hear, comrade, Engels talks about battalions!) whose discipline, while wretched, was surely not more wretched than that of the remnants of the old, and in the main disintegrated, Spanish army. The only dependable government troops were the gendarmes (*guardias civiles*), and these were scattered all over the country. It was primarily a question of preventing a concentration of the gendarme detachments, and this could be brought about only by assuming the *offensive* and the *hazard* of open battle . . . (attention, comrades, attention!). For any one who sought victory, there was no other means. . . ." Engels then goes on to take to task the Bakuninists, who proclaimed as their principle that which could have been avoided: "the splitting up and isolation of the revolutionary forces, which permitted the same government troops to quell one uprising after another" (see Engels's *The Bakuninists at Work*).[8]

This is what the celebrated Marxist, Frederick Engels, says. . . .

Organised battalions, the policy of offensive, organs-ing insurrection, uniting the separate insurrection — that, in Engels's opinion, is needed to ensure the victory of an insurrection.

It appears then that N. H. is a Marxist, but Engels is a Blanquist! Poor Engels!

As you see, N. H. is not familiar with the views of Marx and Engels on insurrection.

That would not be so bad. We declare that the tactics advocated by N. H. belittle and actually deny the importance of arming, of Red detachments, and of military knowledge. His are the tactics of unarmed insurrection. His tactics push us towards the "December defeat." Why did we have no arms, no detachments, no military knowledge and so forth in December? Because the tactics advocated by comrades like N. H. were widely accepted in the Party. . . .

But both Marxism and real life reject such unarmed tactics.

That is what the facts say.

Akhali Tskhovreba
(*New Life*), No. 19,
July 13, 1906
Signed: *Koba*
Translated from the Georgian

---

8 See Frederick Engels, *Die Bakunisten an der Arbeit*, Moskau 1941, S. 16-17.

INTERNATIONAL COUNTER-REVOLUTION

In many ways, present-day Russia reminds us of France in the period of the great revolution. This similarity finds expression, among other things, in that in our country, as in France, counter-revolution is spreading and, overflowing its own frontiers, is entering into an alliance with counter-revolution in other countries—it is gradually assuming an international character. In France, the old government concluded an alliance with the Austrian Emperor and the King of Prussia, called their troops to its aid, and launched an offensive against the people's revolution. In Russia, the old government is concluding an alliance with the German and Austrian emperors—it wants to call their troops to its aid and to drown the people's revolution in blood.

Only a month ago definite rumours were afloat to the effect that "Russia" and "Germany" were conducting secret negotiations (see *Severnaya Zemlya*,[1] No. 3). Later these rumours spread more persistently. And now things have reached such a pitch that the Black-Hundred newspaper *Rossiya*[2] openly states that the blame for "Russia's" (i.e., the counter-revolution's) present difficulties rests upon the revolutionary elements. "The Imperial German government," says that newspaper, "is fully aware of this situation and has therefore undertaken a series of appropriate measures which will certainly lead to the desired results." It transpires that these measures amount to preparations by "Austria" and "Germany" to send troops to assist "Russia" in the event of the Russian revolution proving successful. They have already reached agreement on that point, and have decided that "under certain

---

1 **Original editor:** *Severnaya Zemlya* (*Northern Land*)—a legal Bolshevik daily newspaper published in St. Petersburg from June 23 to 28, 1906.

2 **Original editor:** *Rossiya* (*Russia*)—a daily newspaper expressing the views of the police and the Black Hundreds, published from November 1905 to April 1914. Organ of the Ministry of the Interior.

conditions active intervention in the internal affairs of Russia with the object of suppressing, or curbing, the revolutionary movement may be desirable and beneficial. . . ."

So says *Rossiya*.

As you see, international counter-revolution has long been making extensive preparations. It is well known that for a long time past it has been rendering counterrevolutionary Russia financial assistance in the struggle against the revolution. But it has not confined itself to this. Now, it appears, it has decided to come to the aid of counter-revolutionary Russia also with troops.

After that, even a child can easily understand the real significance of the dissolution of the Duma, as well as the significance of Stolypin's "new" orders[3] and Trepov's "old" pogroms.[4] . . . It must be assumed that now the false hopes entertained by various liberals and other naive people will be dispelled, and that they will at last become convinced that we have no "constitution," that we have civil war, and that the struggle must be waged on military lines. . . .

But present-day Russia resembles France of that time also in another respect. At that time, international counter-revolution caused an expansion of the revolution; the revolution overflowed the borders of France and swept through Europe in a mighty flood. The "crowned heads" of Europe united in a common alliance, but the peoples of Europe also extended their hands to one another. We see the same thing in Russia today. "The old mole is grubbing well." . . . By uniting with the European counter-revolution the Russian counterrevolution is steadily expanding the revolution, uniting the proletarians of all countries, and laying the foundations for the international revolution. The Russian proletariat is marching at the head of the *democratic* revolution and is extending a fraternal hand to, is uniting with, the European proletariat, which will begin the *socialist* revolution. As is well known, after the January 9 action, mass meetings were held all over Europe. The December action evoked demonstrations in Germany and France.

---

3 In June and July 1906, P. A. Stolypin, the Minister of the Interior, issued an order to the local authorities demanding the ruthless suppression by armed force of the revolutionary movement of the workers and peasants and the revolutionary organisations.

4 D. Trepov—the Governor-General of St. Petersburg, who directed the suppression of the 1905 Revolution.

There can be no doubt that the impending action of the Russian revolution will still more vigorously rouse the European proletariat for the struggle. International counter-revolution will only strengthen and deepen, intensify and firmly establish, international revolution. The slogan "Workers of all countries, unite!" will find its true expression.

So go on, gentlemen, keep it up! The Russian revolution, which is expanding, will be followed by the European revolution—and then ... and then the last hour will strike not only for the survivals of serfdom, but also for your beloved capitalism.

Yes, you are "grubbing well," Messieurs counterrevolutionaries.

Akhali Tskhovreba
(New Life), No. 20,
July 14, 1906
Signed: *Koba*
Translated from the Georgian

THE PRESENT SITUATION AND THE UNITY CONGRESS OF THE WORKERS' PARTY[1]

I

What we have been waiting for so impatiently has come to pass — the Unity Congress has ended peacefully, the Party has avoided a split, the amalgamation of the groups has been officially sealed, and the foundation of the political might of the Party has thereby been laid.

We must now take account of, and study more closely, the complexion of the congress and soberly weigh up its good and bad sides.

What has the congress done?

What should the congress have done?

The first question is answered by the resolutions of the congress. To be able to answer the second question one must know the situation in which the congress was opened, and the tasks with which the present situation confronted it.

Let us start with the second question.

---

1 **Original editor:** J. V. Stalin's work *The Present Situation and the Unity Congress of the Workers' Party* was published in the Georgian language in Tiflis in 1906 by Proletariat Publishers. An appendix to the pamphlet contained the three draft resolutions submitted by the Bolsheviks to the Fourth ("Unity") Congress: 1) "The Present Situation in the Democratic Revolution" (see V. I. Lenin, Works, 4th Russ. ed., Vol. 10, pp. 130-31), 2) "The Class Tasks of the Proletariat in the Present Situation in the Democratic Revolution" (see *Resolutions and Decisions of C.P.S.U.(B.) Congresses, Conferences and Central Committee Plenums*, Part I, 6th Russ. ed., 1940, p. 65), 3) "Armed Insurrection" (see V. I. Lenin, *Works*, 4th Russ. ed., Vol. 10, pp. 131-33), and also the draft resolution on the State Duma submitted to the congress on behalf of the Bolsheviks by V. I. Lenin (see V. I. Lenin, Works, 4th Russ. ed., Vol. 10, pp. 266-67). The appendix also contained the resolution adopted by the congress on armed insurrection, and also the draft resolution of the Mensheviks on "The Present Situation in the Revolution and the Tasks of the Proletariat."

It is now clear that the people's revolution has not perished, that in spite of the "December defeat" it is growing and swiftly rising to its peak. We say that this is as it should be: the driving forces of the revolution still live and operate, the industrial crisis which has broken out is becoming increasingly acute, and famine, which is utterly ruining the countryside, is growing worse every day—and this means that the hour is near when the revolutionary anger of the people will burst out in a menacing flood. The facts tell us that a new action is maturing in the social life of Russia—more determined and mighty than the December action. We are on the eve of an uprising.

On the other hand, the counter-revolution, which the people detest, is mustering its forces and is gradually gaining strength. It has already succeeded in organising a camarilla, it is rallying all the dark forces under its banner, it is taking the lead of the Black-Hundred "movement"; it is preparing to launch another attack upon the people's revolution; it is rallying around itself the bloodthirsty landlords and factory owners—consequently, it is preparing to crush the people's revolution.

And the more events develop, the more sharply is the country becoming divided into two hostile camps—the camp of the revolution and the camp of counter-revolution—the more threateningly do the two leaders of the two camps—the proletariat and the tsarist government—confront each other, and the clearer does it become that all the bridges between them have been burnt. One of two things: *either* the victory of the revolution and the sovereignty of the people, *or* the victory of the counter-revolution and the tsarist autocracy. Whoever tries to sit between two stools betrays the revolution. Those who are not for us are against us! That is exactly what has happened to the miserable Duma and its miserable Cadets: they have become stuck between these two stools. The Duma wants to reconcile the revolution with the counter-revolution, it wants the lion and the lamb to lie down together —and in that way to suppress the revolution "at one stroke." That is why the Duma is engaged to this day only in collecting water with a sieve, that is why it has failed to rally any people around itself. Having no ground to stand on, it is dangling in the air.

The chief arena of the struggle is still the street. That is what the facts say. The facts say that it is in the present-day struggle, in street fighting, and not in that talking-shop the Duma, that the forces of the counter-revolution are daily becoming more feeble and disunited, whereas the forces of the revolution are growing and mobilising; that the revolutionary forces are being welded and organised under the leadership of the advanced workers and not of the bourgeoisie. And this means that the victory of the present revolution, and its consummation, is quite *possible*. But it is possible only *if* it continues to be led by the advanced workers, *if* the class-conscious proletariat *worthily* fulfils the task of leading the revolution.

Hence, the tasks with which the present situation confronted the congress, and what the congress should have done, are clear.

Engels said that the workers' party "is the conscious exponent of an unconscious process," i.e., that the party must consciously take the path along which life itself is proceeding unconsciously; that it must consciously express the ideas which unconsciously spring from tempestuous life.

The facts say that tsarism has failed to crush the people's revolution, that, on the contrary, it is growing day by day, rising higher, and marching towards another action. Consequently, it is the Party's task consciously to prepare for this action and to carry the people's revolution through to the end.

Clearly, the congress should have pointed to this task and should have made it incumbent upon the members of the Party honestly to carry it out.

The facts say that conciliation between the revolution and counter-revolution is impossible; that having taken the path of conciliation from the very outset the Duma can do nothing; that *such* a Duma can never become the political centre of the country, cannot rally the people around itself, and will be compelled to become an appendage of the reaction. Consequently, it is the Party's task to dispel the false hopes that have been reposed in the Duma, to combat political illusions among the people and to proclaim to the whole world that the *chief* arena of the revolution is the street and not the Duma; that the victory of the people must be achieved *mainly* in the street, by street fighting and not by the Duma, not by talking in the Duma.

Clearly, the Unity Congress should also have pointed to this task in its resolutions, in order thereby clearly to define the trend of the Party's activities.

The facts say that it is possible to achieve the victory of the revolution, to carry it to the end and to establish the sovereignty of the people, *only* if the class-conscious workers come out at the head of the revolution, if the revolution is led by Social-Democracy and not by the bourgeoisie. Hence it is the Party's task to dig the grave of the hegemony of the bourgeoisie, to rally the revolutionary elements of town and country around itself, to be at the head of their revolutionary struggle, to lead their actions from now on, and thereby strengthen the ground for the hegemony of the proletariat.

Clearly, the Unity Congress should have drawn special attention to this third and main task in order thereby to indicate to the Party its enormous importance.

That is what the present situation demanded of the Unity Congress, and that is what the congress should have done.

Did the congress carry out these tasks?

II

To obtain an answer to the foregoing question it is necessary to study the complexion of the congress.

The congress dealt with numerous questions at its sittings; but the main question, around which all the other questions revolved, was the question of the present situation. *The present situation in the democratic revolution and the class tasks of the proletariat*—that is the question in which all our disagreements on tactics became entangled as in a knot.

In the towns the crisis is growing more acute, said the Bolsheviks; in the countryside the famine is growing more intense; the government is rotting to its foundation, the anger of the people is rising day by day. Consequently, far from subsiding, the revolution is growing day by day, and is preparing for another offensive. Hence, the task is to help on the growing revolution, to carry it to the end and crown it with the sovereignty of the people (see the resolution proposed by the Bolsheviks : "The Present Situation . . .").

The Mensheviks said almost the same thing.

But *how* is the present revolution to be carried to the end; *what* conditions are needed for this?

In the opinion of the Bolsheviks, the present revolution can be carried to the end and crowned with the sovereignty of the people *only if* the class-conscious workers are at the head of this revolution, only if the leadership of the revolution is concentrated in the hands of the socialist proletariat and not of the bourgeois democrats. The Bolsheviks said : "Only the proletariat is capable of carrying the democratic revolution to the end, *provided however, that it . . . carries with it* the masses of the peasantry and introduces political consciousness into their spontaneous struggle. . . ." If the proletariat fails to do this, it will be compelled to abandon the role of "leader of the people's revolution" and will find itself "at the tail of the liberal-monarchist bourgeoisie," which will never strive to carry the revolution to the end (see resolution "The Class Tasks of the Proletariat . . ."). Of course, our revolution is a bourgeois revolution, and in this respect it resembles the Great French Revolution, the fruits of which were reaped by the bourgeoisie. But it is also clear that there is a great difference between these two revolutions. At the time of the French revolution, large-scale machine production, such as we have in our country today, did not exist, and class antagonisms were not so sharp and distinct as they are in our country today; hence, the proletariat there was weak, whereas here it is stronger and more united. We must also take into account the fact that there the proletariat did not have its own party, whereas here it has its own party, with its own programme and tactics. It is not surprising that the French revolution was headed by the bourgeois democrats and that the workers dragged at the tail of these gentlemen; that "the workers did the fighting, while the bourgeoisie achieved power." On the other hand, it can be readily understood that the proletariat of Russia is not content with dragging at the tail of the liberals, that it comes out as the leader of the revolution and is rallying all the "oppressed and dispossessed" to its banner. This is where our revolution has the advantage over the Great French Revolution, and this is why we think that our revolution can be carried to the end and be crowned with the sovereignty of the people. All that is needed is that we should consciously further the hegemony of the proletariat, rally the militant people around it, and *thereby make it possible* for the present revolution to be carried to the end. But the revolution must be carried to the end in order that the fruits of this revolution shall not be reaped by the bourgeoisie alone, and in order that the working class, in addition to achieving political freedom, shall achieve the eight-hour day, and better conditions of labour, and shall fully carry out its minimum programme, thereby hewing a path to socialism. Hence, whoever champions the interests of the proletariat, whoever does not want the proletariat to become a hanger-on of the bourgeoisie, pulling the chestnuts out of the fire for it, whoever is fighting to convert the proletariat into an independent force and wants it to utilise the present revolution for its own purpose—must openly condemn the hegemony of the bourgeois democrats, must strengthen the ground for the hegemony of the socialist proletariat in the present revolution.

That is how the Bolsheviks argued.

The Mensheviks said something entirely different. Of course, the revolution is growing, they said, and it must be carried to the end, but the hegemony of the socialist proletariat is not at all needed for that—let the bourgeois democrats act as the leaders of the revolution Why? What is the point? the Bolsheviks asked. Because the present revolution is a bourgeois revolution, and therefore, the bourgeoisie should act as its leader — answered the Mensheviks. What is the function of the proletariat, then? It must follow in the wake of the bourgeois democrats, "prod them on," and thereby "push the bourgeois revolution forward." This was said by Martynov, the leader of the Mensheviks, whom they put up as their "reporter." The same idea was expressed, although not so distinctly, in the Mensheviks' resolution on "The Present Situation." But already in his *Two Dictatorships* Martynov had said that "the hegemony of the proletariat is a dangerous utopia," a fantasy; that the bourgeois revolution "must be led by the extreme democratic opposition" and not by the socialist proletariat; that the militant proletariat "must march behind bourgeois democracy" and prod it along the path to freedom (see Martynov's well-known pamphlet *Two Dictatorships*). He expressed this idea again at the Unity Congress. In his opinion, the Great French Revolution was the original, whereas our revolution is a faint copy of this original; and, as the revolution in France was first headed by the National Assembly and later by the National Convention in which the bourgeoisie predominated, so, in our country, the leader of the revolution which rallies the people around itself should be first the State Duma, and later some other representative body which will be more revolutionary than the Duma. Both in the Duma and in this future representative body the bourgeois democrats are to predominate—hence, we need the hegemony of bourgeois democracy and not of the socialist proletariat. All we need to do is to *follow* the bourgeoisie step by step and prod it further forward towards genuine freedom. It is characteristic that the Mensheviks greeted Martynov's speech with loud applause. It is also characteristic that *in none of their resolutions* do they refer to the necessity of the hegemony of the proletariat—the term "hegemony of the proletariat" has been completely expunged from their resolutions, as well as from the resolutions of the congress (see the resolutions of the congress).

Such was the stand the Mensheviks took at the congress.

As you see, here we have two mutually exclusive standpoints, and this is the source of all the other disagreements.

If the class-conscious proletariat is the leader of the present revolution and the bourgeois Cadets predominate in the present Duma, it is self-evident that the present Duma cannot become the "political centre of the country," it cannot unite the revolutionary people around itself and become the leader of the growing revolution, no matter what efforts it exerts. Further, if the class-conscious proletariat is the leader of the revolution and the revolution cannot be led from the Duma—it is self-evident that the street and not the floor of the Duma must, at the present time, become the *chief arena* of our activities. Further, if the class-conscious proletariat is the leader of the revolution and the street is the chief arena of the struggle—it is self-evident that our task is to take an active part in organising the struggle in the street, to give *concentrated* attention to the task of arming, to augment the Red detachments and disseminate military knowledge among the advanced elements. Lastly, if the advanced proletariat is the leader of the revolution, and if it must take an active part in organising the uprising—then it is self-evident that we cannot wash our hands of and remain aloof from the provisional revolutionary government; that we must conquer political power in conjunction with the peasantry and take part in the provisional government[2]: the leader of the revolutionary street must also be the leader in the revolution's government.

Such was the stand taken by the Bolsheviks.

If, on the other hand, as the Mensheviks think, the bourgeois democrats will lead the revolution, and the Cadets in the Duma "approximate to this type of democrat," then it is self-evident that the present Duma can become the "political centre of the country," the present Duma can unite the revolutionary people around itself, become their leader and serve as the chief arena of the struggle. Further, if the Duma can become the chief arena of the struggle, there is no need to give *concentrated* attention to the task of arming and organising Red detachments; it is not our business to devote *special* attention to organising the struggle in the street, and still less is it our business to conquer political power in conjunction with the peasantry and to take part in the provisional government—let the bourgeois democrats worry about that for they will be the leaders of the revolution. Of course, it would not be bad to have arms and Red detachments, in fact they are actually necessary, but they are not so important as the Bolsheviks imagine.

Such was the stand taken by the Mensheviks.

The congress took the second path, i.e., it rejected the hegemony of the socialist proletariat and endorsed the stand taken by the Mensheviks.

The congress thereby clearly proved that it failed to understand the urgent requirements of the present situation.

This was the fundamental mistake the congress made, and from it necessarily followed all the other mistakes.

---

2 We are not dealing here with the principle underlying this question.

III

After the congress rejected the idea of the hegemony of the proletariat it became clear how it would settle the other questions: "the attitude to be taken towards the State Duma," "armed insurrection," etc.

Let us pass to these questions.

Let us begin with the question of the State Duma.

We shall not discuss the question as to which tactics were more correct—the boycott or participation in the elections. We shall note only the following: today, the Duma does nothing but talk; it lies stranded between the revolution and counter-revolution. This shows that the advocates of participation in the elections were mistaken when they called upon the people to go to the polls and thereby roused false hopes among them. But let us leave this aside. The point is that at the time the congress was in session the elections were already over (except in the Caucasus and in Siberia); we already had the returns and, consequently, the only point of discussion was the *Duma itself*, which was to meet within a few days. Clearly, the congress could not turn to the past; it had to devote its attention mainly to the question as to what the Duma was, and what our attitude towards it should be.

And so, what is the present Duma, and what should be our attitude towards it?

It was already known from the Manifesto of October 17 that the Duma would not have particularly great powers: it is an assembly of deputies who "have the right" to deliberate, but "have no right" to overstep the existing "fundamental laws." The Duma is supervised by the State Council, which "has the right" to veto any of its decisions. And on guard, armed to the teeth, stands the tsarist government, which "has the right" to disperse the Duma if it does not rest content with its deliberative role.

As regards the Duma's complexion, we knew before the congress what its composition would be; we knew that it would consist largely of Cadets. We do not wish to say that the Cadets by themselves would have constituted the majority in the Duma—we only say that out of approximately five hundred members of the Duma, one third would be

Cadets while another third would consist of the intermediary groups and the Rights (the "Party of Democratic Reform,"[3] the moderate elements among the non-party deputies, the Octobrists,[4] etc.) who, when it came to clashes with the extreme Lefts (the workers' group and the group of revolutionary peasants) would unite around the Cadets and vote with them; consequently, the Cadets would be the masters of the situation in the Duma.

What are the Cadets? Can they be called revolutionaries? Of course, not! What, then, are the Cadets? The Cadets are a *party of compromisers*: they want to restrict the powers of the tsar, but not because they are in favour of the victory of the people, as they claim—the Cadets want to replace the autocracy of the tsar by the autocracy of the bourgeoisie, not the sovereignty of the people (see their programme)—but in order that the people should moderate its revolutionary spirit, withdraw its revolutionary demands and come to some arrangement with the tsar; the Cadets want a compromise between the tsar and the people.

As you see, the majority of the Duma was bound to consist of compromisers and not of revolutionaries. This was already self-evident in the early part of April.

Thus, on the one hand, the Duma was a boycotted and impotent body with insignificant rights; on the other hand, it was a body in which the majority was non-revolutionary and in favour of a compromise. The weak usually take the path of compromise in any case; if in addition their strivings are non-revolutionary, they are all the more likely to slip into the path of compromise. That is exactly what was bound to happen with the State Duma. It could not entirely take the side of the tsar because it wished to limit the tsar's powers; but it could not go over to the side of the people because the people were making revolutionary demands. Hence, it had to take a stand between the tsar and the people and endeavour to reconcile the two, that is, to busy

---

3 **Original editor:** The Party of Democratic Reform—a party of the liberal monarchist bourgeoisie, was formed during the election of the First State Duma in 1906.

4 **Original editor:** The Octobrists, or Union of October Seventeenth—the counter-revolutionary party of the big commercial and industrial bourgeoisie and big landowners, was formed in November 1905. It fully supported the Stolypin regime, the home and foreign policy of tsarism.

itself collecting water with a sieve. On the one hand, it had to try to persuade the people to abandon their "excessive demands" and somehow reach an understanding with the tsar; but on the other hand, it had to act as a go-between, and go to the tsar to plead that he should make some slight concession to the people and thereby put a stop to the "revolutionary unrest."

That is the kind of Duma the Unity Congress of the Party had to deal with.

What should have been the Party's attitude towards such a Duma? Needless to say, the Party could not undertake to support such a Duma, because to support the Duma means supporting a compromising policy; but a compromising policy fundamentally contradicts the task of intensifying the revolution, and the workers' party must not accept the role of pacifier of the revolution. Of course, the Party had to utilise the Duma itself as well as the conflicts between the Duma and the government, but that does not mean that it must support the non-revolutionary tactics of the Duma. On the contrary, to expose the two-faced character of the Duma, ruthlessly to criticise it, to drag its treacherous tactics into the light of day—such should be the Party's attitude towards the State Duma.

And if that is the case, it is clear that the Cadet Duma does not express the will of the people, that it cannot fulfil the role of representative of the people, that it cannot become the political centre of the country and unite the people around itself.

Under these circumstances, it was the Party's duty to dispel the false hopes that had been reposed in the Duma and to declare publicly that the Duma does not express the will of the people and, therefore, cannot become a weapon of the revolution; that the chief arena of the struggle today is the street and not the Duma.

At the same time it was clear that the peasant "Group of Toil"[5] in the Duma, small in numbers compared with the Cadets, could not

---

5 Trudoviks, or Group of Toil—a group of petty-bourgeois democrats formed in April 1906, consisting of the peasant deputies in the First State Duma. They demanded the abolition of all caste and national restrictions, the democratisation of the rural and municipal local government bodies, universal suffrage for the election of the State Duma and, above all, the solution of the agrarian problem.

follow the compromising tactics of the Cadets to the end and would very soon have to begin to fight them as the betrayers of the people and take the path of revolution. It was the Party's duty to support the "Group of Toil" in its struggle against the Cadets, to develop its revolutionary tendencies to the full, to contrast its revolutionary tactics to the non-revolutionary tactics of the Cadets, and thereby to expose still more clearly the treacherous tendencies of the Cadets.

How did the congress act? What did the congress say in its resolution on the State Duma?

The resolution of the congress says that the Duma is an institution that has sprung "from the depths of the nation." That is to say, notwithstanding its defects, the Duma, nevertheless, expresses the will of the people.

Clearly, the congress failed to give a correct appraisal of the Cadet Duma; the congress forgot that the majority in the Duma consists of compromisers; that compromisers who reject the revolution cannot express the will of the people and, consequently, we have no right to say that the Duma has sprung "from the depths of the nation."

What did the Bolsheviks say on this question at the congress?

They said that "the State Duma, which it is already evident has now become Cadet (predominantly) in composition, *cannot under any circumstances fulfil* the role of a genuine representative of the people." That is to say, the present Duma has not sprung from the depths of the people, it is against the people and, therefore, does not express the will of the people (see the resolution of the Bolsheviks).

On this question the congress rejected the stand taken by the Bolsheviks.

The resolution of the congress says that "the Duma," notwithstanding its "pseudo-constitutional" character, nevertheless, "will become a weapon of the revolution" . . . its conflicts with the government may grow to such dimensions "as will make it possible to use them as the starting point for broad mass movements directed towards the overthrow of the present political system." This is as much as to say that the Duma may become a political centre, rally the revolutionary people around itself and raise the standard of revolution.

Do you hear, workers? The compromising Cadet Duma, it appears, may become the centre of the revolution and find itself at its head—a dog, it appears, can give birth to a lamb! There is no need for you to worry—henceforth the hegemony of the proletariat and the rallying of the people around the proletariat are no longer necessary: the *non-revolutionary* Duma will of its own accord rally the *revolutionary* people around itself and everything will be in order! Do you see how simple it is to make a revolution? Do you see how the present revolution is to be carried to the end?

Obviously, the congress failed to realise that the two-faced Duma, with its two-faced Cadets, must inevitably get stuck between two stools, will try to make peace between the tsar and the people and then, like all two-faced people, will be obliged to swing over towards the side which promises most!

What did the Bolsheviks say on this point at the congress?

They said that "the conditions are not yet at hand for our Party to take the parliamentary path," i.e., we cannot yet enter into tranquil parliamentary life; the chief arena of the struggle is still the street, and not the Duma (see the resolution of the Bolsheviks).

On this point, too, the congress rejected the resolution of the Bolsheviks.

The resolution of the congress says nothing definite about the fact that in the Duma there are representatives of the revolutionary peasantry (the "Group of Toil") who remain a minority, and who will be obliged to reject the compromising tactics of the Cadets and take the path of the revolution; and it says nothing about it being necessary to encourage them and support them in their struggle against the Cadets or to help them to set their feet still more firmly on the revolutionary path.

Obviously, the congress failed to understand that the proletariat and the peasantry are the two principal forces in the present revolution; that at the present time the proletariat, as the leader of the revolution, must support the revolutionary peasants in the street as well as in the Duma, provided they wage a struggle against the enemies of the revolution.

What did the Bolsheviks say on this point at the congress?

They said that Social-Democracy must ruthlessly expose "the inconsistency and vacillation of the Cadets, while watching with special attention the elements of peasant revolutionary democracy, uniting them, contrasting them to the Cadets and supporting those of their actions which conform to the interests of the proletariat" (see resolution).

The congress also failed to accept this proposal of the Bolsheviks. Probably, that was because it too vividly expressed the leading role of the proletariat in the present struggle; for the congress, as we have seen above, regarded the hegemony of the proletariat with distrust — the peasantry, it said in effect, must rally around the Duma, and not around the proletariat!

That is why the bourgeois newspaper *Nasha Zhizn*[6] praises the resolution of the congress; that is why the Cadets of *Nasha Zhizn* began to shout in one voice: At last the Social-Democrats have come to their senses and have abandoned Blanquism (see *Nasha Zhizn*, No. 432).

Obviously, it is not for nothing that the enemies of the people — the Cadets — are praising the resolution of the congress. And it was not for nothing that Bebel said: What pleases our enemies is harmful to us!

IV

Let us pass to the question of an armed uprising.

It is no longer a secret to anybody today that action by the people is inevitable. Since the crisis and famine are growing in town and country, since unrest among the proletariat and the peasantry is increasing day by day, since the tsarist government is decaying, and since, therefore, the revolution is on the upgrade—it is self-evident that life is

---

6 **Original editor:** *Nasha Zhizn (Our Life)*—a liberal-bourgeois newspaper published in St. Petersburg with interruptions from November 1904 to December 1906.

preparing another action by the people, wider and more powerful than the October and December actions. It is quite useless to discuss today whether this new action is desirable or undesirable, good or bad: it is not a matter of what we desire; the fact is that action by the people is maturing of its own accord, and that it is inevitable.

But there is action and action. Needless to say, the January general strike in St. Petersburg (1905) was an action by the people. So also was the October general political strike an action by the people, as also was the "December clash" in Moscow, and the clash in Latvia. It is clear that there were also differences between these actions. Whereas in January (1905), the chief role was played by the strike, in December the strike served only as a beginning and then grew into an armed uprising, which assumed the principal role. The actions in January, October and December showed that however "peacefully" you may start a general strike, however "delicately" you may behave in presenting your demands, and even if you come on to the battle-field unarmed, it must all end in a clash (recall January 9 in St. Petersburg, when the people marched with crosses and portraits of the tsar); the government will, nevertheless, resort to guns and rifles; the people will, nevertheless, take to arms, and thus, the general strike will, nevertheless, grow into an armed uprising. What does that prove? Only that the impending action of the people will not be simply a demonstration, but must necessarily assume an *armed* character; thus, the decisive role will be played by *armed* insurrection. It is useless discussing whether bloodshed is desirable or undesirable, good or bad: we repeat—it is not a matter of what we desire; the fact is that *armed* insurrection will undoubtedly take place, and it will be impossible to avert it.

Our task today is to achieve the sovereignty of the people. We want the reins of government to be transferred to the hands of the proletariat and the peasantry. Can this object be achieved by means of a general strike? The facts say that it cannot (recall what we said above). Or perhaps the Duma with its grandiloquent Cadets will help us, perhaps the sovereignty of the people will be established with its aid? The facts tell us that this, too, is impossible; for the Cadet Duma wants the autocracy of the big bourgeoisie and not the sovereignty of the people (recall what we said above).

Clearly, the only sure path is an armed uprising of the proletariat and the peasantry. Only by means of an armed uprising can the rule of the tsar be overthrown and the rule of the people be established, if, of course, this uprising ends in victory. That being the case, since the victory of the people is impossible today without the victory of the uprising, and since, on the other hand, life itself is preparing the ground for armed action by the people and, since this action is inevitable—it is self-evident that the task of Social-Democracy is consciously to prepare for this action, consciously to prepare the ground for its victory. One of two things: either we must reject the sovereignty of the people (a democratic republic) and rest content with a constitutional monarchy—and in that case we shall be right in saying that it is not our business to organise an armed uprising; or we must continue to have as our present aim the sovereignty of the people (a democratic republic) and emphatically reject a constitutional monarchy—and in that case we shall be wrong in saying that it is not our business consciously to organise the spontaneously growing action.

But how should we prepare for an armed uprising? How can we facilitate its victory?

The December action showed that, in addition to all our other sins, we Social-Democrats are guilty of another great sin against the proletariat. This sin is that we failed to take the trouble, or took too little trouble, to arm the workers and to organise Red detachments. Recall December. Who does not remember the excited people who rose to the struggle in Tiflis, in the west Caucasus, in the south of Russia, in Siberia, in Moscow, in St. Petersburg and in Baku? Why did the autocracy succeed in dispersing these infuriated people so easily? Was it because the people were not yet convinced that the tsarist government was no good? Of course not! Why was it, then?

First of all because the people had no arms, or too few of them. However great your consciousness may be, you cannot stand up against bullets with bare hands! Yes, they were quite right when they cursed us and said: You take our money, but where are the arms?

Secondly, because we had no trained Red detachments capable of leading the rest, of procuring arms by force of arms and of arming the people. The people are heroes in street fighting, but if they are not led by their armed brothers and are not set an example, they can turn into a mob.

Thirdly, because the uprising was sporadic and unorganised. While Moscow was fighting at the barricades, St. Petersburg was silent. Tiflis and Kutais were preparing for an assault when Moscow was already "subdued." Siberia took to arms when the South and the Letts were already "vanquished." That shows that the fighting proletariat entered the uprising split up into groups, as a consequence of which the government was able to inflict "defeat" upon it with comparative ease.

Fourthly, because our uprising adhered to the policy of the defensive and not of the offensive. The government itself provoked the December uprising. The government attacked us; it had a plan, whereas we met the government's attack unprepared; we had no thought-out plan, we were obliged to adhere to the policy of self-defence and thus dragged at the tail of events. Had the people of Moscow, from the very outset, chosen the policy of attack, they would have immediately captured the Nikolayevsky Railway Station, the government would have been unable to transport troops from St. Petersburg to Moscow, and thus, the Moscow uprising would have lasted longer. That would have exerted corresponding influence upon other towns. The same must be said about the Letts; had they taken the path of attack at the very outset, they would first of all have captured artillery and would thus have sapped the forces of the government.

It was not for nothing that Marx said :

". . . The insurrectionary career once entered upon, act with the greatest determination, and *on the offensive. The defensive is the death of every armed rising.* . . . Surprise your antagonists while their forces are scattering, prepare new successes, however small, but daily; keep up the moral ascendant which the first successful rising has given to you; rally thus those vacillating elements to your side which always follow the strongest impulse and which always look out for the safer side; force your enemies to a retreat before they can collect their strength against you; in the words of Danton, the greatest master of revolutionary policy yet known: de l'audace, de l'audace, encore de l'audace!" (See K.

Marx, *Historical Sketches*, p. 95.)

It was precisely this "audacity" and the policy of an offensive that the December uprising lacked.

We shall be told: these are not the only reasons for the December "defeat"; you have forgotten that in December the peasantry failed to unite with the proletariat, and that, too, was one of the main reasons for the December retreat. This is the downright truth, and we do not intend to forget it. But why did the peasantry fail to unite with the proletariat? What was the reason? We shall be told: lack of political consciousness. Granting that, how should we make the peasants politically conscious? By distributing pamphlets? This is not enough, of course! Then how? By fighting, by drawing them into the struggle, and by leading them during the struggle. Today it is the mission of the town to lead the countryside, it is the mission of the workers to lead the peasants; and if an uprising is not organised in the towns, the peasantry will never march with the advanced proletariat in this action.

Such are the facts.

Hence, the attitude the congress should have adopted towards the armed uprising and the slogans it should have issued to the Party comrades are self-evident.

The Party was weak in the matter of arming, and arming was a neglected matter in the Party—consequently, the congress should have said to the Party: arm, give concentrated attention to the matter of arming, so as to meet the impending action at least to some extent prepared.

Further. The Party was weak in the matter of organising armed detachments; it did not pay due attention to the task of augmenting the number of Red detachments. Consequently, the congress should have said to the Party: *form Red detachments, disseminate military knowledge among the people*, give concentrated attention to the task of organising Red detachments, so as to be able later on to procure arms by force of arms and extend the uprising.

Further. The December uprising found the proletariat disunited; nobody thought seriously of organising the uprising—consequently, it

was the duty of the congress to issue a slogan to the Party urging it en-
ergetically to proceed to unite the militant elements, to bring them into
action according to a single plan, and actively to organise the armed
uprising.

Further. The proletariat, adhered to a defensive policy in the
armed uprising; it never took the path of the offensive; that is what
prevented the victory of the uprising. Consequently, it was the duty of
the congress to point out to the Party comrades that the moment of
victory of the uprising was approaching and that it was *necessary to pass
to the policy of offensive.*

How did the congress act, and what slogans did it issue to the
Party?

The congress said that ". . . the Party's main task at the present
moment is to develop the revolution by expanding and intensifying
agitation activities among broad sections of the proletariat, the peasantry, the urban petty bourgeoisie and among the armed forces, and by
drawing them into the active struggle against the government through
the constant intervention of Social-Democracy, and of the proletariat
which it leads, in all manifestations of political life in the country." The
Party "cannot undertake the obligation of arming the people, which
can only rouse false hopes, and must restrict its tasks to facilitating
the self-arming of the population and the organisation and arming of
fighting squads. . . ." "It is the Party's duty to counteract all attempts
to draw the proletariat into an armed collision under unfavourable circumstances . . ." etc., etc. (see resolution of the congress).

It appears, then, that *today, at the present moment*, when we are on the
threshold of another action by the people, the *main thing for achieving the
victory of the uprising is agitation*, while the arming and organising of Red
detachments is something unimportant, something which we must not
get enthusiastic about, and in relation to which we must "restrict" our
activities to "facilitating." As regards the necessity of organising the
uprising, of not carrying it out with scattered forces, and the necessity of adopting an offensive policy (recall the words of Marx)—the
congress said not a word. Clearly, it did not regard these questions as
important.

The facts say: Arm and do everything to strengthen the Red detachments. The congress, however, answers: Do not get too enthusiastic about arming and organising Red detachments, "restrict" your activities in this matter, because the most important thing is agitation.

One would think that until now we have been busy arming, that we have armed a vast number of comrades and have organised a large number of detachments, but have neglected agitation—and so the congress admonishes us: Enough of arming, you have paid quite enough attention to that; the main thing is agitation!

It goes without saying that agitation is always and everywhere one of the Party's main weapons; but will agitation decide the question of victory in the forthcoming uprising? Had the congress said this four years ago, when the question of an uprising was not yet on the order of the day, it would have been understandable; but today, when we are on the threshold of an armed uprising, when the question of an uprising is on the order of the day, when it may start independently and in spite of us—what can "mainly" agitation do? What can be achieved by means of this "agitation"?

Or consider this. Let us assume that we have expanded our agitation; let us assume that the people have risen. What then? How can they fight without arms? Has not enough blood of unarmed people been shed? And besides, of what use are arms to the people if they are unable to wield them, if they have not a sufficient number of Red detachments? We shall be told: But we do not reject arming and Red detachments. Very well, but if you fail to devote due attention to the task of arming, if you neglect it—it shows that actually you do reject it.

We shall not go into the point that the congress did not even hint at the necessity of *organising* the uprising and of adhering to an *offensive* policy. It could not have been otherwise, because the resolution of the congress lags four or five years behind life, and because, to the congress, an uprising was still a theoretical question.

What did the Bolsheviks say on this question at the congress?

They said that ". . . in the Party's propaganda and agitation activities *concentrated attention must be given* to studying the practical experience of the December uprising, to criticising it from the military point of view, and to drawing direct lessons from it for the future," that "*still more energetic activity must be developed* in augmenting the number of fighting squads, in improving their organisation and supplying them with weapons of all kinds and, in conformity with the lessons of experience, not only should Party fighting squads be organised, but also squads of sympathisers with the Party, and even of non-Party people . . ." that "in view of the growing peasant movement, which may flare up into a whole uprising in the very near future, it is desirable to exert efforts to *unite the activities of the workers and peasants for the purpose of organising, as far as possible, joint and simultaneous military operations . . .*" that, consequently, ". . . in view of the growth and intensification of another political crisis, the prospect is opening for the *transition from defensive to offensive forms of armed struggle . . .*" that it is necessary, jointly with the soldiers, to launch ". . . *most determined offensive operations against the government . . .*" etc. (see the resolution of the Bolsheviks).

That is what the Bolsheviks said.

But the congress rejected the stand taken by the Bolsheviks.

After this, it is not difficult to understand why the resolutions of the congress were welcomed with such enthusiasm by the liberal-Cadets (see *Nasha Zhizn*, No. 432): they realised that *these resolutions* lag several years behind the present revolution, that these resolutions totally fail to express the class tasks of the proletariat, that *these resolutions*, if applied, would make the proletariat an appendage of the liberals rather than an independent force—they realised all this, and that is why they were so loud in their praise of them.

It is the duty of the Party comrades to adopt a critical attitude towards the resolutions of the congress and, at the proper time, introduce the necessary amendments.

It is precisely this duty that we had in mind when we sat down to write this pamphlet.

True, we have here touched upon only two resolutions: "On the Attitude To Be Taken Towards the State Duma," and "On Armed Insurrection," but these two resolutions are, undoubtedly, the main resolutions, which most distinctly express the congress's position on tactics.

Thus, we have arrived at the main conclusion, viz., that the question that confronts the Party is: *should the class-conscious proletariat be the leader in the present revolution, or should it drag at the tail of the bourgeois democrats?*

We have seen that the settlement of this question one way or another will determine the settlement of all the other questions.

All the more carefully, therefore, should the comrades weigh the essence of these two positions.

Reprinted from the pamphlet
issued by *Proletariat* Publishers
in 1906
Signed: *Comrade K.*
Translated from the Georgian

THE CLASS STRUGGLE

"The unity of the bourgeoisie can be shaken only by the unity of the proletariat."
Karl Marx

Present-day society is extremely complex! It is a motley patchwork of classes and groups—the big, middle and petty bourgeoisie; the big, middle and petty feudal landlords; journeymen, unskilled labourers and skilled factory workers; the higher, middle and lower clergy; the higher, middle and minor bureaucracy; a heterogeneous intelligentsia, and other groups of a similar kind. Such is the motley picture our society presents!

But it is also obvious that the further society develops the more clearly two main trends stand out in this complexity, and the more sharply this complex society divides up into two opposite camps— the capitalist camp and the proletarian camp. The January economic strikes (1905) clearly showed that Russia is indeed divided into two camps. The November strikes in St. Petersburg (1905) and the June-July strikes all over Russia (1906), brought the leaders of the two camps into collision and thereby fully exposed the present-day class antagonisms. Since then the capitalist camp has been wide awake. In that camp feverish and ceaseless preparation is going on; local associations of capitalists are being formed, the local associations combine to form regional associations and the regional associations combine in all-Russian associations; funds and newspapers are being started, and all-Russian congresses and conferences of capitalists are being convened. . . .

Thus, the capitalists are organising in a separate class with the object of curbing the proletariat.

On the other hand, the proletarian camp is wide awake too. Here, too, feverish preparations for the impending struggle are being made. In spite of persecution by the reaction, here, too, local trade unions are being formed, the local unions combine to form regional unions, trade union funds are being started, the trade union press is growing, and all-Russian congresses and conferences of workers' unions are being held. . . .

It is evident that the proletarians are also organising in a separate class with the object of curbing exploitation.

There was a time when "peace and quiet" reigned in society. At that time there was no sign of these classes and their class organisations. A struggle went on at that time too, of course, but that struggle bore a local and not a general class character; the capitalists had no associations of their own, and each capitalist was obliged to deal with "his" workers by himself. Nor did the workers have any unions and, consequently, the workers in each factory were obliged to rely only on their own strength. True, local Social-Democratic organisations led the workers' economic struggle, but everybody will agree that this leadership was weak and casual; the Social-Democratic organisations could scarcely cope with their own Party affairs.

The January economic strikes, however, marked a turning point. The capitalists got busy and began to organise local associations. The capitalist associations in St. Petersburg, Moscow, Warsaw, Riga and other towns were brought into being by the January strikes. As regards the capitalists in the oil, manganese, coal and sugar industries, they converted their old, "peaceful" associations into "fighting" associations, and began to fortify their positions. But the capitalists were not content with this. They decided to form an all-Russian association, and so, in March 1905, on the initiative of Morozov, they gathered at a general congress in Moscow. That was the first all-Russian congress of capitalists. Here they concluded an agreement, by which they pledged themselves not to make any concessions to the workers without previous arrangement among themselves and, in "extreme" cases—to declare a *lockout*.[1] That was the starting point of a fierce struggle between the

---

1 *Lockout*—a strike of employers, during which the employers deliberately shut down their factories in order to break the resistance of the workers and to frustrate their demands.

capitalists and the proletarians. It marked the opening of a series of big lockouts in Russia. To conduct a big struggle a strong association is needed, and so the capitalists decided to meet once again to form a still more closely-knit association. Thus, three months after the first congress (in July 1905), the second all-Russian congress of capitalists was convened in Moscow. Here they reaffirmed the resolutions of the first congress, reaffirmed the necessity of lockouts, and elected a committee to draft the rules and to arrange for the convocation of another congress. Meanwhile, the resolutions of the congresses were put into effect. Facts have shown that the capitalists are carrying out these resolutions to the letter. If you recall the lockouts the capitalists declared in Riga, Warsaw, Odessa, Moscow, and other large cities; if you recall the November days in St. Petersburg, when 72 capitalists threatened 200,000 St. Petersburg workers with a cruel lockout, then you will easily understand what a mighty force the all-Russian association of capitalists represents, and how punctiliously they are carrying out the decisions of their association. Then, after the second congress, the capitalists arranged another congress (in January 1906), and finally, in April this year, the all-Russian inaugural congress of the capitalists took place, at which uniform rules were adopted and a Central Bureau was elected. As the newspapers report, these rules have already been sanctioned by the government.

Thus, there can be no doubt that the Russian big bourgeoisie has already organised in a separate class, that it has its own local, regional and central organisations, and can rouse the capitalists of the whole of Russia in conformity with a single plan.

To reduce wages, lengthen the working day, weaken the proletariat and smash its organisations—such are the objects of the general association of capitalists.

Meanwhile, the workers' trade union movement has been growing and developing. Here, too, the influence of the January economic strikes (1905) made itself felt. The movement assumed a mass character; its needs grew wider and, in the course of time, it became evident that the Social-Democratic organisations could not conduct both Party and trade union affairs. Something in the nature of a division of labour between the Party and the trade unions was needed. Party affairs had to be directed by the Party organisations, and trade union affairs by trade unions. And so the organisation of trade unions began. Trade unions were formed all over the country—in Moscow, St. Petersburg, Warsaw, Odessa, Riga, Kharkov and Tiflis. True, the reactionaries placed obstacles in the way, but in spite of that the needs of the movement gained the upper hand and the unions grew in number. Soon the appearance of local unions was followed by the appearance of regional unions and, finally, things reached the stage when, in September last year, an all-Russian conference of trade unions was convened. That was the first conference of workers' unions. The upshot of that conference was, among other things, that it drew together the unions in the different towns and finally elected a Central Bureau to prepare for the convocation of a general congress of trade unions. The October days arrived—and the trade unions became twice as strong as they were before. Local and, finally, regional unions grew day by day. True, the "December defeat" appreciably checked the rate of formation of trade unions, but later the trade union movement recovered and things went so well that in February of this year the second conference of trade unions was called, and it was more widely and fully representative than the first conference. The conference recognised the necessity of forming local, regional and all-Russian centres, elected an "organising commission" to make arrangements for the forthcoming all-Russian congress, and passed appropriate resolutions on current questions affecting the trade union movement.

Thus, there can be no doubt that, notwithstanding the reaction that is raging, the proletariat is also organising in a separate class, is steadily strengthening its local, regional and central trade union organisations, and is also steadily striving to unite its innumerable fellow-workers against the capitalists.

To secure higher wages, a shorter working day, better conditions of labour, to curb exploitation and to thwart the capitalist associations —such are the objects of the workers' trade unions.

Thus, present-day society is splitting up into two big camps; each camp is organising in a separate class; the class struggle that has flared up between them is expanding and growing more intense every day, and all other groups are gathering around these two camps.

Marx said that every class struggle is a political struggle. This means that, if the proletarians and capitalists are waging an economic struggle against each other today, they will be compelled to wage a political struggle tomorrow and thus protect their respective class interests in a struggle that bears two forms. The capitalists have their particular business interests. And it is to protect these interests that their economic organisations exist. But in addition to their particular business interests, they also have common class interests, namely, to strengthen capitalism. And it is to protect these common interests that they must wage a political struggle and need a political party. The Russian capitalists solved this problem very easily: they realised that the only party which "straightforwardly and fearlessly" championed their interests was the *Octobrist Party*, and they therefore resolved to rally around that party and to accept its ideological leadership. Since then the capitalists have been waging their political struggle under the ideological leadership of this party; with its aid they exert influence on the present government (which suppresses the workers' unions but hastens to sanction the formation of capitalist associations), they secure the election of its candidates to the Duma, etc., etc.

Thus, economic struggle with the aid of associations, and general political struggle under the ideological leadership of the Octobrist Party—that is the form the class struggle waged by the big bourgeoisie is assuming today.

On the other hand, similar phenomena are also observed in the proletarian class movement today. To protect the trade interests of the proletarians trade unions are being formed, and these fight for higher wages, a shorter working day, etc. But in addition to trade interests, the proletarians have also common class interests, namely, the socialist revolution and the establishment of socialism. It is impossible, however, to achieve the socialist revolution until the proletariat conquers political power as a united and indivisible class. That is why the proletariat must wage the political struggle, and why it needs a political party that will act as the ideological leader of its political movement. Most of the workers' unions are, of course, non-party and neutral; but this merely means that they are independent of the party only in financial and organisational matters, i.e., they have their own separate funds, their own leading bodies, call their own congresses and, officially, are not bound by the decisions of political parties. As regards the *ideological* dependence of the trade unions upon any given political party, such dependence must undoubtedly exist and cannot help existing, because, apart from everything else, members of different parties belong to the unions and inevitably carry their political convictions into them. Clearly, if the proletariat cannot dispense with the political struggle, it cannot dispense with the ideological leadership of some political party. More than that. It must itself seek a party which will worthily lead its unions to the "promised land," to socialism. But here the proletariat must be on the alert and act with circumspection. It must carefully examine the ideological stock-in-trade of the political parties and freely accept the ideological leadership of the party that will courageously and consistently champion its class interests, hold aloft the Red Flag of the proletariat, and boldly lead it to political power, to the socialist revolution.

Until now this role has been carried out by the *Russian Social-Democratic Labour Party* and, consequently, it is the task of the trade unions to accept its ideological leadership.

It is common knowledge that they actually do so.

Thus, economic clashes with the aid of trade unions, political attacks under the ideological leadership of Social-Democracy — that is the form the class struggle of the proletariat has assumed today.

There can be no doubt that the class struggle will flare up with increasing vigour. The task of the proletariat is to introduce the system and the spirit of organisation into its struggle. To accomplish this, it is necessary to strengthen the unions and to unite them, and in this the all-Russian congress of trade unions can render a great service. Not a "non-party workers' congress," but a congress of workers' trade unions is what we need today in order that the proletariat shall be organised in a united and indivisible class. At the same time, the proletariat must exert every effort to strengthen and fortify the party which will act as the ideological and political leader of its class struggle.

Akhali Droyeba
(*New Times*),[279]
November 14, 1906
Signed: *Ko...*
Translated from the Georgian

---

2 **Original editor**: *Akhali Droyeba* (*New Times*)—a trade union weekly newspaper published legally in the Georgian language in Tiflis from November 14, 1906, to January 8, 1907, under the directorship of J. V. Stalin, M. Tskhakaya, and M. Davitashvili. Was suppressed by order of the Governor of Tiflis.

"FACTORY LEGISLATION"
AND THE PROLETARIAN STRUGGLE
(CONCERNING THE TWO LAWS OF NOVEMBER 15)

There was a time when our labour movement was in its initial stages. At that time the proletariat was split up into separate groups and did not think of waging a common struggle. Railway workers, miners, factory workers, artisans, shop assistants, and clerks—such were the groups into which the Russian proletariat was divided. Moreover, the workers in each group, in their turn, were split up according to the towns, big or small, they lived and worked in, with no link, either party or trade union, between them. Thus, there was no sign of the proletariat as a united and indivisible class. Consequently, there was no sign of the proletarian struggle, as a general class offensive. That is why the tsarist government was able calmly to pursue its "traditional" policy. That is why, when the "Workers' Insurance Bill" was introduced in the State Council in 1893, Pobedonostsev, the inspirer of the reaction, jeered at the sponsors and said with aplomb : "Gentlemen, you have taken all this trouble for nothing; I assure you that *there is no labour problem in our country*. . . ."

But time passed, the economic crisis drew near, strikes became more frequent, and the disunited proletariat gradually organised itself in a united class. The strikes of 1903 already showed that "there is a labour problem in our country," and that it had existed for a long time. The strikes in January and February 1905 proclaimed to the world for the first time that the proletariat, as a united class, was growing and becoming mature in Russia. Then, the general strikes in October-December 1905, and the "ordinary" strikes in June and July 1906, actually drew together the proletarians in the different towns, actually welded together the shop assistants, clerks, artisans and industrial workers in a united class, and thereby loudly proclaimed to the world that the forces of the once disunited proletariat had now taken the path of union and were organising themselves in a united class. The effect of the general political strike as a method of waging the common proletarian struggle against the present system also made itself felt. . . . Now it was no longer possible to deny the existence of the "labour problem," now the tsarist government was already obliged to reckon with the movement. And so, the reactionaries gathered in their offices and began to set up different commissions and to draft "factory laws": the Shidlovsky Commission,[1] the Kokov-tsev Commission,[2] the Associations Act[3] (see the "Manifesto" of October 17), the Witte-Durnovo circulars,[4] various projects and plans, and lastly the two laws of November 15 applying to artisans and commercial employees.

---

1 The commission headed by Senator Shidlovsky was set up by the tsar's ukase of January 29, 1905, ostensibly "for the purpose of urgently investigating the causes of discontent among the workers of the city of St. Petersburg and its suburbs." It was intended to include in the commission delegates elected by the workers. The Bolsheviks regarded this as an attempt on the part of the tsarist government to divert the workers from the revolutionary struggle and therefore proposed that advantage be taken of the election of delegates to this commission to present political demands to the government. After the government rejected these demands the worker-electors refused to elect their representatives to the commission and called upon the workers of St. Petersburg to come out on strike. Mass political strikes broke out the very next day. On February 20, 1905, the tsarist government was obliged to dissolve the Shidlovsky Commission.

2 The function of the commission headed by V. N. Kokovtsev, the Minister of Finance, set up in February 1905, was, like that of the Shidlovsky Commission, to investigate the labour problem, but without the participation of workers' representatives. The commission remained in existence until the summer of 1905.

3 The Associations Act of March 4, 1906, granted right of legal existence to societies and unions, provided they registered their rules with the government. Notwithstanding the numerous restrictions imposed upon the activities of various associations and the fact that they were held criminally liable for infringements of the law, the workers made extensive use of the rights granted them in order to form proletarian industrial organisations. In the period of 1905-07 mass trade unions were formed in Russia for the first time, and these waged an economic and political struggle under the leadership of revolutionary Social-Democracy.

4 After the promulgation of the tsar's Manifesto of October 17, 1905, S. J. Witte, the President of the Council of Ministers, and P. N. Durnovo, the Minister of the Interior, notwithstanding the official proclamation of "freedom," issued a series of circulars and telegrams to provincial governors and city governors, calling upon them to disperse meetings and assemblies by armed force, to suppress newspapers, to take stringent measures against trade unions, and summarily exile all persons suspected of conducting revolutionary activities, etc.

So long as the movement was weak, so long as it lacked a mass character, the reaction employed only one method against the proletariat—imprisonment, Siberia, the whip and the gallows. Always and everywhere the reaction pursues one object: to split the proletariat into small groups, to smash its vanguard, to intimidate and win over to its side the neutral masses, and thus create confusion in the proletarian camp. We have seen that it achieved this object famously with the aid of whips and prisons.

But things took an entirely different turn when the movement assumed a mass character. Now the reaction had no longer to deal only with "ringleaders"—it was faced by countless masses in all their revolutionary grandeur. And it had to reckon precisely with these masses. But it is impossible to hang the masses; you cannot banish them to Siberia, there are not enough prisons to hold them. As for lashing them with whips, that is not always to the advantage of the reaction now that the ground under its feet has long been shaken. Clearly, in addition to the old methods, a new, "more cultured" method had to be employed, which, in the opinion of the reaction, might aggravate the disagreements in the camp of the proletariat, rouse false hopes among the backward section of the workers, induce them to abandon the struggle and rally around the government.

"Factory legislation" is precisely this new method.

Thus, while still adhering to the old methods, the tsarist government wants, at the same time, to utilise "factory legislation" and, consequently, to solve the "burning labour problem" by means of both the whip and the law. By means of promises of a shorter working day, the protection of child and female labour, improvement in sanitary conditions, workers' insurance, abolition of fines, and other benefits of a similar kind, it seeks to win the confidence of the backward section of the workers and thereby dig the grave of proletarian class unity. The tsarist government knows very well that it was never so necessary for it to engage in such "activity" as it is now, at this moment when the October general strike has united the proletarians in the different industries and has struck at the roots of reaction, when a future general strike may grow into an armed struggle and overthrow the old system, and when, consequently, the reaction must, for its very life, provoke confusion in the labour camp, win the confidence of the backward workers, and win them over to its side.

In this connection it is extremely interesting to note that, with its laws of November 15, the reaction graciously turned its gaze only upon *shop assistants and artisans*, whereas it sends the best sons of the *industrial* proletariat to prison and to the gallows. But this is not surprising when you come to think of it. Firstly, shop assistants, artisans and employees in commercial establishments are not concentrated in big factories and mills as the industrial workers are; they are scattered among small enterprises, they are relatively less class conscious and, consequently, can be more easily deceived than the others. Secondly, shop assistants, office clerks and artisans constitute a large section of the proletariat of present-day Russia and, consequently, their desertion of the militant proletarians would appreciably weaken the forces of the proletariat both in the present elections and in the forthcoming action. Lastly, it is common knowledge that the urban petty bourgeoisie is of great importance in the present revolution; that Social-Democracy must revolutionise it under the hegemony of the proletariat; and that nobody can win over the petty bourgeoisie so well as the artisans, shop assistants and office clerks who stand closer to it than the rest of the proletarians. Clearly, if the shop assistants and artisans desert the proletariat the petty bourgeoisie will turn away from it too, and the proletariat will be doomed to isolation in the towns, which is exactly what the tsarist government wants. In the light of these facts, the reason why the reaction concocted the laws of November 15, which affect only artisans, shop assistants and office clerks, becomes self-evident. The industrial proletariat will not trust the government whatever it may do, so "factory legislation" would be wasted on it. Maybe only bullets can bring the proletariat to its senses. What laws cannot do, bullets must do! . . .

That is what the tsarist government thinks.

And that is the opinion not only of our government, but also of every other anti-proletarian government — irrespective of whether it is feudal-autocratic, bourgeois-monarchist or bourgeois-republican. The fight against the proletariat is waged by means of bullets and laws everywhere, and that will go on until the socialist revolution breaks out, until socialism is established. Recall the years 1824 and 1825 in constitutional England, when the law granting freedom to strike was being drafted, while at the same time the prisons were crammed with workers on strike. Recall republican France in the forties of last century, when there was talk about "factory legislation," while at the same time the streets of Paris ran with workers' blood. Recall all these and numerous other cases of the same kind and you will see that it is precisely as we have said.

That, however, does not mean that the proletariat cannot utilise such laws. True, in passing "factory laws" the reaction has its own plans in view—it wants to curb the proletariat: but step by step life is frustrating the reaction's plans, and under such circumstances clauses beneficial to the proletariat always creep into the laws. This happens because no "factory law" comes into being without a reason, without a struggle; the government does not pass a single "factory law" until the workers come out to fight, until the government is compelled to satisfy the workers' demands. History shows that every "factory law" is preceded by a partial or general strike. The law of June 1882 (concerning the employment of children, the length of the working day for them, and the institution of factory inspection), was preceded by strikes in Narva, Perm, St. Petersburg and Zhirardov in that same year. The laws of June-October 1886 (on fines, pay-books, etc.) were the direct result of the strikes in the central area in 1885-86. The law of June 1897 (shortening the working day) was preceded by the strikes in St. Petersburg in 1895-96. The laws of 1903 (concerning "employers' liability" and "shop stewards") were the direct result of the "strikes in the south" in the same year Lastly, the laws of November 15, 1906 (on a shorter working day and Sunday rest for shop assistants, office clerks and artisans), are the direct result of the strikes that took place all over Russia in June and July this year.

As you see, every "factory law" was preceded by a movement of the masses who in one way or another achieved the satisfaction of their demands, if not in full, then at least in part. It is self-evident, therefore, that however bad a "factory law" may be, it, nevertheless, contains several clauses which the proletariat can utilise for the purpose of intensifying its struggle. Needless to say, it must grasp such clauses and use them as instruments with which still further to strengthen its organisations and to stir up more fiercely the proletarian struggle, the struggle for the socialist revolution. Bebel was right when he said: "The devil's head must be cut off with his own sword". . . .

In this respect, both laws of November 15 are extremely interesting. Of course, they contain numerous bad clauses, but they also contain clauses which the reaction introduced unconsciously, but which the proletariat must utilise *consciously*.

Thus, for example, although both laws are called laws "for the protection of labour," they contain atrocious clauses which completely nullify all "protection of labour," and which, here and there, even the employers will shrink from utilising. Both laws establish a twelve-hour day in commercial establishments and artisans' workshops, in spite of the fact that in many places the twelve-hour day has already been abolished and a ten- or an eight-hour day has been introduced. Both laws permit two hours overtime per day (making a fourteen-hour day) over a period of forty days in commercial establishments, and sixty days in workshops, in spite of the fact that nearly everywhere all overtime has been abolished. At the same time, the employers are granted the right, "by agreement with the workers," i.e., by coercing the workers, to increase overtime and lengthen the working day to seventeen hours, etc., etc.

The proletariat will not, of course, surrender to the employers a single shred of the rights they have already won, and the fables in the above-mentioned laws will remain the ridiculous fables they really are.

On the other hand, the laws contain clauses which the proletariat can make good use of to strengthen its position. Both laws say that where the working day is not less than eight hours, *the workers must be given a two hours' break for dinner*. It is well known that at present artisans, shop assistants and office clerks do not everywhere enjoy a two hours' break. Both laws also say that *persons under seventeen have the right, in addition to these two hours, to absent themselves from the shop or workshop for another three hours a day to attend school*, which of course will be a great relief for our young comrades. . . .

There can be no doubt that the proletariat will make fitting use of such clauses in the laws of November 15, will duly intensify its proletarian struggle, and show the world once again that the devil's head must be cut off with his own sword.

Akhali Droveba
(*New Times*), No. 4,
December 4, 1906
Signed: *Ko.* . . .
Translated from the Georgian

ANARCHISM OR SOCIALISM?[1]

The hub of modern social life is the class struggle. In the course of this struggle each class is guided by its own ideology. The bourgeoisie has its own ideology—so-called *liberalism*. The proletariat also has its own ideology—this, as is well known, is *socialism*.

Liberalism must not be regarded as something whole and indivisible: it is subdivided into different trends, corresponding to the different strata of the bourgeoisie.

---

1 **Original editor:** At the end of 1905 and the beginning of 1906, a group of Anarchists in Georgia, headed by the well-known Anarchist and follower of Kropotkin, V. Cherkezishvili and his supporters Mikhako Tsereteli (Bâton), Shalva Gogelia (Sh. G.) and others conducted a fierce campaign against the Social-Democrats. This group published in Tiflis the newspapers *Nobati, Musha* and others. The Anarchists had no support among the proletariat, but they achieved some success among the declassed and petty-bourgeois elements. J. V. Stalin wrote a series of articles against the Anarchists under the general title of *Anarchism or Socialism?* The first four instalments appeared in *Akhali Tskhovreba* in June and July 1906. The rest were not published as the newspaper was suppressed by the authorities. In December 1906 and on January 1, 1907, the articles that were published in *Akhali Tskhovreba* were reprinted in *Akhali Droyeba*, in a slightly revised form, with the following editorial comment: "Recently, the Office Employees' Union wrote to us suggesting that we should publish articles on anarchism, socialism, and cognate questions (see *Akhali Droyeba*, No. 3). The same wish was expressed by several other comrades. We gladly meet these wishes and publish these articles. Regarding them, we think it necessary to mention that some have already appeared in the Georgian press (but for reasons over which the author had no control, they were not completed). Nevertheless we considered it necessary to reprint all the articles in full and requested the author to rewrite them in a more popular style, and this he gladly did." This explains the two versions of the first four instalments of Anarchism or Socialism? They were continued in the newspapers *Chveni Tskhovreba* in February 1907, and in *Dro* in April 1907. The first version of the articles *Anarchism or Socialism?* as published in *Akhali Tskhovreba* is given as an appendix to the present volume.

Chveni Tskhovreba (*Our Life*)—a daily Bolshevik newspaper published legally in Tiflis under the direction of J. V. Stalin, began publication on February 18, 1907. In all, thirteen numbers were issued. It was suppressed on March 6, 1907, for its "extremist trend."

Dro (*Time*)—a daily Bolshevik newspaper published in Tiflis after the suppression of *Chveni Tskhovreba*, ran from March 11 to April 15, 1907, under the direction of J. V. Stalin. M. Tskhakaya and M. Davitashvili were members of the editorial board. In all, thirty-one numbers were issued.

Nor is socialism whole and indivisible: in it there are also different trends.

We shall not here examine liberalism—that task had better be left for another time. We want to acquaint the reader only with socialism and its trends. We think that he will find this more interesting.

Socialism is divided into three main trends: *reformism, anarchism and Marxism.*

Reformism (Bernstein and others), which regards socialism as a remote goal and nothing more, reformism, which actually repudiates the socialist revolution and aims at establishing socialism by peaceful means, reformism, which advocates not class struggle but class collaboration—this reformism is decaying day by day, is day by day losing all semblance of socialism and, in our opinion, it is totally unnecessary to examine it in these articles when defining socialism.

It is altogether different with Marxism and anarchism: both are at the present time recognised as socialist trends, they are waging a fierce struggle against each other, both are trying to present themselves to the proletariat as genuinely socialist doctrines, and, of course, a study and comparison of the two will be far more interesting for the reader.

We are not the kind of people who, when the word "anarchism" is mentioned, turn away contemptuously and say with a supercilious wave of the hand: "Why waste time on that, it's not worth talking about!" We think that such cheap "criticism" is undignified and useless.

Nor are we the kind of people who console themselves with the thought that the Anarchists "have no masses behind them and, therefore, are not so dangerous." It is not who has a larger or smaller "mass" following today, but the essence of the doctrine that matters. If the "doctrine" of the Anarchists expresses the truth, then it goes without saying that it will certainly hew a path for itself and will rally the masses around itself. If, however, it is unsound and built up on a false foundation, it will not last long and will remain suspended in mid-air. But the unsoundness of anarchism must be proved.

Some people believe that Marxism and anarchism are based on the same principles and that the disagreements between them concern only tactics, so that, in the opinion of these people, it is quite impossible to draw a contrast between these two trends.

This is a great mistake.

We believe that the Anarchists are real enemies of Marxism. Accordingly, we also hold that a real struggle must be waged against real enemies. Therefore, it is necessary to examine the "doctrine" of the Anarchists from beginning to end and weigh it up thoroughly from all aspects.

The point is that Marxism and anarchism are built up on entirely different principles, in spite of the fact that both come into the arena of the struggle under the flag of socialism. The cornerstone of anarchism is the *individual*, whose emancipation, according to its tenets, is the principal condition for the emancipation of the masses, the collective body. According to the tenets of anarchism, the emancipation of the masses is impossible until the individual is emancipated. Accordingly, its slogan is: "Everything for the individual." The cornerstone of Marxism, however, is the masses, whose emancipation, according to its tenets, is the principal condition for the emancipation of the individual. That is to say, according to the tenets of Marxism, the emancipation of the individual is impossible until the masses are emancipated. Accordingly, its slogan is: "Everything for the masses."

Clearly, we have here two principles, one negating the other, and not merely disagreements on tactics.

The object of our articles is to place these two opposite principles side by side, to compare Marxism with anarchism, and thereby throw light on their respective virtues and defects. At this point we think it necessary to acquaint the reader with the plan of these articles.

We shall begin with a description of Marxism, deal, in passing, with the Anarchists' views on Marxism, and then proceed to criticise anarchism itself. Namely: we shall expound the dialectical method, the Anarchists' views on this method, and our criticism; the materialist theory, the Anarchists' views and our criticism (here, too, we shall discuss the socialist revolution, the socialist dictatorship, the minimum programme, and tactics generally); the philosophy of the Anarchists and our criticism; the socialism of the Anarchists and our criticism;

anarchist tactics and organisation—and, in conclusion, we shall give our deductions.

We shall try to prove that, as advocates of small community socialism, the Anarchists are not genuine Socialists.

We shall also try to prove that, in so far as they repudiate the dictatorship of the proletariat, the Anarchists are also not genuine revolutionaries. . . .

And so, let us proceed with our subject.

I

THE DIALECTICAL METHOD

Everything in the world is in motion...
Life changes, productive forces grow, old
relations collapse.

Karl Marx

Marxism is not only the theory of socialism, it is an integral world outlook, a philosophical system, from which Marx's proletarian socialism logically follows. This philosophical system is called dialectical materialism.

Hence, to expound Marxism means to expound also dialectical materialism.

Why is this system called dialectical materialism?

Because its *method* is dialectical, and its *theory* is materialistic.

What is the dialectical method?

It is said that social life is in continual motion and development. And that is true: life must not be regarded as something immutable and static; it never remains at one level, it is in eternal motion, in an eternal process of destruction and creation. Therefore, life always contains the *new* and the *old*, the *growing* and the *dying*, the revolutionary and the counter-revolutionary.

The dialectical method tells us that we must regard life as it actually is. We have seen that life is in continual motion; consequently, we must regard life in its motion and ask: Where is life going? We have seen that life presents a picture of constant destruction and creation; consequently, we must examine life in its process of destruction and creation and ask: What is being destroyed and what is being created in life?

That which in life is born and grows day by day is invincible, its progress cannot be checked. That is to say, if, for example, in life the proletariat as a class is born and grows day by day, no matter how weak and small in numbers it may be *today*, in the long run it must triumph. Why? Because it is growing, gaining strength and marching forward. On the other hand, that which in life is growing old and advancing to its grave must inevitably suffer defeat, even if *today* it represents a titanic force. That is to say, if, for example, the bourgeoisie is gradually losing ground and is slipping farther and farther back every day, then, no matter how strong and numerous it may be today, it must, in the long run, suffer defeat. Why? Because as a class it is decaying, growing feeble, growing old, and becoming a burden to life.

Hence arose the well-known dialectical proposition: all that which really exists, i.e., all that which grows day by day is rational, and all that which decays day by day is irrational and, consequently, cannot avoid defeat.

For example. In the eighties of the last century a great controversy flared up among the Russian revolutionary intelligentsia. The Narodniks asserted that the main force that could undertake the task of "emancipating Russia" was the petty bourgeoisie, rural and urban. Why?—the Marxists asked them. Because, answered the Narodniks, the rural and urban petty bourgeoisie now constitute the majority and, moreover, they are poor, they live in poverty.

To this the Marxists replied: It is true that the rural and urban petty bourgeoisie now constitute the majority and are really poor, but is that the point? The petty bourgeoisie has long constituted the majority, but up to now it has displayed no initiative in the struggle for "freedom" without the assistance of the proletariat. Why? Because the petty bourgeoisie as a class is not growing; on the contrary, it is disintegrating day by day and breaking up into bourgeois and proletarians. On the other hand, nor is poverty of decisive importance here, of course: "tramps" are poorer than the petty bourgeoisie, but nobody will say that they can undertake the task of "emancipating Russia."

As you see, the point is not which class today constitutes the majority, or which class is poorer, but which class is gaining strength and which is decaying.

And as the proletariat is the only class which is steadily growing and gaining strength, which is pushing social life forward and rallying all the revolutionary elements around itself, our duty is to regard it as the main force in the present-day movement, join its ranks and make its progressive strivings our strivings.

That is how the Marxists answered.

Obviously the Marxists looked at life dialectically, whereas the Narodniks argued metaphysically—they pictured social life as having become static at a particular stage.

That is how the dialectical method looks upon the development of life.

But there is movement and movement. There was movement in social life during the "December days," when the proletariat, straightening its back, stormed arms depots and launched an attack upon reaction. But the movement of preceding years, when the proletariat, under the conditions of "peaceful" development, limited itself to individual strikes and the formation of small trade unions, must also be called social movement.

Clearly, movement assumes different forms.

And so the dialectical method says that movement has two forms: the evolutionary and the revolutionary form.

Movement is evolutionary when the progressive elements spontaneously continue their daily activities and introduce minor, *quantitative* changes into the old order.

Movement is revolutionary when the same elements combine, become imbued with a single idea and sweep down upon the enemy camp with the object of uprooting the old order and of introducing *qualitative* changes in life, of establishing a new order.

Evolution prepares for revolution and creates the ground for it; revolution consummates the process of evolution and facilitates its further activity.

Similar processes take place in nature. The history of science shows that the dialectical method is a truly scientific method: from astronomy to sociology, in every field we find confirmation of the idea that nothing is eternal in the universe, everything changes, everything develops. Consequently, everything in nature must be regarded from the point of view of movement, development. And this means that the spirit of dialectics permeates the whole of present-day science.

As regards the forms of movement, as regards the fact that according to dialectics, minor, *quantitative* changes sooner or later lead to major, *qualitative* changes—this law applies with equal force to the history of nature Mendeleyev's "periodic system of elements" clearly shows how very important in the history of nature is the emergence of qualitative changes out of quantitative changes. The same thing is shown in biology by the theory of neo-Lamarckism, to which neo-Darwinism is yielding place.

We shall say nothing about other facts, on which F. Engels has thrown sufficiently full light in his *Anti-Dühring*.

Such is the content of the dialectical method.

*   *   *

How do the Anarchists look upon the dialectical method?

Everybody knows that Hegel was the father of the dialectical method. Marx purged and improved this method. The Anarchists are aware of this, of course. They know that Hegel was a conservative, and so, taking advantage of this, they vehemently revile Hegel as a supporter of "restoration," they try with the utmost zeal to "prove" that "Hegel is a philosopher of restoration . . . that he eulogizes bureaucratic constitutionalism in its absolute form, that the general idea of his philosophy of history is subordinate to and serves the philosophical trend of the period of restoration," and so on and so forth (see *Nobati*,[2] No. 6. Article by V. Cherkezishvili.)

The well-known Anarchist Kropotkin tries to "prove" the same thing in his works (see, for example, his *Science and Anarchism*, in Russian).

Our Kropotkinites, from Cherkezishvili right down to Sh. G., all with one voice echo Kropotkin (see *Nobati*).

True, nobody contests what they say on this point; on the contrary, everybody agrees that Hegel was not a revolutionary. Marx and Engels themselves proved before anybody else did, in their *Critique of Critical Criticism*, that Hegel's views on history fundamentally contradict the idea of the sovereignty of the people. But in spite of this, the Anarchists go on trying to "prove," and deem it necessary to go on day in and day out trying to "prove," that Hegel was a supporter of "restoration." Why do they do this? Probably, in order by all this to discredit Hegel and make their readers feel that the "reactionary" Hegel's method also cannot be other than "repugnant" and unscientific.

The Anarchists think that they can refute the dialectical method in this way.

We affirm that in this way they can prove nothing but their own ignorance. Pascal and Leibnitz were not revolutionaries, but the mathematical method they discovered is recognised today as a scientific method. Mayer and Helmholtz were not revolutionaries, but their discoveries in the field of physics became the basis of science. Nor were Lamarck and Darwin revolutionaries, but their evolutionary method put biological science on its feet. . . . Why, then, should the fact not be admitted that, in spite of his conservatism, Hegel succeeded in working out a scientific method which is called the dialectical method?

No, *in this way* the Anarchists will prove nothing but their own

2 *Nobati* (*The Call*)—a weekly newspaper published by the Georgian Anarchists in Tiflis in 1906.

ignorance.

To proceed. In the opinion of the Anarchists, "dialectics is meta-physics," and as they "want to free science from metaphysics, philoso-phy from theology," they repudiate the dialectical method (see *Nobati*, Nos. 3 and 9. Sh. G. See also Kropotkin's *Science and Anarchism*).

Oh, those Anarchists! As the saying goes: "Blame others for your own sins." Dialectics matured in the struggle against metaphysics and gained fame in this struggle; but according to the Anarchists, dialectics is metaphysics!

Dialectics tells us that nothing in the world is eternal, everything in the world is transient and mutable; nature changes, society changes, habits and customs change, conceptions of justice change, truth itself changes—that is why dialectics regards everything critically; that is why it denies the existence of a once-and-for-all established truth. Con-sequently, it also repudiates abstract "dogmatic propositions, which, once discovered, had merely to be learned by heart" (see F. Engels, *Ludwig Feuerbach*).[3]

Metaphysics, however, tells us something altogether different. From its standpoint the world is something eternal and immutable (see F. Engels, *Anti-Dühring*), it has been once and for all determined by someone or something—that is why the metaphysicians always have "eternal justice" or "immutable truth" on their lips.

Proudhon, the "father" of the Anarchists, said that there existed in the world an *immutable justice determined once and for all*, which must be made the basis of future society. That is why Proudhon has been called a metaphysician. Marx fought Proudhon with the aid of the dialectical method and proved that since everything in the world changes, "jus-tice" must also change, and that, consequently, "immutable justice" is metaphysical nonsense (see K. Marx, *The Poverty of Philosophy*). The Georgian disciples of the metaphysician Proudhon, however, keep re-iterating that "Marx's dialectics is metaphysics"!

Metaphysics recognises various nebulous dogmas, such as, for ex-ample, the "unknowable," the "thing-in-itself," and, in the long run,

---

3 Karl Marx and Frederick Engels, *Selected Works*, Vol. II, Moscow 1951, p; 328.

passes into empty theology. In contrast to Proudhon and Spencer, Engels combated these dogmas with the aid of the dialectical method (see *Ludwig Feuerbach*); but the Anarchists—the disciples of Proudhon and Spencer—tell us that Proudhon and Spencer were scientists, whereas Marx and Engels were metaphysicians!

One of two things: either the Anarchists are deceiving themselves, or else they do not know what they are talking about.

At all events, it is beyond doubt that the Anarchists confuse Hegel's *metaphysical* system with his *dialectical* method.

Needless to say, Hegel's *philosophical system*, which rests on the immutable idea, is from beginning to end *metaphysical*. But it is also clear that Hegel's *dialectical method*, which repudiates all immutable ideas, is from beginning to end *scientific* and *revolutionary*.

That is why Karl Marx, who subjected Hegel's metaphysical system to devastating criticism, at the same time praised his dialectical method, which, as Marx said, "lets nothing impose upon it, and is in its essence critical and revolutionary" (see *Capital*, Vol. I. Preface).

That is why Engels sees a big difference between Hegel's method and his *system*. "Whoever placed the chief emphasis on the Hegelian system could be fairly conservative in both spheres; whoever regarded the dialectical *method* as the main thing could belong to the most extreme opposition, both in politics and religion" (see *Ludwig Feuerbach*).

The Anarchists fail to see this difference and thoughtlessly maintain that "dialectics is metaphysics."

To proceed. The Anarchists say that the dialectical method is "subtle word-weaving," "the method of sophistry," "logical somersaults" (see *Nobati*, No. 8. Sh. G.), "with the aid of which both truth and falsehood are proved with equal facility" (see *Nobati*, No. 4. Article by V. Cherkezishvili).

Thus, in the opinion of the Anarchists, the dialectical method proves both truth and falsehood.

At first sight it would seem that the accusation advanced by the Anarchists has some foundation. Listen, for example, to what Engels says about the follower of the metaphysical method:

". . . His communication is: 'Yea, yea; nay, nay, for whatsoever is more than these cometh of evil.' For him a thing either exists, or it does not exist; it is equally impossible for a thing to be itself and at the same time something else. Positive and negative absolutely exclude one another . . ." (see *Anti-Dühring*. Introduction).

How is that?—the Anarchists cry heatedly. Is it possible for a thing to be good and bad at the same time?! That is "sophistry," "juggling with words," it shows that "you want to prove truth and falsehood with equal facility"! . . .

Let us, however, go into the substance of the matter.

Today we are demanding a democratic republic. Can we say that a democratic republic is good in all respects, or bad in all respects? No we cannot! Why? Because a democratic republic is good only in one respect: when it destroys the feudal system; but it is bad in another respect: when it strengthens the bourgeois system. Hence we say: in so far as the democratic republic destroys the feudal system it is good— and we fight for it; but in so far as it strengthens the bourgeois system it is bad—and we fight against it.

So the same democratic republic can be "good" and "bad" at the same time—it is "yes" and "no."

The same thing may be said about the eight-hour day, which is good and bad at the same time: "good" in so far as it strengthens the proletariat, and "bad" in so far as it strengthens the wage system.

It was *facts* of this kind that Engels had in mind when he characterised the dialectical method in the words we quoted above.

The Anarchists, however, fail to understand this, and an absolutely clear idea seems to them to be nebulous "sophistry."

The Anarchists are, of course, at liberty to note or ignore these *facts*, they may even ignore the sand on the sandy seashore—they have every right to do that. But why drag in the dialectical method, which, unlike anarchism, does not look at life with its eyes shut, which has its finger on the pulse of life and openly says: since life changes and is in motion, every phenomenon of life has two trends: a positive and a negative; the first we must defend, the second we must reject.

To proceed further. In the opinion of our Anarchists, "dialectical development is catastrophic development, by means of which, first the past is utterly destroyed, and then the future is established quite separately. . . . Cuvier's cataclysms were due to unknown causes, but Marx and Engels's catastrophes are engendered by dialectics" (see *Nobati*, No. 8. Sh. G.).

In another place the same author writes: "Marxism rests on Darwinism and treats it uncritically" (see *Nobati*, No. 6).

Now listen!

Cuvier rejects Darwin's theory of evolution, he recognises only cataclysms, and cataclysms are *unexpected* upheavals "due to *unknown* causes." The Anarchists say that the Marxists *adhere to Cuvier's view* and therefore *repudiate Darwinism.*

Darwin rejects Cuvier's cataclysms, he recognises gradual evolution. But the same Anarchists say that "Marxism rests on Darwinism and treats it uncritically," i.e., the Marxists repudiate *Cuvier's cataclysms.*

In short, the Anarchists accuse the Marxists of adhering to Cuvier's view and at the same time reproach them for adhering to Darwin's and not to Cuvier's view.

This is anarchy if you like! As the saying goes: the Sergeant's widow flogged herself! Clearly, Sh. G. of No. 8 of *Nobati* forgot what Sh. G. of No. 6 said.

Which is right: No. 8 or No. 6?

Let us turn to the facts. Marx says:

"At a certain stage of their development, the material productive forces of society come in conflict with the existing relations of production, or—what is but a legal expression for the same thing—with the property relations. . . . Then begins an epoch of social revolution." But "no social order ever perishes before all the productive forces for which there is room in it have developed . . ." (see K. Marx, *A Contribution to the Critique of Political Economy.* Preface).[4]

If this thesis of Marx is applied to modern social life, we shall

---

4 Karl Marx and Frederick Engels, *Selected Works*, Vol. I, Moscow 1951, p; 329.

find that between the present-day productive forces, which are social in character, and the form of appropriation of the product, which is *private* in character, there is a fundamental conflict which must culminate in the socialist revolution (see F. Engels, *Anti-Dühring*, Part III, Chapter II).

As you see, in the opinion of Marx and Engels, revolution is engendered not by Cuvier's "unknown causes," but by very definite and vital social causes called "the development of the productive forces."

As you see, in the opinion of Marx and Engels, revolution comes only when the productive forces have sufficiently matured, and not *unexpectedly*, as Cuvier thought.

Clearly, there is nothing in common between Cuvier's cataclysms and Marx's dialectical method.

On the other hand, Darwinism repudiates not only Cuvier's cataclysms, but also dialectically understood development, which includes revolution; whereas, from the standpoint of the dialectical method, evolution and revolution, quantitative and qualitative changes, are two essential forms of the same motion.

Obviously, it is also wrong to assert that "Marxism . . . treats Darwinism uncritically."

It turns out therefore, that *Nobati* is wrong in both cases, in No. 6 as well as in No. 8.

Lastly, the Anarchists tell us reproachfully that "dialectics . . . provides no possibility of getting, or jumping, out of oneself, or of jumping over oneself" (see *Nobati*, No. 8. Sh. G.).

Now that is the downright truth, Messieurs Anarchists! Here you are absolutely right, my dear sirs: the dialectical method does not, indeed, provide such a possibility. But why not? Because "jumping out of oneself, or jumping over oneself" is an exercise for wild goats, while the dialectical method was created for human beings.

That is the secret! . . .

Such, in general, are the Anarchists' views on the dialectical method.

Clearly, the Anarchists fail to understand the dialectical method of Marx and Engels; they have conjured up their own dialectics, and it is against this dialectics that they are fighting so ruthlessly.

All we can do is to laugh as we gaze at this spectacle, for one cannot help laughing when one sees a man fighting his own imagination, smashing his own inventions, while at the same time heatedly asserting that he is smashing his opponent.

II

THE MATERIALIST THEORY

"It is not the consciousness of men that determines their being, but, on the contrary, their social being that determines their consciousness."

Karl Marx

We already know what the dialectical method is. What is the materialist theory?

Everything in the world changes, everything in life develops, but *how* do these changes take place and *in what form* does this development proceed?

We know, for example, that the earth was once an incandescent, fiery mass; then it gradually cooled, plants and animals appeared, the development of the animal kingdom was followed by the appearance of a certain species of ape, and all this was followed by the appearance of man.

This, broadly speaking, is the way nature developed.

We also know that social life did not remain static either. There was a time when men lived on a primitive-communist basis; at that time they gained their livelihood by primitive hunting; they roamed through the forests and procured their food in that way. There came a time when primitive communism was superseded by the matriarchate

—at that time men satisfied their needs mainly by means of primitive agriculture. Later the matriarchate was superseded by the patriarchate, under which men gained their livelihood mainly by cattle-breeding. The patriarchate was later superseded by the slave-owning system — at that time men gained their livelihood by means of relatively more developed agriculture. The slave-owning system was followed by feudalism, and then, after all this, came the bourgeois system.

That, broadly speaking, is the way social life developed.

Yes, all this is well known. . . . But *how* did this development take place; did consciousness call forth the development of "nature" and of "society," or, on the contrary, did the development of "nature" and "society" call forth the development of consciousness?

This is how the materialist theory presents the question.

Some people say that "nature" and "social life" were preceded by the universal idea, which subsequently served as the basis of their development, so that the development of the phenomena of "nature" and of "social life" is, so to speak, the external form, merely the expression of the development of the universal idea.

Such, for example, was the doctrine of the *idealists*, who in the course of time split up into several trends.

Others say that from the very beginning there have existed in the world two mutually negating forces—idea and matter, consciousness and being, and that correspondingly, phenomena also fall into two cate-gories—the ideal and the material, which negate each other, and contend against each other, so that the development of nature and society is a constant struggle between ideal and material phenomena.

Such, for example, was the doctrine of the *dualists*, who in the course of time, like the idealists, split up into several trends.

The materialist theory utterly repudiates both dualism and idealism.

Of course, both ideal and material phenomena exist in the world, but this does not mean that they negate each other. On the contrary, the ideal and the material sides are two different forms of one and the same nature or society, the one cannot be conceived without the other, they exist together, develop together, and, consequently, we have no grounds whatever for thinking that they negate each other.

Thus, so-called dualism proves to be unsound.

A single and indivisible nature expressed in two different forms—material and ideal; a single and indivisible social life expressed in two different forms—material and ideal—that is how we should regard the development of nature and of social life.

Such is the monism of the materialist theory.

At the same time, the materialist theory also repudiates idealism.

It is wrong to think that in its development the ideal side, and consciousness in general, precedes the development of the material side. So called external "non-living" nature existed before there were any living beings. The first living matter possessed no consciousness, it possessed only *irritability* and the first rudiments of *sensation*. Later, animals gradually developed the power of sensation, which slowly passed into *consciousness*, in conformity with the development of the structure of their organisms and nervous systems. If the ape had always walked on all fours, if it had never stood upright, its descendant—man—would not have been able freely to use his lungs and vocal chords and, therefore, would not have been able to speak; and that would have fundamentally retarded the development of his consciousness. If, furthermore, the ape had not risen up on its hind legs, its descendant—man—would have been compelled always to walk on all fours, to look downwards and obtain his impressions only from there; he would have been unable to look up and around himself and, consequently, his brain would have obtained no more impressions than the brain of a quadruped. All this would have fundamentally retarded the development of human consciousness.

It follows, therefore, that the development of consciousness needs a particular structure of the organism and development of its nervous system.

It follows, therefore, that the development of the ideal side, the development of consciousness, is *preceded* by the development of the material side, the development of the external conditions: first the external conditions change, first the material side changes, and *then* consciousness, the ideal side, changes accordingly.

Thus, the history of the development of nature utterly refutes so-called idealism.

The same thing must be said about the history of the development of human society.

History shows that if at different times men were imbued with different ideas and desires, the reason for this is that at different times men fought nature in different ways to satisfy their needs and, accordingly, their economic relations assumed different forms. There was a time when men fought nature collectively, on the basis of primitive communism; at that time their property was communist property and, therefore, at that time they drew scarcely any distinction between "mine" and "thine," their consciousness was communistic. There came a time when the distinction between "mine" and "thine" penetrated the process of production; at that time property, too, assumed a private, individualist character and, therefore, the consciousness of men became imbued with the sense of private property. Then came the time, the present time, when production is again assuming a social character and, consequently, property, too, will soon assume a social character—and this is precisely why the consciousness of men is gradually becoming imbued with socialism.

Here is a simple illustration. Let us take a shoemaker who owned a tiny workshop, but who, unable to withstand the competition of the big manufacturers, closed his workshop and took a job, say, at Adelkhanov's shoe factory in Tiflis. He went to work at Adelkhanov's factory not with the view to becoming a permanent wage-worker, but with the object of saving up some money, of accumulating a little capital to enable him to reopen his workshop. As you see, the position of this shoemaker is *already* proletarian, but his consciousness is *still* non-proletarian, it is thoroughly petty-bourgeois. In other words, this shoemaker has *already* lost his petty-bourgeois position, it has gone, but his petty-bourgeois consciousness has *not yet* gone, it has lagged behind his actual position.

Clearly, here too, in social life, first the external conditions change, first the conditions of men change and then their consciousness changes accordingly.

But let us return to our shoemaker. As we already know, he intends to save up some money and then reopen his workshop. This proletarianised shoemaker goes on working, but finds that it is a very difficult matter to save money, because what he earns barely suffices to maintain an existence. Moreover, he realises that the opening of a private workshop is after all not so alluring: the rent he will have to pay for the premises, the caprices of customers, shortage of money, the competition of the big manufacturers and similar worries—such are the many troubles that torment the private workshop owner. On the other hand, the proletarian is relatively freer from such cares; he is not troubled by customers, or by having to pay rent for premises. He goes to the factory every morning, "calmly" goes home in the evening, and as calmly pockets his "pay" on Saturdays. Here, for the first time, the wings of our shoemaker's petty-bourgeois dreams are clipped; here for the first time proletarian strivings awaken in his soul.

Time passes and our shoemaker sees that he has not enough money to satisfy his most essential needs, that what he needs very badly is a rise in wages. At the same time, he hears his fellow-workers talking about unions and strikes. Here our shoemaker realises that in order to improve his conditions he must fight the masters and not open a workshop of his own. He joins the union, enters the strike movement, and soon becomes imbued with socialist ideas. . . .

Thus, *in the long run*, the change in the shoemaker's material conditions was followed by a change in his consciousness: first his material conditions changed, and then, after a time, his consciousness changed accordingly.

The same must be said about classes and about society as a whole.

In social life, too, first the external conditions change, first the material conditions change, and then the ideas of men, their habits, customs and their world outlook change accordingly.

That is why Marx says:

"It is not the consciousness of men that determines their being, but, on the contrary, their social being that determines their consciousness."

If we can call the material side, the external conditions, being, and other phenomena of the same kind, the *content*, then we can call the ideal side, consciousness and other phenomena of the same kind, the *form*. Hence arose the well-known materialist proposition: in the process of development content precedes form, form lags behind content.

And as, in Marx's opinion, economic development is the "material foundation" of social life, its *content*, while legal-political and religious-philosophical development is the "ideological form" of this content, its "superstructure," Marx draws the conclusion that: "With the change of the economic foundation the entire immense superstructure is *more or less rapidly* transformed."

This, of course, does not mean that in Marx's opinion content is possible without form, as Sh. G. imagines (see *Noboati*, No. 1. "A Critique of Monism"). Content is impossible without form, but the point is that since a given form lags behind its content, it never *fully* corresponds to this content; and so the new content is "obliged" to clothe itself for a time in the old form, and this causes a conflict between them. At the present time, for example, the form of appropriation of the product, which is *private* in character, does not correspond to the *social* content of production, and this is the basis of the present-day social "conflict."

On the other hand, the idea that consciousness is a form of being does not mean that by its nature consciousness, too, is matter. That was the opinion held only by the vulgar materialists (for example, Büchner and Moleschott), whose theories fundamentally contradict Marx's materialism, and whom Engels rightly ridiculed in his *Ludwig Feuerbach*. According to Marx's materialism, consciousness and being, idea and matter, are two different forms of the same phenomenon, which, broadly speaking, is called nature, or society. Consequently, they do not negate each other[5]; nor are they one and the same phenome-

---

5 This does not contradict the idea that there is a conflict between form and content. The point is that the conflict is not between content and form in general, but between the old form and the new content, which is seeking a new form and is

non. The only point is that, in the development of nature and society, consciousness, i.e., what takes place in our heads, is preceded by a corresponding material change, i.e., what takes place outside of us; any given material change is, sooner or later, inevitably followed by a corresponding ideal change.

Very well, we shall be told, perhaps this is true as applied to the history of nature and society. But how do different conceptions and ideas arise in our heads at the present time? Do so-called external conditions really exist, or is it only our conceptions of these external conditions that exist? And if external conditions exist, to what degree are they perceptible and cognizable?

On this point the materialist theory says that our conceptions, our "self," exist only in so far as external conditions exist that give rise to impressions in our "self." Whoever unthinkingly says that nothing exists but our conceptions, is compelled to deny the existence of all external conditions and, consequently, must deny the existence of all other people and admit the existence only of his own "self," which is absurd, and utterly contradicts the principles of science.

Obviously, external conditions do actually exist; these conditions existed before us, and will exist after us; and the more often and the more strongly they affect our consciousness, the more easily perceptible and cognizable do they become.

As regards the question as to how different conceptions and ideas arise in our heads *at the present time*, we must observe that here we have a repetition in brief of what takes place in the history of nature and society. In this case, too, the object outside of us preceded our conception of it; in this case, too, our conception, the form, lags behind the object—behind its content. When I look at a tree and see it—that only shows that this tree existed even before the conception of a tree arose in my head, that it was this tree that aroused the corresponding conception in my head. . . .

Such, in brief, is the content of Marx's materialist theory.

The importance of the materialist theory for the practical activi-

---

striving towards it.

ties of mankind can be readily understood.

If the economic conditions change *first* and the consciousness of men undergoes a corresponding change *later*, it is clear that we must seek the grounds for a given ideal not in the minds of men, not in their imaginations, but in the development of their economic conditions. Only that ideal is good and acceptable which is based on a study of economic conditions. All those ideals which ignore economic conditions and are not based upon their development are useless and unacceptable.

Such is the first practical conclusion to be drawn from the materialist theory.

If the consciousness of men, their habits and customs, are determined by external conditions, if the unsuitability of legal and political forms rests on an economic content, it is clear that we must help to bring about a radical change in economic relations in order, with this change, to bring about a radical change in the habits and customs of the people, and in their political system.

Here is what Karl Marx says on that score:

"No great acumen is required to perceive the necessary interconnection of materialism with . . . socialism. If man constructs all his knowledge, perceptions, etc., from the world of sense . . . then it follows that it is a question of so arranging the empirical world that he experiences the truly human in it, that he becomes accustomed to experiencing himself as a human being. . . . If man is unfree in the materialist sense—that is, is free not by reason of the negative force of being able to avoid this or that, but by reason of the positive power to assert his true individuality, then one should not punish individuals for crimes, but rather destroy the anti-social breeding places of crime. . . . If man is moulded circumstances, then the circumstances must be moulded humanly" (see *Ludwig Feuerbach*, Appendix: "Karl Marx on the History of French Materialism of the XVIII Century").[6]

Such is the second practical conclusion to be drawn from the ma-

---

6 **Original editor:** See Karl Marx and Friedrich Engels, *Die heilige Familie, "Kritische Schlacht gegen den französischen Materialismus."* (Marx-Engels, *Gesamtausgabe*, Erste Abteilung, Band 3, S. 307-08.)

terialist theory.

*   *   *

What is the anarchist view of the materialist theory of Marx and Engels?

While the dialectical method originated with Hegel, the materialist theory is a further development of the materialism of Feuerbach. The Anarchists know this very well, and they try to take advantage of the defects of Hegel and Feuerbach to discredit the dialectical materialism of Marx and Engels. We have already shown with reference to Hegel and the dialectical method that these tricks of the Anarchists prove nothing but their own ignorance. The same must be said with reference to their attacks on Feuerbach and the materialist theory.

For example. The Anarchists tell us with great aplomb that "Feuerbach was a pantheist . . ." that he "deified man . . ." (see *Nobati*, No. 7. D. Delendi), that "in Feuerbach's opinion man is what he eats . . ." alleging that from this Marx drew the following conclusion: "Consequently, the main and primary thing is economic conditions . . ." (see *Nobati*, No. 6, Sh. G.).

True, nobody has any doubts about Feuerbach's pantheism, his deification of man, and other errors of his of the same kind. On the contrary, Marx and Engels were the first to reveal Feuerbach's errors. Nevertheless, the Anarchists deem it necessary once again to "expose" the already exposed errors. Why? Probably because, in reviling Feuerbach, they want indirectly to discredit the materialist theory of Marx and Engels. Of course, if we examine the subject impartially we shall certainly find that in addition to erroneous ideas, Feuerbach gave utterance to correct ideas, as has been the case with many scholars in history. Nevertheless, the Anarchists go on "exposing." . . .

We say again that by tricks of this kind they prove nothing but their own ignorance.

It is interesting to note (as we shall see later on) that the Anarchists took it into their heads to criticise the materialist theory from hearsay, without any acquaintance with it. As a consequence, they often contradict and refute each other, which, of course, makes our "critics" look ridiculous. If, for example, we listen to what Mr. Cherkezishvili has to say, it would appear that Marx and Engels detested monistic materialism, that their materialism was vulgar and not monistic materialism :

"The great science of the naturalists, with its system of evolution, transformism and monistic materialism, which *Engels so heartily detested . . .* avoided dialectics," etc. (see *Nobati*, No. 4. V. Cherkezishvili).

It follows, therefore, that natural-scientific materialism, which Cherkezishvili approves of and which Engels "detested," was monistic materialism and, *therefore*, deserves approval, whereas the materialism of Marx and Engels is not monistic and, of course, does not deserve recognition.

Another Anarchist, however, says that the materialism of Marx and Engels is monistic and therefore should be rejected.

"Marx's conception of history is a throwback to Hegel. The monistic materialism of absolute objectivism in general, and Marx's economic monism in particular, are impossible in nature and fallacious in theory. . . . Monistic materialism is poorly disguised dualism and a compromise between metaphysics and science . . . " (see *Nobati*, No. 6. Sh. G.).

It would follow, therefore, that monistic materialism is unacceptable, that Marx and Engels do not detest it, but, on the contrary, are themselves monistic materialists—and therefore, monistic materialism must be rejected.

They are all at sixes and sevens. Try and make out which of them is right, the former or the latter! They have not yet agreed among themselves about the merits and demerits of Marx's materialism, they have not yet understood whether it is monistic or not, and have not yet made up their minds themselves as to which is the more acceptable, vulgar or monistic materialism—but they already deafen us with their boastful claims to have shattered Marxism!

Well, well, if Messieurs the Anarchists continue to shatter each other's views as zealously as they are doing now, we need say no more, the future belongs to the Anarchists. . . .

No less ridiculous is the fact that certain "celeblated" Anarchists, notwithstanding their "celebrity," have not yet made themselves familiar with the different trends in science. It appears that they are ignorant of the fact that there are various kinds of materialism in science which differ a great deal from each other: there is, for example, vulgar materialism, which denies the importance of the ideal side and the effect it has upon the material side; but there is also so-called monistic materialism—the materialist theory of Marx—which scientifically examines the interrelation between the ideal and the material sides. But the Anarchists *confuse* these different kinds of materialism, fail to see even the obvious differences between them, and at the same time affirm with great aplomb that they are regenerating science!

P. Kropotkin, for example, smugly asserts in his "philosophical" works that anarcho-communism rests on "contemporary materialist philosophy," but he does not utter a single word to explain on which "materialist philosophy" anarcho-communism rests: on vulgar, monistic, or some other. Evidently he is ignorant of the fact that there are fundamental contradictions between the different trends of materialism, and he fails to understand that to confuse these trends means not "regenerating science," but displaying one's own downright ignorance (see Kropotkin, *Science and Anarchism*, and also *Anarchy and Its Philosophy*).

The same thing must be said about Kropotkin's Georgian disciples. Listen to this:

"In the opinion of Engels, and also of Kautsky, Marx rendered mankind a great service in that he. . ." among other things, discovered the "materialist conception. Is this true? We do not think so, for we know . . . that all the historians, scientists and philosophers who adhere to the view that the social mechanism is set in motion by geographic, climatic and telluric, cosmic, anthropological and biological conditions — *are all materialists*" (see *Nobati*, No. 2).

It follows, therefore, that there is no difference whatever between the "materialism" of Aristotle and Holbach, or between the "materialism" of Marx and Moleschott! This is criticism if you like! And people whose knowledge is on such a level have taken it into their heads to renovate science! Indeed, it is an apt saying: "It's a bad lookout when a cobbler begins to bake pies! . . ."

To proceed. Our "celebrated" Anarchists heard somewhere that Marx's materialism was a "belly theory," and so they rebuke us, Marxists, saying :

"In the opinion of Feuerbach, man is what he eats. This formula had a magic effect on Marx and Engels," and, as a consequence, Marx drew the conclusion that "the main and primary thing is economic conditions, relations of production. . . ." And then the Anarchists proceed to instruct us in a philosophical tone: "It would be a mistake to say that the *sole* means of achieving this object of social life) is *eating* and economic production. . . . If *ideology were determined* mainly, monistically, by *eating* and economic conditions—then some gluttons would be geniuses" (see *Nobati*, No. 6. Sh. G.).

You see how easy it is to refute the materialism of Marx and Engels! It is sufficient to hear some gossip in the street from some schoolgirl about Marx and

Engels, it is sufficient to repeat that street gossip with philosophical aplomb in the columns of a paper like *Nobati*, to leap into fame as a "critic" of Marxism!

But tell me, gentlemen: Where, when, on which planet, and which Marx did you hear say that "*eating determines ideology*"? Why did you not cite a single sentence, a single word from the works of Marx to back your assertion? True, Marx said that the economic conditions of men determine their consciousness, their ideology, but who told you that eating and economic conditions are the same thing? Don't you really know that physiological phenomena, such as *eating*, for example, differ fundamentally from sociological phenomena, such as the *economic conditions* of men, for example? One can forgive a schoolgirl, say, for confusing these two different phenomena; but how is it that you, the "vanquishers of Social-Democracy," "regenerators of science," so carelessly repeat the mistake of a schoolgirl?

How, indeed, can eating determine social ideology? Ponder over what you yourselves have said: eating, the form of eating, does not change; in ancient times people ate, masticated and digested their food in the same way as they do now, but ideology changes all the time. Ancient, feudal, bourgeois and proletarian — such are the forms of ideology. Is it conceivable that *that which does not change* can determine *that which is constantly changing?*

To proceed further. In the opinion of the Anarchists, Marx's materialism "is parallelism. . . ." Or again: "monistic materialism is poorly disguised dualism and a compromise between metaphysics and science. . . ." "Marx drops into dualism because he depicts relations of production as material, and human striving and will *as an illusion and a utopia,* which, even though it exists, is *of no importance*" (see *Nobati,* No. 6. Sh. G.).

Firstly, Marx's monistic materialism has nothing in common with silly parallelism. From the standpoint of this materialism, the material side, content, necessarily *precedes* the ideal side, form. Parallelism, however, repudiates this view and emphatically affirms that neither the material nor the ideal *comes first,* that both develop together, side by side.

Secondly, even if Marx had in fact "depicted relations of production as material, and human striving and will as an illusion and a utopia having no importance," does that mean that Marx was a dualist? The dualist, as is well known, ascribes *equal* importance to the ideal and material sides as two opposite principles. But if, as you say, Marx attaches higher importance to the material side and no importance to the ideal side because it is a "utopia," how do you make out that Marx was a dualist, Messieurs "Critics"?

Thirdly, what connection can there be between materialist monism and dualism, when even a child knows that monism springs from *one principle*—nature, or being, which has a material and an ideal form, whereas dualism springs from *two principles*—the material and the ideal, which, according to dualism, negate each other?

Fourthly, when did Marx depict "human striving and will as a utopia and an illusion"? True, Marx explained "human striving and will" by economic development, and when the strivings of certain armchair philosophers failed to harmonise with economic conditions he called them utopian. But does this mean that Marx believed that human striving in general is utopian? Does this, too, really need explanation? Have you really not read Marx's statement that: *"mankind always sets itself only such tasks as it can solve"* (see Preface to *A Contribution to the Critique of Political Economy*), i.e., that, generally speaking, mankind does not pursue utopian aims? Clearly, either our "critic" does not know what he is talking about, or he is deliberately distorting the facts.

Fifthly, who told you that in the opinion of Marx and Engels "human striving and will are of no importance"? Why do you not point to the place where they say that? Does not Marx speak of the importance of "striving and will" in his *Eighteenth Brumaire of Louis Bonaparte*, in his *Class Struggles in France*, in his *Civil War in France*, and in other pamphlets of the same kind? Why then did Marx try to develop the proletarians' "will and striving" in the socialist spirit, why did he conduct propaganda among them if he attached no importance to "striving and will"? Or, what did Engels talk about in his well-known articles of 1891-94 if not the "importance of will and striving"? True, in Marx's opinion human "will and striving" acquire their content from economic conditions, but does that mean that they themselves exert no influence on the development of economic relations? Is it really so difficult for the Anarchists to understand such a simple idea?

Here is another "accusation" Messieurs the Anarchists make: "form is inconceivable without content . . ." therefore, one cannot say that "form *comes after* content (lags behind content. K.) . . . they 'co-exist.'. . . Otherwise, monism would be an absurdity" (see *Nobati*, No. 1. Sh. G.).

Our "scholar" is somewhat confused again. It is quite true that content is inconceivable without form. But it is also true that the *existing form* never fully corresponds to the *existing content*: the former lags behind the latter, to a certain extent the new content is always clothed in the old form and, as a consequence, there is always a conflict between the old form and the new content. It is precisely on this ground that revolutions occur, and this, among other things, expresses the revolutionary spirit of Marx's materialism. The "celebrated" Anarchists, however, have failed to understand this, and for this they themselves and not the materialist theory are to blame, of course.

Such are the views of the Anarchists on the materialist theory of Marx and Engels, that is, if they can be called views at all.

III

PROLETARIAN SOCIALISM

We are now familiar with Marx's theoretical doctrine; we are familiar with his *method* and also with his *theory*.

What practical conclusions must we draw from this doctrine?

What connection is there between dialectical materialism and proletarian socialism?

The dialectical method affirms that only that class which is growing day by day, which always marches forward and fights unceasingly for a better future, can be progressive to the end, only that class can smash the yoke of slavery. We see that the only class which is steadily growing, which always marches forward and is fighting for the future is the urban and rural proletariat. Therefore, we must serve the proletariat and place our hopes on it.

Such is the first practical conclusion to be drawn from Marx's theoretical doctrine.

But there is service and service. Bernstein also "serves" the proletariat when he urges it to forget about socialism. Kropotkin also "serves" the proletariat when he offers it community "socialism," which is scattered and has no broad industrial base. And Karl Marx serves the proletariat when he calls it to proletarian socialism, which will rest on the broad basis of modern large-scale industry.

What must we do in order that our activities may benefit the proletariat? How should we serve the proletariat?

The materialist theory affirms that a given ideal may be of direct service to the proletariat only if it does not run counter to the economic development of the country, if it fully answers to the requirements of that development. The economic development of the capitalist system shows that present-day production is assuming a social character, that the social character of production is a fundamental negation of existing capitalist property; consequently, our main task is to help to abolish capitalist property and to establish socialist property. And that means that the doctrine of Bernstein, who urges that socialism should be forgotten, fundamentally contradicts the requirements of economic development—it is harmful to the proletariat.

Further, the economic development of the capitalist system shows that present-day production is expanding day by day; it is not confined within the limits of individual towns and provinces, but constantly overflows these limits and embraces the territory of the whole state—consequently, we must welcome the expansion of production and regard as the basis of future socialism not separate towns and communities, but the entire and indivisible territory of the whole state which, in future, will, of course, expand more and more. And this means that the doctrine advocated by Kropotkin, which confines future socialism within the limits of separate towns and communities, is contrary to the interests of a powerful expansion of production—it is harmful to the proletariat.

Fight for a *broad* socialist life as the *principal* goal—this is how we should serve the proletariat.

Such is the second practical conclusion to be drawn from Marx's theoretical doctrine.

Clearly, proletarian socialism is the logical deduction from dialectical materialism.

What is proletarian socialism?

The present system is a capitalist system. This means that the world is divided up into two opposing camps, the camp of a small handful of capitalists and the camp of the majority—the proletarians. The proletarians work day and night, nevertheless they remain poor. The capitalists do not work, nevertheless they are rich. This takes place not because the proletarians are unintelligent and the capitalists are geniuses, but because the capitalists appropriate the fruits of the labour of the proletarians, because the capitalists exploit the proletarians.

Why are the fruits of the labour of the proletarians appropriated by the capitalists and not by the proletarians? Why do the capitalists exploit the proletarians and not vice versa?

Because the capitalist system is based on commodity production: here everything assumes the form of a commodity, everywhere the principle of buying and selling prevails. Here you can buy not only articles of consumption, not only food products, but also the labour power of men, their blood and their consciences. The capitalists know all this and purchase the labour power of the proletarians, they hire them. This means that the capitalists become the owners of the labour power they buy. The proletarians, however, lose their right to the labour power which they have sold. That is to say, what is produced by that labour power no longer belongs to the proletarians, it belongs only to the capitalists and goes into their pockets. The labour power which you have sold may produce in the course of a day goods to the value of 100 rubles, but that is not your business, those goods do not belong to you, it is the business only of the capitalists, and the goods belong to them—all that you are due to receive is your daily wage which, perhaps, may be sufficient to satisfy your essential needs if, of course, you live frugally. Briefly: the capitalists buy the labour power of the proletarians, they hire the proletarians, and this is precisely why the capitalists appropriate the fruits of the labour of the proletarians, this is precisely why the capitalists exploit the proletarians and not vice versa.

But why is it precisely the capitalists who buy the labour power of the proletarians? Why do the capitalists hire the proletarians and not vice versa?

Because the principal basis of the capitalist system is the private ownership of the instruments and means of production. Because the factories, mills, the land and minerals, the forests, the railways, machines and other means of production have become the private property of a small handful of capitalists. Because the proletarians lack all this. That is why the capitalists hire proletarians to keep the factories and mills going—if they did not do that their instruments and means of production would yield no profit. That is why the proletarians sell their labour power to the capitalists—if they did not, they would die of starvation.

All this throws light on the general character of capitalist production. Firstly, it is self-evident that capitalist production cannot be united and organised: it is all split up among the private enterprises of individual capitalists. Secondly, it is also clear that the immediate purpose of this scattered production is not to satisfy the needs of the people, but to produce goods for sale in order to increase the profits of the capitalists. But as every capitalist strives to increase his profits, each one tries to produce the largest possible quantity of goods and, as a result, the market is soon glutted, prices fall and—a general crisis sets in.

Thus, crises, unemployment, suspension of production, anarchy of production, and the like, are the direct results of present-day unorganised capitalist production.

If this unorganised social system still remains standing, if it still firmly withstands the attacks of the proletariat, it is primarily because it is protected by the capitalist state, by the capitalist government.

Such is the basis of present-day capitalist society.

*   *   *

There can be no doubt that future society will be built on an entirely different basis.

Future society will be socialist society. This means primarily, that there will be no classes in that society; there will be neither capitalists nor proletarians and, consequently, there will be no exploitation. In that society there will be only workers engaged in collective labour.

Future society will be socialist society. This means also that, with the abolition of exploitation commodity production and buying and selling will also be abolished and, therefore, there will be no room for buyers and sellers of labour power, for employers and employed— there will be only free workers.

Future society will be socialist society. This means, lastly, that in that society the abolition of wage-labour will be accompanied by the complete abolition of the private ownership of the instruments and means of production; there will be neither poor proletarians nor rich capitalists—there will be only workers who collectively own all the land and minerals, all the forests, all the factories and mills, all the railways, etc.

As you see, the main purpose of production in the future will be to satisfy the needs of society and not to produce goods for sale in order to increase the profits of the capitalists. Where there will be no room for commodity production, struggle for profits, etc.

It is also clear that future production will be socialistically organised, highly developed production, which will take into account the needs of society and will produce as much as society needs. Here there will be no room whether for scattered production, competition, crises, or unemployment.

Where there are no classes, where there are neither rich nor poor, there is no need for a state, there is no need either for political power, which oppresses the poor and protects the rich. Consequently, in socialist society there will be no need for the existence of political power.

That is why Karl Marx said as far back as 1846:

"The working class in the course of its development will substitute for the old bourgeois society an *association* which will exclude classes and their antagonism, and there will be *no more political power properly so-called . . .*" (see *The Poverty of Philosophy*).[7]

That is why Engels said in 1884:

"The state, then, has not existed from all eternity. There have been societies that did without it, that had no conception of the state and state power. At a certain stage of economic development, which was necessarily bound up with the cleavage of society into classes, the state became a necessity. . . . We are now rapidly approaching a stage in the development of production at which the existence of these classes not only will have ceased to be a necessity, but will become a positive hindrance to production. They will fall as inevitably as they arose at an

---

7 **Original editor:** See Karl Marx, *Misère de la Philosophie.* (Marx-Engels, *Gesamtausgabe*, Erste Abteilung, Band 6, S. 227.)

earlier stage. *Along with them the state will inevitably fall.* The society that will organise production on the basis of a free and equal association of the producers will put the whole machinery of state where it will then belong: into the Museum of Antiquities, by the side of the spinning wheel and the bronze axe" (see *The Origin of the Family, Private Property and the State*).[8]

At the same time, it is self-evident that for the purpose of administering public affairs there will have to be in socialist society, in addition to local offices which will collect all sorts of information, a central statistical bureau, which will collect information about the needs of the whole of society, and then distribute the various kinds of work among the working people accordingly. It will also be necessary to hold conferences, and particularly congresses, the decisions of which will certainly be binding upon the comrades in the minority until the next congress is held.

Lastly, it is obvious that free and comradely labour should result in an equally comradely, and complete, satisfaction of all needs in the future socialist society. This means that if future society demands from each of its members as much labour as he can perform, it, in its turn, must provide each member with all the products he needs. From each according to his ability, to each according to his needs!—such is the basis upon which the future collectivist system must be created. It goes without saying that in the *first* stage of socialism, when elements who have not yet grown accustomed to work are being drawn into the new way of life, when the productive forces also will not yet have been sufficiently developed and there will still be "dirty" and "clean" work to do, the application of the principle: "to each according to his needs," will undoubtedly be greatly hindered and, as a consequence, society will be obliged *temporarily* to take some other path, a middle path. But it is also clear that when future society runs into its groove, when the survivals of capitalism will have been eradicated, the only principle that will conform to socialist society will be the one pointed out above.

That is why Marx said in 1875 :

---

8 **Original editor:** See Karl Marx and Frederick Engels, *Selected Works*, Vol. II, Moscow 1951, p. 292.

"In a higher phase of communist (i.e., socialist) society, after the enslaving subordination of the individual to the division of labour, and therewith also the antithesis between mental and physical labour, has vanished; after labour has become not only a means of livelihood but life's prime want; after the productive forces have also increased with the all-round development of the individual . . . only then can the narrow horizon of bourgeois law be crossed in its entirety and society inscribe on its banners: 'From each according to his ability, to each according to his needs'" (see *Critique of the Gotha Programme*).[9]

Such, in general, is the picture of future socialist society according to the theory of Marx.

This is all very well. But is the achievement of socialism conceivable? Can we assume that man will rid himself of his "savage habits"?

Or again: if everybody receives according to his needs, can we assume that the level of the productive forces of socialist society will be adequate for this?

Socialist society presupposes an adequate development of productive forces and socialist consciousness among men, their socialist enlightenment. At the present time the development of productive forces is hindered by the existence of capitalist property, but if we bear in mind that this capitalist property will not exist in future society, it is self-evident that the productive forces will increase tenfold. Nor must it be forgotten that in future society the hundreds of thousands of present-day parasites, and also the unemployed, will set to work and augment the ranks of the working people; and this will greatly stimulate the development of the productive forces. As regards men's "savage" sentiments and opinions, these are not as eternal as some people imagine; there was a time, under primitive communism, when man did not recognise private property; there came a time, the time of individualistic production, when private property dominated the hearts and minds of men; a new time is coming, the time of socialist production—will it be surprising if the hearts and minds of men become imbued with socialist strivings? Does not being determine the "sentiments" and opinions of men?

---

9 See Karl Marx and Frederick Engels, *Selected Works*, Vol. II, Moscow 1951, p. 23.

But what proof is there that the establishment of the socialist system is inevitable? Must the development of modern capitalism inevitably be followed by socialism? Or, in other words: How do we know that Marx's proletarian socialism is not merely a sentimental dream, a fantasy? Where is the scientific proof that it is not?

History shows that the form of property is directly determined by the form of production and, as a consequence, a change in the form of production is sooner or later inevitably followed by a change in the form of property. There was a time when property bore a communistic character, when the forests and fields in which primitive men roamed belonged to all and not to individuals. Why did communist property exist at that time? Because production was communistic, labour was performed in common, collectively—all worked together and could not dispense with each other. A different period set in, the period of petty-bourgeois production, when property assumed an individualistic (private) character, when everything that man needed (with the exception, of course, of air, sunlight, etc.) was regarded as private property. Why did this change take place? Because production became individualistic; each one began to work for himself, stuck in his own little corner. Finally there came a time, the time of large-scale capitalist production, when hundreds and thousands of workers gather under one roof, in one factory, and engage in collective labour. Here you do not see the old method of working individually, each pulling his own way—here every worker is closely associated in his work with his comrades in his own shop, and all of them are associated with the other shops. It is sufficient for one shop to stop work for the workers in the entire plant to become idle. As you see, the process of production, labour, has already assumed a social character, has acquired a socialist hue. And this takes place not only in individual factories, but in entire branches of industry, and between branches of industry; it is sufficient for the railwaymen to go on strike for production to be put in difficulties, it is sufficient for the production of oil and coal to come to a standstill for whole factories and mills to close down after a time. Clearly, here the process of production has assumed a social, collective character. As, however, the private character of appropriation does not correspond to the social character of production, as present-day collective labour must inevitably lead to collective property, it is self-evident that the socialist system will follow capitalism as inevitably as day follows night.

That is how history proves the inevitability of Marx's proletarian socialism.

*   *   *

History teaches us that the class or social group which plays the principal role in social production and performs the main functions in production must, in the course of time, inevitably take control of that production. There was a time, under the matriarchate, when women were regarded as the masters of production. Why was this? Because under the kind of production then prevailing, primitive agriculture, women played the principal role in production, they performed the main functions, while the men roamed the forests in quest of game. Then came the time, under the patriarchate, when the predominant position in production passed to men. Why did this change take place? Because under the kind of production prevailing at that time, stock-raising, in which the principal instruments of production were the spear, the lasso and the bow and arrow, the principal role was played by men. . . . There came the time of large-scale capitalist production, in which the proletarians begin to play the principal role in production, when all the principal functions in production pass to them, when without them production cannot go on for a single day (let us recall general strikes), and when the capitalists, far from being needed for production, are even a hindrance to it. What does this signify? It signifies either that all social life must collapse entirely, or that the proletariat, sooner or later, but inevitably, must take control of modern production, must become its sole owner, its socialistic owner.

Modern industrial crises, which sound the death knell of capitalist property and bluntly put the question: capitalism *or* socialism, make this conclusion absolutely obvious; they vividly reveal the parasitism of the capitalists and the inevitability of the victory of socialism.

That is how history further proves the inevitability of Marx's proletarian socialism.

Proletarian socialism is based not on sentiment, not on abstract "justice," not on love for the proletariat, but on the scientific grounds referred to above.

That is why proletarian socialism is also called "scientific socialism."

Engels said as far back as 1877:

"If for the imminent overthrow of the present mode of distribution of the products of labour . . . we had no better guarantee than the consciousness that this mode of distribution is unjust, and that justice must eventually triumph, we should be in a pretty bad way, and we might have a long time to wait. . . ." The most important thing in this is that "the productive forces created by the modern capitalist mode of production and the system of distribution of goods established by it have come into crying contradiction with that mode of production itself, and in fact to such a degree that, if the whole of modern society is not to perish, a revolution of the mode of production and distribution must take place, a revolution which will put an end to all class divisions. On this tangible, material fact . . . and not on the conceptions of justice and injustice held by any armchair philosopher, is modern socialism's confidence of victory founded" (see *Anti-Dühring*).[10]

That does not mean, of course, that since capitalism is decaying the socialist system can be established any time we like. Only Anarchists and other petty-bourgeois ideologists think that. The socialist ideal is not the ideal of all classes. It is the ideal only of the proletariat; not all classes are directly interested in its fulfilment the proletariat alone is so interested. This means that as long as the proletariat constitutes a small section of society the establishment of the socialist system is impossible. The decay of the old form of production, the further concentration of capitalist production, and the proletarianisation of the majority in society—such are the conditions needed for the achievement of socialism. But this is still not enough. The majority in society may already be proletarianised, but socialism may still not be

---

10 See Frederick Engels, *Herr Eugen Dühring's Revolution in Science (Anti-Dühring)*, Moscow 1947, pp. 233-35.

achievable. This is because, in addition to all this, the achievement of socialism calls for class consciousness, the unity of the proletariat and the ability of the proletariat to manage its own affairs. In order that all this may be acquired, what is called political freedom is needed, i.e., freedom of speech, press, strikes and association, in short, freedom to wage the class struggle. But political freedom is not equally ensured everywhere. Therefore, the conditions under which it is obliged to wage the struggle: under a feudal autocracy (Russia), a constitutional monarchy (Germany), a big-bourgeois republic (France), or under a democratic republic (which Russian Social-Democracy is demanding), are not a matter of indifference to the proletariat. Political freedom is best and most fully ensured in a democratic republic, that is, of course, in so far as it can be ensured under capitalism at all. Therefore, all advocates of proletarian socialism necessarily strive for the establishment of a democratic republic as the best "bridge" to socialism.

That is why, under present conditions, the Marxist programme is divided into two parts: the *maximum programme*, the goal of which is socialism, and the *minimum programme*, the object of which is to lay the road to socialism through a democratic republic.

*   *   *

What must the proletariat do, what path must it take in order consciously to carry out its programme, to overthrow capitalism and build socialism?

The answer is clear: the proletariat cannot achieve socialism by making peace with the bourgeoisie—it must unfailingly take the path of struggle, and this struggle must be a class struggle, a struggle of the entire proletariat against the entire bourgeoisie. Either the bourgeoisie and its capitalism, or the proletariat and its socialism! That must be the basis of the proletariat's actions, of its class struggle.

But the proletarian class struggle assumes numerous forms. A strike, for example—whether partial or general makes no difference —is class struggle. Boycott and sabotage are undoubtedly class struggle. Meetings, demonstrations, activity in public representative bodies, etc.—whether national parliaments or local government bodies makes no difference—are also class struggle. All these are different forms of the same class struggle. We shall not here examine which form of struggle is more important for the proletariat in its class struggle, we shall merely observe that, in its proper time and place, each is undoubtedly needed by the proletariat as essential means for developing its class consciousness and organisation; and the proletariat needs class consciousness and organisation as much as it needs air. It must also be observed, however, that for the proletariat, all these forms of struggle are merely *preparatory* means, that not one of them, taken separately, constitutes the *decisive* means by which the proletariat can smash capitalism. Capitalism cannot be smashed by the general strike alone: the general strike can only create some of the conditions that are necessary for the smashing of capitalism. It is inconceivable that the proletariat should be able to overthrow capitalism merely by its activity in parliament: parliamentarism can only prepare some of the conditions that are necessary for overthrowing capitalism.

What, then, is the *decisive* means by which the proletariat will overthrow the capitalist system?

The *socialist revolution* is this means.

Strikes, boycott, parliamentarism, meetings and demonstrations are all good forms of struggle as means for preparing and organising the proletariat. But not one of these means is capable of abolishing existing inequality. All these means must be concentrated in one principal and decisive means; the proletariat must rise and launch a determined attack upon the bourgeoisie in order to destroy capitalism to its foundations. This principal and decisive means is the socialist revolution.

The socialist revolution must not be conceived as a sudden and short blow, it is a prolonged struggle waged by the proletarian masses, who inflict defeat upon the bourgeoisie and capture its positions. And as the victory of the proletariat will at the same time mean domination over the vanquished bourgeoisie, as, *in a collision of classes*, the defeat of one class signifies the domination of the other, the first stage of the socialist revolution will be the political domination of the proletariat

over the bourgeoisie. The socialist *dictatorship of the proletariat*, capture
of power by the proletariat—this is what the socialist revolution must
start with.

This means that *until the bourgeoisie is completely vanquished*, until its
wealth has been confiscated, the proletariat must without fail possess a
military force, it must without fail have its "proletarian guard," with the
aid of which it will repel the counter-revolutionary attacks of the dying
bourgeoisie, exactly as the Paris proletariat did during the Commune.

The socialist dictatorship of the proletariat is needed to enable
the proletariat to expropriate the bourgeoisie, to enable it to confiscate
the land, forests, factories and mills, machines, railways, etc., from the
entire bourgeoisie.

The expropriation of the bourgeoisie—this is what the socialist
revolution must lead to.

This, then, is the principal and decisive means by which the proletariat will overthrow the present capitalist system.

That is why Karl Marx said as far back as 1847 :

". . . The first step in the revolution by the working class, is to raise
the proletariat to the position of ruling class. . . . The proletariat will
use its political supremacy to wrest, by degrees, all capital from the
bourgeoisie, to centralise all instruments of production in the hands . .
. of the proletariat organised as the ruling class . . ." (see the *Communist
Manifesto*).

That is how the proletariat must proceed if it wants to bring about
socialism.

From this general principle emerge all the other views on tactics.
Strikes, boycott, demonstrations, and parliamentarism are important
only in so far as they help to organise the proletariat and to strengthen
and enlarge its organisations for accomplishing the socialist revolution.

*   *   *

Thus, to bring about socialism, the socialist revolution is needed, and the socialist revolution must begin with the dictatorship of the proletariat, i.e., the proletariat must capture political power as a means with which to expropriate the bourgeoisie.

But to achieve all this the proletariat must be organised, the proletarian ranks must be closely-knit and united, strong proletarian organisations must be formed, and these must steadily grow.

What forms must the proletarian organisations assume?

The most widespread, mass organisations are trade unions and workers' co-operatives (mainly producers' and consumers' co-operatives). The object of the trade unions is to fight (mainly) against industrial capital to improve the conditions of the workers within the limits of the present capitalist system. The object of the co-operatives is to fight (mainly) against merchant capital to secure an increase of consumption among the workers by reducing the prices of articles of prime necessity, also within the limits of the capitalist system, of course. The proletariat undoubtedly needs both trade unions and co-operatives as means of organising the proletarian masses. Hence, from the point of view of the proletarian socialism of Marx and Engels, the proletariat must utilise both these forms of organisation and reinforce and strengthen them, as far as this is possible under present political conditions, of course.

But trade unions and co-operatives alone cannot satisfy the organisational needs of the militant proletariat. This is because the organisations mentioned cannot go beyond the limits of capitalism, for their object is to improve the conditions of the workers under the capitalist system. The workers, however, want to free themselves entirely from capitalist slavery, they want to smash these limits, and not merely operate within the limits of capitalism. Hence, in addition, an organisation is needed that will rally around itself the class-conscious elements of the workers of *all* trades, that will transform the proletariat into a conscious class and make it its chief aim to smash the capitalist system, to prepare for the socialist revolution.

Such an organisation is the Social-Democratic Party of the proletariat.

This Party must be a class party, and it must be quite independent of other parties—and this is because it is the party of the proletarian class, the emancipation of which can be brought about only by this class itself.

This Party must be a revolutionary party—and this because the workers can be emancipated only by revolutionary means, by means of the socialist revolution.

This Party must be an international party, the doors of the Party must be open to all class-conscious proletarians—and this because the emancipation of the workers is not a national but a social question, equally important for the Georgian proletarians, for the Russian proletarians, and for the proletarians of other nations.

Hence, it is clear, that the more closely the proletarians of the different nations are united, the more thoroughly the national barriers which have been raised between them are demolished, the stronger will the Party of the proletariat be, and the more will the organisation of the proletariat in one indivisible class be facilitated.

Hence, it is necessary, as far as possible, to introduce the principle of centralism in the proletarian organisations as against the looseness of federation—irrespective of whether these organisations are party, trade union or co-operative.

It is also clear that all these organisations must be built on a democratic basis, in so far as this is not hindered by political or other conditions, of course.

What should be the relations between the Party on the one hand and the co-operatives and trade unions on the other? Should the latter be party or non-party? The answer to this question depends upon where and under what conditions the proletariat has to fight. At all events, there can be no doubt that the friendlier the trade unions and co-operatives are towards the socialist party of the proletariat, the more fully will both develop. And this is because both these economic organisations, if they are not closely connected with a strong socialist party, often become petty, allow narrow craft interests to obscure general class interests and thereby cause great harm to the proletariat. It is therefore necessary, in all cases, to ensure that the trade unions and co-operatives are under the ideological and political influence of the Party. Only if this is done will the organisations mentioned be transformed into a socialist school that will organise the proletariat—at present split up into separate groups—into a conscious class.

Such, in general, are the characteristic features of the proletarian socialism of Marx and Engels.

*   *   *

How do the Anarchists look upon proletarian socialism?

First of all we must know that proletarian socialism is not simply a philosophical doctrine. It is the doctrine of the proletarian masses, their banner; it is honoured and "revered" by the proletarians all over the world. Consequently, Marx and Engels are not simply the founders of a philosophical "school"—they are the living leaders of the living proletarian movement, which is growing and gaining strength every day. Whoever fights against this doctrine, whoever wants to "overthrow" it, must keep all this well in mind so as to avoid having his head cracked for nothing in an unequal struggle. Messieurs the Anarchists are well aware of this. That is why, in fighting Marx and Engels, they resort to a most unusual and, in its way, a new weapon.

What is this new weapon? A new investigation of capitalist production? A refutation of Marx's *Capital*? Of course not! Or perhaps, having armed themselves with "new facts" and the "inductive" method, they "scientifically" refute the "Bible" of Social-Democracy—the *Communist Manifesto* of Marx and Engels? Again no! Then what is this extraordinary weapon?

It is the accusation that Marx and Engels indulged in "plagiarism"! Would you believe it? It appears that Marx and Engels wrote nothing original, that scientific socialism is a pure fiction, because the *Communist Manifesto* of Marx and Engels was, from beginning to end, "stolen" from the *Manifesto* of Victor Considerant. This is quite ludicrous, of course, but V. Cherkezishvili, the "incomparable leader" of the Anarchists, relates this amusing story with such aplomb, and a certain Pierre Ramus, Cherkezishvili's foolish "apostle," and our homegrown

Anarchists repeat this "discovery" with such fervour, that it is worth while dealing at least briefly with this "story."

Listen to Cherkezishvili :

"The entire theoretical part of the *Communist Manifesto*, namely, the first and second chapters . . . are taken from V. Considerant. Consequently, the *Manifesto* of Marx and Engels—that Bible of legal revolutionary democracy—is nothing but a clumsy paraphrasing of V. Considerant's *Manifesto*. Marx and Engels not only appropriated the contents of Considerant's *Manifesto* but even . . . borrowed some of its chapter headings" (see the symposium of articles by Cherkezishvili, Ramus and Labriola, published in German under the title of *The Origin of the "Communist Manifesto,"* p. 10).

This story is repeated by another Anarchist, P. Ramus :

"It can be emphatically asserted that their (Marx-Engels's) major work (the *Communist Manifesto*) is simply theft (a plagiary), shameless theft; they did not, however, copy it word for word as ordinary thieves do, but stole only the ideas and theories . . ." (*ibid.*, p. 4).

This is repeated by our Anarchists in *Nobati, Musha,*[11] *Khma,*[12] and other papers.

Thus it appears that scientific socialism and its theoretical principles were "stolen" from Considerant's Manifesto.

Are there any grounds for this assertion?

What was V. Considerant?

What was Karl Marx?

V. Considerant, who died in 1893, was a disciple of the utopian Fourier and remained an incorrigible *utopian*, who placed his hopes for the "salvation of France" on the *conciliation* of classes.

Karl Marx, who died in 1883, was a materialist, an *enemy of the utopians*. He regarded the development of the productive forces and the

---

11 *Musha (The Worker)*—a daily newspaper published by the Georgian Anarchists in Tiflis in 1906.

12 *Khma (The Voice)*—a daily newspaper published by the Georgian Anarchists in Tiflis in 1906.

struggle between classes as the guarantee of the liberation of mankind.

Is there anything in common between them?

The *theoretical* basis of scientific socialism is the materialist theory of Marx and Engels. From the standpoint of this theory the development of social life is wholly determined by the development of the productive forces. If the feudal-landlord system was superseded by the bourgeois system, the "blame" for this rests upon the development of the productive forces, which made the rise of the bourgeois system inevitable. Or again: if the present bourgeois system will inevitably be superseded by the socialist system, it is because this is called for by the development of the modern productive forces. Hence the historical necessity of the destruction of capitalism and the establishment of socialism. Hence the Marxist proposition that we must seek our ideals in the history, of the development of the productive forces and not in the minds of men.

Such is the theoretical basis of the *Communist Manifesto* of Marx and Engels (see the *Communist Manifesto*, Chapters I and II).

Does V. Considerant's *Democratic Manifesto* say anything of the kind? Did Considerant accept the materialist point of view?

We assert that neither Cherkezishvili, nor Ramus, nor our *Nobatists* quote a *single* statement, or a single word from Considerant's *Democratic Manifesto* which would confirm that Considerant was a materialist and based the evolution of social life upon the development of the productive forces. On the contrary, we know very well that Considerant is known in the history of socialism as an idealist utopian (see Paul Louis, *The History of Socialism in France*).

What, then, induces these queer "critics" to indulge in this idle chatter? Why do they undertake to criticise Marx and Engels when they are even unable to distinguish idealism from materialism? Is it only to amuse people? . . .

The *tactical* basis of scientific socialism is the doctrine of uncompromising class struggle, for this is the *best* weapon the proletariat possesses. The proletarian class struggle is the weapon by means of which the proletariat will capture political power and then expropriate the bourgeoisie in order to establish socialism.

Such is the *tactical* basis of scientific socialism as expounded in the *Manifesto* of Marx and Engels.

Is anything like this said in Considerant's *Democratic Manifesto*? Did Considerant regard the class struggle as the best weapon the proletariat possesses?

As is evident from the articles of Cherkezishvili and Ramus (see the above-mentioned symposium), there is not a word about this in Considerant's *Manifesto*—it merely notes the class struggle as a deplorable fact. As regards the class struggle as a means of smashing capitalism, Considerant spoke of it in his *Manifesto* as follows :

"Capital, labour and talent—such are the three basic elements of production, the three sources of wealth, the three wheels of the industrial mechanism. . . . The three classes which represent them have 'common interests'; their function is to make the machines work for the capitalists and for the people. . . . Before them . . . is the great goal of organising *the association of classes within the unity of the nation . . .*" (see K. Kautsky's pamphlet *The Communist Manifesto—A Plagiary*, p. 14, where this passage from Considerant's *Manifesto* is quoted).

All classes, unite!—this is the slogan that V. Considerant proclaimed in his *Democratic Manifesto*.

What is there in common between these tactics of class *conciliation* and the tactics of uncompromising class *struggle* advocated by Marx and Engels, whose resolute call was: *Proletarians of all countries, unite against all anti-proletarian classes*?

There is nothing in common between them, of course!

Why, then, do Messieurs Cherkezishvili and their foolish followers talk this rubbish? Do they think we are dead? Do they think we shall not drag them into the light of day?!

And lastly, there is one other interesting point. V. Considerant lived right up to 1893. He published his *Democratic Manifesto* in 1843. At the end of 1847 Marx and Engels wrote their *Communist Manifesto*. After that the Manifesto of Marx and Engels was published over and over again in all European languages. Everybody knows that the *Manifesto* of Marx and Engels was an epoch-making document. Nevertheless, nowhere did Considerant or his friends ever state during the lifetime of Marx and Engels that the latter had stolen "socialism" from Considerant's *Manifesto*. Is this not strange, reader?

What, then, impels the "inductive" upstarts—I beg your pardon, "scholars"—to talk this rubbish? In whose name are they speaking? Are they more familiar with Considerant's *Manifesto* than was Considerant himself? Or perhaps they think that V. Considerant and his supporters had not read the *Communist Manifesto*?

But enough. . . . Enough because the Anarchists themselves do not take seriously the Quixotic crusade launched by Ramus and Cherkezishvili: the inglorious end of this ridiculous crusade is too obvious to make it worthy of much attention. . . .

Let us proceed to the actual criticism.

*   *   *

The Anarchists suffer from a certain ailment: they are very fond of "criticising" the parties of their opponents, but they do not take the trouble to make themselves in the least familiar with these parties. We have seen the Anarchists behave precisely in this way when "criticising" the dialectical method and the materialist theory of the Social-Democrats (see Chapters I and II). They behave in the same way when they deal with the theory of scientific socialism of the Social-Democrats.

Let us, for example, take the following fact. Who does not know that fundamental disagreements exist between the Socialist-Revolutionaries and the Social-Democrats? Who does not know that the former repudiate Marxism, the materialist theory of Marxism, its dialectical method, its programme and the class struggle—whereas the Social-Democrats take their stand entirely on Marxism? These fundamental disagreements must be self-evident to anybody who has heard anything, if only with half an ear, about the controversy between *Revolutsionnaya Rossiya* (the organ of the Socialist-Revolutionaries) and *Iskra* (the organ of the Social-Democrats). But what will you say about those "critics" who fail to see this difference between the two and shout that both the Socialist Revolutionaries and the Social-Democrats are Marxists? Thus, for example, the Anarchists assert that both *Revolutsionnaya Rossiya* and *Iskra* are Marxist organs (see the Anarchists' symposium *Bread and Freedom*, p. 202).

That shows how "familiar" the Anarchists are with the principles of Social-Democracy!

After this, the soundness of their "scientific criticism" will be self-evident. . . .

Let us examine this "criticism."

The Anarchists' principal "accusation" is that they do not regard the Social-Democrats as genuine *Socialists*—you are not Socialists, you are enemies of socialism, they keep on repeating.

This is what Kropotkin writes on this score:

". . . We arrive at conclusions different from those arrived at by the majority of the Economists . . . of the Social-Democratic school. . . . We . . . arrive at free communism, whereas the majority of Socialists (meaning Social-Democrats too—*The Author*) arrive at state capitalism and collectivism (see Kropotkin, *Modern Science and Anarchism*, pp. 74-75).

What is this "state capitalism" and "collectivism" of the Social-Democrats?

This is what Kropotkin writes about it :

"The German Socialists say that all accumulated wealth must be concentrated in the hands of the state, which will place it at the disposal of workers' associations, organise production and exchange, and control the life and work of society" (see Kropotkin, *The Speeches of a Rebel*, p. 64).

And further :

"In their schemes . . . the collectivists commit . . . a double mistake. They want to abolish the capitalist system, but they preserve the two institutions which constitute the foundations of this system: represen-

tative government and wage-labour" (see *The Conquest of Bread*, p. 148).
... "Collectivism, as is well known ... preserves ... wage-labour. Only
... representative government ... takes the place of the employer. ..
." The representatives of this government "retain the right to utilise in
the interests of all the surplus value obtained from production. Moreover, in this system a distinction is made ... between the labour of
the common labourer and that of the trained man: the labour of the
unskilled worker, in the opinion of the collectivists, is *simple* labour,
whereas the skilled craftsman, engineer, scientist and so forth perform
what Marx calls *complex* labour and have the right to higher wages"
(*ibid.*, p. 52). Thus, the workers will receive their necessary products not
according to their needs, but "in proportion to the services they render
society" (*ibid.*, p. 157).

The Georgian Anarchists say the same thing only with greater
aplomb. Particularly outstanding among them for the recklessness of
his statements is Mr. Baton. He writes :

"What is the collectivism of the Social-Democrats? Collectivism,
or more correctly, state capitalism, is based on the following principle:
each must work as much as he likes, or as much as the state determines,
and receives in reward the value of his labour in the shape of goods. .
.." Consequently, here "there is needed a legislative assembly ... there
is needed (also) an executive power, i.e., ministers, all sorts of adminis-
trators, gendarmes and spies and, perhaps, also troops, if there are too
many discontented" (see *Nobati*, No. 5, pp. 68-69).

Such is the first "accusation" of Messieurs the Anarchists against
Social-Democracy.

*   *   *

Thus, from the arguments of the Anarchists it follows that :

1. In the opinion of the Social-Democrats, socialist society is impossible without a government which, in the capacity of principal master, will hire workers and will certainly have "ministers ... gendarmes
and spies." 2. In socialist society, in the opinion of the Social-Demo-

crats, the distinction between "dirty" and "clean" work will be retained, the principle "to each according to his needs" will be rejected, and another principle will prevail, viz., "to each according to his services."

Those are the two points on which the Anarchists' "accusation" against Social-Democracy is based.

Has this "accusation" advanced by Messieurs the Anarchists any foundation?

We assert that everything the Anarchists say on this subject is either the result of stupidity, or it is despicable slander.

Here are the facts.

As far back as 1846 Karl Marx said : "The working class in the course of its development will substitute for the old bourgeois society an *association* which will exclude classes and their antagonism, and there will be *no more political power properly so-called . . .*" (see *Poverty of Philosophy*).

A year later Marx and Engels expressed the same idea in the *Communist Manifesto* (*Communist Manifesto*, Chapter II).

In 1877 Engels wrote: "The first act in which the state really comes forward as the representative of society as a whole—the taking possession of the means of production in the name of society—is at the same time its last independent act as a state. The interference of the state power in social relations becomes superfluous in one sphere after another, and then ceases of itself. . . . The state is not 'abolished,' it *withers away*" (*Anti-Dühring*).

In 1884 the same Engels wrote: "The state, then, has not existed from all eternity. There have been societies that did without it, that had no conception of the state. . . . At a certain stage of economic development, which was necessarily bound up with the cleavage of society into classes, the state became a necessity. . . . We are now rapidly approaching a stage in the development of production at which the existence of these classes not only will have ceased to be a necessity, but will become a positive hindrance to production. They will fall as inevitably as they arose at an earlier stage. *Along with them the state will inevitably fall.* The society that will organise production on the basis of a free and equal association of the producers will put the whole machinery of state where it will then belong: into the Museum of Antiquities, by the side of the spinning wheel and the bronze axe" (see *Origin of the Family, Private Property and the State*).

Engels said the same thing again in 1891 (see his Introduction to *The Civil War in France*).

As you see, in the opinion of the Social-Democrats, socialist society is a society in which there will be no room for the so-called state, political power, with its ministers, governors, gendarmes, police and soldiers. The last stage in the existence of the state will be the period of the socialist revolution, when the proletariat will capture political power and set up its own government (dictatorship) for the final abolition of the bourgeoisie. But when the bourgeoisie is abolished, when classes are abolished, when socialism becomes firmly established, there will be no need for any political power—and the so-called state will retire into the sphere of history.

As you see, the above-mentioned "accusation" of the Anarchists is mere tittle-tattle devoid of all foundation.

As regards the second point in the "accusation," Karl Marx says the following about it :

"In a higher phase of communist (i.e., socialist) society, after the enslaving subordination of the individual to the division of labour, and therewith also the *antithesis* between *mental* and *physical labour, has vanished*; after labour has become . . . life's prime want; after the productive forces have also increased with the all-round development of the individual . . . only then can the narrow horizon of bourgeois law be crossed in its entirety and society inscribe on its banners: '*From each according to his ability, to each according to his needs*'" (*Critique of the Gotha Programme*).

As you see, in Marx's opinion, the higher phase of communist (i.e., socialist) society will be a system under which the division of work into "dirty" and "clean," and the contradiction between mental and physical labour will be completely abolished, labour will be equal, and in society the genuine communist principle will prevail: from each according to his ability, to each according to his needs. Here there is no room for wage-labour.

Clearly this "accusation" is also devoid of all foundation.

One of two things: either Messieurs the Anarchists have never seen the above-mentioned works of Marx and Engels and indulge in "criticism" on the basis of hearsay, or they are familiar with the above-mentioned works of Marx and Engels and are deliberately lying.

Such is the fate of the first "accusation."

*   *   *

The second "accusation" of the Anarchists is that they deny that Social-Democracy is *revolutionary*. You are not revolutionaries, you repudiate violent revolution, you want to establish socialism only by means of ballot papers—Messieurs the Anarchists tell us.

Listen to this:

". . . Social-Democrats . . . are fond of declaiming on the theme of 'revolution,' 'revolutionary struggle,' 'fighting with arms in hand.' . . . But if you, in the simplicity of your heart, ask them for arms, they will solemnly hand you a ballot paper to vote in elections. . . ." They affirm that "the only expedient tactics befitting revolutionaries are peaceful and legal parliamentarism, with the oath of allegiance to capitalism, to established power and to the entire existing bourgeois system" (see symposium *Bread and Freedom*, pp. 21, 22-23).

The Georgian Anarchists say the same thing, with even greater aplomb, of course. Take, for example, Baton, who writes :

"The whole of Social-Democracy . . . openly asserts that fighting with the aid of rifles and weapons is a bourgeois method of revolution, and that only by means of ballot papers, only by means of general elections, can parties capture power, and then, by means of a parliamentary majority and legislation, reorganise society" (see *The Capture of Political Power*, pp. 3-4).

That is what Messieurs the Anarchists say about the Marxists.

Has this "accusation" any foundation? We affirm that here, too, the Anarchists betray their ignorance and their passion for slander.

Here are the facts.

As far back as the end of 1847, Karl Marx and Frederick Engels wrote:

"The Communists disdain to conceal their views and aims. They openly declare that their *ends can be obtained only by the forcible overthrow* of all existing social conditions. Let the ruling classes tremble at a Communistic Revolution. The proletarians have nothing to lose but their chains. They have a world to win. *Working men of all countries, unite!*" (See the *Manifesto of the Communist Party*. In some of the legal editions several words have been omitted in the translation.)

In 1850, in anticipation of another outbreak in Germany, Karl Marx wrote to the German comrades of that time as follows:

"Arms and ammunition must not be surrendered on any pretext . . . the *workers* must . . . *organise themselves independently as a proletarian guard with commanders . . . and with a general staff. . . .*" And this "you must keep in view during and after the impending insurrection" (see *The Cologne Trial*. Marx's Address to the Communists).[13]

In 1851-52 Karl Marx and Frederick Engels wrote:

". . . The insurrectionary career once entered upon, *act with the greatest determination, and on the offensive.* The defensive is the death of every armed rising. . . . Surprise your antagonists while their forces are scattering, prepare new successes, however small, but daily . . . force your enemies to a retreat before they can collect their strength against you; in the words of Danton, the greatest master of revolutionary policy yet known: de l'audace, de l'audace, encore de l'audace!" (*Revolution and Counter-revolution in Germany.*)

We think that something more than "ballot papers" is meant here.

Lastly, recall the history of the Paris Commune, recall how peace-

---

13 Karl Marx, *The Cologne Trial of the Communists*, published by Molot Publishers, St. Petersburg, 1906, p. 113 (IX. Appendix. *Address of the Central Committee to the Communist League*, March, 1850). (See Karl Marx and Frederick Engels, *Selected Works*, Vol. I, Moscow 1951, pp. 104-05.)

fully the Commune acted, when it was content with the victory in Paris and refrained from attacking Versailles, that hotbed of counter-revolution. What do you think Marx said at that time? Did he call upon the Parisians to go to the ballot box? Did he express approval of the complacency of the Paris workers (the whole of Paris was in the hands of the workers), did he approve of the good nature they displayed towards the vanquished Versaillese? Listen to what Marx said:

"What elasticity, what historical initiative, what a capacity for sacrifice in these Parisians! After six months of hunger . . . they rise, beneath Prussian bayonets. . . . History has no like example of like greatness! If they are defeated only their 'good nature' will be to blame. *They should have marched at once on Versailles*, after first Vinoy and then the reactionary section of the Paris National Guard had themselves retreated. They missed their opportunity because of conscientious scruples. They did not want to *start a civil war*, as if that mischievous abortion Thiers had not already started the civil war with his attempt to disarm Paris!" (*Letters to Kugelmann*.)[14]

That is how Karl Marx and Frederick Engels thought and acted.

That is how the Social-Democrats think and act.

But the Anarchists go on repeating: Marx and Engels and their followers are interested only in ballot papers—they repudiate violent revolutionary action!

As you see, this "accusation" is also slander, which exposes the Anarchists' ignorance about the essence of Marxism.

Such is the fate of the second "accusation."

*   *   *

The third "accusation" of the Anarchists consists in denying that Social-Democracy is a popular movement, describing the Social-Democrats as bureaucrats, and affirming that the Social-Democratic plan for the dictatorship of the proletariat spells death to the revolution,

---

14 See Karl Marx and Frederick Engels, *Selected Works*, Vol. II, Moscow 1951, p. 420.

and since the Social-Democrats stand for such a dictatorship they actually want to establish not the dictatorship of the proletariat, but their own dictatorship over the proletariat.

Listen to Mr. Kropotkin:

"We Anarchists have pronounced final sentence upon dictatorship. . . . We know that every dictatorship, no matter how honest its intentions, will lead to the death of the revolution. We know . . . that the idea of dictatorship is nothing more or less than the pernicious product of governmental fetishism which . . . has always striven to perpetuate slavery" (see Kropotkin, *The Speeches of a Rebel*, p. 131). The Social-Democrats not only recognise revolutionary dictatorship, they also "advocate dictatorship over the proletariat. . . . The workers are of interest to them only in so far as they are a disciplined army under their control. . . . Social-Democracy strives through the medium of the proletariat to capture the state machine" (see *Bread and Freedom*, pp. 62, 63).

The Georgian Anarchists say the same thing:

"The dictatorship of the proletariat in the direct sense of the term is utterly impossible, because the advocates of dictatorship are state men, and their dictatorship will be not the free activities of the entire proletariat, but the establishment at the head of society of the same representative government that exists today" (see Baton, *The Capture of Political Power*, p. 45). The Social-Democrats stand for dictatorship not in order to facilitate the emancipation of the proletariat, but in order . . . "*by their own rule to establish a new slavery*" (see *Nobati*, No. 1, p. 5. Baton).

Such is the third "accusation" of Messieurs the Anarchists.

It requires no great effort to expose this, one of the regular slanders uttered by the Anarchists with the object of deceiving their readers.

We shall not analyse here the deeply mistaken view of Kropotkin, according to whom every dictatorship spells death to revolution. We shall discuss this later when we discuss the Anarchists' tactics. At present we shall touch upon only the "accusation" itself.

As far back as the end of 1847 Karl Marl and Frederick Engels said that to establish socialism the proletariat must achieve political dictatorship in order, with the aid of this dictatorship, to repel the counter-revolutionary attacks of the bourgeoisie and to take from it the means of production; that this dictatorship must be not the dictatorship of a few individuals, but the dictatorship of the entire proletariat as a class:

"The proletariat will use its political supremacy to wrest, by degrees, all capital from the bourgeoisie, to centralise all instruments of production in the hands . . . of the proletariat organised as the ruling class . . ." (see the *Communist Manifesto*).

That is to say, the dictatorship of the proletariat will be a dictatorship of the entire proletariat as a class over the bourgeoisie and not the domination of a few individuals over the proletariat.

Later they repeated this same idea in nearly all their other works, such as, for example, *The Eighteenth Brumaire of Louis Bonaparte, The Class Struggles in France, The Civil War in France, Revolution and Counterrevolution in Germany, Anti-Dühring,* and other works.

But this is not all; To ascertain how Marx and Engels conceived of the dictatorship of the proletariat, to ascertain to what extent they regarded this dictatorship as possible, for all this it is very interesting to know their attitude towards the Paris Commune. The point is that the dictatorship of the proletariat is denounced not only by the Anarchists but also by the urban petty bourgeoisie, including all kinds of butchers and tavern-keepers—by all those whom Marx and Engels called philistines. This is what Engels said about the dictatorship of the proletariat, addressing such philistines:

"Of late, the German philistine has once more been filled with wholesome terror at the words: *Dictatorship of the Proletariat.* Well and good, gentlemen, do you want to know what this dictatorship looks like? Look at the Paris Commune. That was the Dictatorship of the Proletariat" (see *The Civil War in France*, Introduction by Engels).[15]

As you see, Engels conceived of the dictatorship of the proletariat

---

15 The author quotes this passage from Karl Marx's pamphlet *The Civil War in France*, with a preface by F. Engels, Russian translation from the German edited by N. Lenin, 1905 (see Karl Marx and Frederick Engels, *Selected Works*, Vol. I, Moscow 1951, p. 440).

in the shape of the Paris Commune.

Clearly, everybody who wants to know what the dictatorship of the proletariat is as conceived of by Marxists must study the Paris Commune. Let us then turn to the Paris Commune. If it turns out that the Paris Commune was indeed the dictatorship of a few individuals over the proletariat, then—down with Marxism, down with the dictatorship of the proletariat! But if we find that the Paris Commune was indeed the dictatorship of the proletariat over the bourgeoisie, then . . . we shall laugh heartily at the anarchist slanderers who in their struggle against the Marxists have no alternative but to invent slander.

The history of the Paris Commune can be divided into two periods: the first period, when affairs in Paris were controlled by the well-known "Central Committee," and the second period, when, after the authority of the "Central Committee" had expired, control of affairs was transferred to the recently elected Commune. What was this "Central Committee," what was its composition? Before us lies Arthur Arnould's *Popular History of the Paris Commune* which, according to Arnould, briefly answers this question. The struggle had only just commenced when about 300,000 Paris workers, organised in companies and battalions, elected delegates from their ranks. In this way the "Central Committee" was formed.

"All these citizens (members of the "Central Committee") elected during partial elections by their companies or battalions," says Arnould, "were known only to the small groups whose delegates they were. Who were these people, what kind of people were they, and what did they want to do?" This was "an anonymous government consisting almost exclusively of common workers and minor office employees, the names of three fourths of whom were unknown outside their streets or offices. . . . Tradition was upset. Something unexpected had happened in the world. There was not a single member of the ruling classes among them. A revolution had broken out which was not represented by a single *lawyer, deputy, journalist* or *general*. Instead, there was a *miner* from Creusot, a *bookbinder*, a *cook*, and so forth" (see *A Popular History of the Paris Commune*, p. 107).

Arthur Arnould goes on to say :

"The members of the 'Central Committee' said: 'We are obscure bodies, humble tools of the attacked people. . . . Instruments of the people's will, we are here to be its echo, to achieve its triumph. The people want a Commune, and we shall remain in order to proceed to the election of the Commune.' Neither more nor less. These dictators do not put themselves above nor stand aloof from the masses. One feels that they are living with the masses, in the masses, by means of the masses, that they consult with them every second, that they listen and convey all they hear, striving only, in a concise form . . . to convey the opinion of three hundred thousand men" (*ibid.*, p. 109).

That is how the Paris Commune behaved in the first period of its existence.

Such was the Paris Commune.

Such is the dictatorship of the proletariat.

Let us now pass to the second period of the Commune, when the Commune functioned in place of the "Central Committee." Speaking of these two periods, which lasted two months, Arnould exclaims with enthusiasm that this was a real dictatorship of the people. Listen:

"The magnificent spectacle which this people presented during those two months imbues us with strength and hope . . . to look into the face of the future. During those two months there was a real dictatorship in Paris, a most complete and uncontested dictatorship not of one man, *but of the entire people* — the sole master of the situation. . . . This dictatorship lasted uninterruptedly for over two months, from March 18 to May 22 (1871). . . ." In itself ". . . the Commune was only a moral power and possessed no other material strength than the universal sympathy . . . of the citizens, *the people were the rulers*, the only rulers, they themselves set up their police and magistracy . . ." (*ibid.*, pp. 242, 244).

That is how the Paris Commune is described by *Arthur Arnould*, a member of the Commune and an active participant in its hand-to-hand fighting.

The Paris Commune is described in the same way by another of its members and equally active participant *Lissagaray* (see his *History of the Paris Commune*).

The people as the "only rulers," "not the dictatorship of one man, but of the whole people"—this is what the Paris Commune was.

"Look at the Paris Commune. That was the dictatorship of the proletariat"—exclaimed Engels for the information of philistines.

So this is the dictatorship of the proletariat as conceived of by Marx and Engels.

As you see, Messieurs the Anarchists know as much about the dictatorship of the proletariat, the Paris Commune, and Marxism, which they so often "criticise," as you and I, dear reader, know about the Chinese language.

Clearly, there are two kinds of dictatorship. There is the dictatorship of the minority, the dictatorship of a small group, the dictatorship of the Trepovs and Ignatyevs, which is directed against the people. This kind of dictatorship is usually headed by a camarilla which adopts secret decisions and tightens the noose around the neck of the majority of the people.

Marxists are the enemies of such a dictatorship, and they fight such a dictatorship far more stubbornly and self-sacrificingly than do our noisy Anarchists.

There is another kind of dictatorship, the dictatorship of the proletarian majority, the dictatorship of the masses, which is directed against the bourgeoisie, against the minority. At the head of this dictatorship stand the masses; here there is no room either for a camarilla or for secret decisions, here everything is done openly, in the streets, at meetings—because it is the dictatorship of the street, of the masses, a dictatorship directed against all oppressors.

Marxists support this kind of dictatorship "with both hands"—and that is because such a dictatorship is the magnificent beginning of the great socialist revolution.

Messieurs the Anarchists confused these two mutually negating dictatorships and thereby put themselves in a ridiculous position: they are fighting not Marxism but the figments of their own imagination, they are fighting not Marx and Engels but windmills, as Don Quixote of blessed memory did in his day. . . .

Such is the fate of the third "accusation."

(TO BE CONTINUED)[16]

Akhali Droyeba (New Times),
Nos. 5, 6, 7 and 8,
December 11, 18,-25, 1906
and January 1, 1907
Chveni Tskhovreba (Our Life),
Nos. 3, 5, 8 and 9,
February 21, 23, 27 and 28, 1907
Dro (Time) Nos. 21, 22, 23 and 26,
April 4, 5, 6 and 10, 1907
Signed: *Ko*. . . .
Translated from the Georgian

---

16   The continuation did not appear in the press because, in the middle of 1907, Comrade Stalin was transferred by the Central Committee of the Party to Baku for Party work, and several months later he was arrested there. His notes on the last chapters of his work *Anarchism or Socialism?* were lost when the police searched his lodgings. — *Ed.*

APPENDIX

ANARCHISM OR SOCIALISM?

THE FIRST VERSION OF THE ARTICLES *ANARCHISM OR SOCIALISM?*
AS PUBLISHED IN *AKHALI TSKHOVREBA*

DIALECTICAL MATERIALISM

I

We are not the kind of people who, when the word "anarchism" is mentioned, turn away contemptuously and say with a supercilious wave of the hand: "Why waste time on that, it's not worth talking about!" We think that such cheap "criticism" is undignified and useless.

Nor are we the kind of people who console themselves with the thought that the Anarchists "have no masses behind them and, therefore, are not so dangerous." It is not who has a larger or smaller "mass" following today, but the essence of the doctrine that matters. If the "doctrine" of the Anarchists expresses the truth, then it goes without saying that it will certainly hew a path for itself and will rally the masses around itself. If, however, it is unsound and built up on a false foundation, it will not last long and will remain suspended in mid-air. But the unsoundness of anarchism must be proved.

We believe that the Anarchists are real enemies of Marxism. Accordingly, we also hold that a real struggle must be waged against real enemies. Therefore, it is necessary to examine the "doctrine" of the Anarchists from beginning to end and weigh it up thoroughly from all aspects.

But in addition to criticising anarchism we must explain our own position and in that way expound in general outline the doctrine of Marx and Engels. This is all the more necessary for the reason that some Anarchists are spreading false conceptions about Marxism and are causing confusion in the minds of readers.

And so, let us proceed with our subject.

*   *   *

> *Everything in the world is in motion. . . .*
> *Life changes, productive forces grow, old*
> *relations collapse. . . . Eternal motion and*
> *eternal destruction and creation—such is*
> *the essence of life.*
>
> Karl Marx
> (See *The Poverty of Philosophy*)

Marxism is not only the theory of socialism, it is an integral world outlook, a philosophical system, from which Marx's proletarian socialism logically follows. This philosophical system is called dialectical materialism. Clearly, to expound Marxism means to expound also dialectical materialism.

Why is this system called dialectical materialism?

Because its *method* is dialectical, and its *theory* is materialistic.

What is the dialectical method? What is the materialist theory?

It is said that life consists in constant growth and development. And that is true: social life is not something immutable and static, it never remains at one level, it is in eternal motion, in an eternal process of destruction and creation. It was with good reason that Marx said that eternal motion and eternal destruction and creation are the essence of life. Therefore, life always contains the *new* and the *old*, the growing and the dying, revolution and reaction—in it something is always dying, and at the same time something is always being born. . . .

The dialectical method tells us that we must regard life as it actually is. Life is in continual motion, and therefore life must be viewed in its motion, in its destruction and creation. Where is life going, what is dying and what is being born in life, what is being destroyed and what is being created?—these are the questions that should interest us first of all.

Such is the first conclusion of the dialectical method.

That which in life is born and grows day by day is invincible, its progress cannot be checked, its victory is inevitable. That is to say, if, for example, in life the proletariat is born and grows day by day, no matter how weak and small in numbers it may be today, in the long run it must triumph On the other hand, that which in life is dying and moving towards its grave must inevitably suffer defeat, i.e., if, for example, the bourgeoisie is losing ground and is slipping farther and farther back every day, then, no matter how strong and numerous it may be today, it must, in the long run, suffer defeat and go to its grave. Hence arose the well-known dialectical proposition: all that which really exists, i.e., all that which grows day by day is rational.

Such is the second conclusion of the dialectical method.

In the eighties of the nineteenth century a famous controversy flared up among the Russian revolutionary intelligentsia The Narodniks asserted that the main force that could undertake the task of "emancipating Russia" was the poor peasantry. Why?—the Marxists asked them. Because, answered the Narodniks, the peasantry is the most numerous and at the same time the poorest section of Russian society. To this the Marxists replied: It is true that today the peasantry constitutes the majority and that it is very poor, but is that the point? The peasantry has long constituted the majority, but up to now it has displayed no initiative in the struggle for "freedom" without the assistance of the proletariat. Why? Because the peasantry as a class is *disintegrating day by day*, it is breaking up into the proletariat and the bourgeoisie, whereas the proletariat as a class *is day by day growing* and gaining strength. Nor is poverty of decisive importance here: tramps are poorer than the peasants, but nobody will say that they can undertake the task of "emancipating Russia." The only thing that matters is: Who is growing and who is becoming aged in life? As the proletariat is the only class which is steadily growing and gaining strength, our duty is to take our place by its side and recognise it as the main force in the Russian revolution — that is how the Marxists answered. As you see, the Marxists lookeda the question from the dialectical standpoint, whereas the Narodniks argued metaphysically, because they regarded the phenomena of life as "immutable, static, given once and for all" (see F. Engels, *Philosophy, Political Economy, Socialism*).

That is how the dialectical method looks upon the movement of life.

But there is movement and movement. There was social movement in the "December days" when the proletariat, straightening its back, stormed arms depots and launched an attack upon reaction. But the movement of preceding years, when the proletariat, under the conditions of "peaceful" development, limited itself to individual strikes and the formation of small trade unions, must also be called social movement. Clearly, movement assumes different forms. And so the dialectical method says that movement has two forms: the evolutionary and the revolutionary form. Movement is evolutionary when the progressive elements spontaneously continue their daily activities and introduce minor, *quantitative* changes in the old order. Movement is revolutionary when the same elements combine, become imbued with a single idea and sweep down upon the enemy camp with the object of uprooting the old order and its *qualitative* features and to establish a new order. Evolution prepares for revolution and creates the ground for it; revolution consummates the process of evolution and facilitates its further activity.

Similar processes take place in nature. The history of science shows that the dialectical method is a truly scientific method: from astronomy to sociology, in every field we find confirmation of the idea that nothing is eternal in the universe, everything changes, everything develops. Consequently, everything in nature must be regarded from the point of view of movement, development. And this means that the spirit of dialectics permeates the whole of present-day science.

As regards the forms of movement, as regards the fact that according to dialectics, minor, *quantitative* changes sooner or later lead to major, *qualitative* changes — this law applies with equal force to the history of nature. Mendeleyev's "periodic system of elements" clearly shows how very important in the history of nature is the emergence of qualitative changes out of quantitative changes. The same thing is shown in biology by the theory of neo-Lamarckism, to which neo-Darwinism is yielding place.

We shall say nothing about other facts, on which F. Engels has thrown sufficiently full light in his *Anti-Dühring*.

*   *   *

Thus, we are now familiar with the dialectical method. We know that according to that method the universe is in eternal motion, in an eternal process of destruction and creation, and that, consequently, all phenomena in nature and in society must be viewed in motion, in process of destruction and creation and not as something static and immobile. We also know that this motion has two forms: evolutionary and revolutionary. . . .

How do our Anarchists look upon the dialectical method?

Everybody knows that Hegel was the father of the dialectical method. Marx merely purged and improved this method. The Anarchists are aware of this; they also know that Hegel was a conservative, and so, taking advantage of the "opportunity," they vehemently revile Hegel, throw mud at him as a "reactionary," as a supporter of restoration, and zealously try to "prove" that "Hegel . . . is a philosopher of restoration . . . that he eulogizes bureaucratic constitutionalism in its absolute form, that the general idea of his philosophy of history is subordinate to and serves the philosophical trend of the period of restoration," and so on and so forth (see *Nobati*, No. 6. Article by V. Cherkezishvili). True, nobody contests what they say on this point; on the contrary, everybody agrees that Hegel was not a revolutionary, that he was an advocate of monarchy, nevertheless, the Anarchists go on trying to "prove" and deem it necessary to go on endlessly trying to "prove" that Hegel was a supporter of "restoration." Why do they do this? Probably, in order by all this to discredit Hegel, to make their readers feel that the method of the "reactionary" Hegel is also "repugnant" and unscientific. If that is so, if Messieurs the Anarchists think they can refute the dialectical method *in this way*, then I must say that *in this way* they can prove nothing but their own simplicity. Pascal and Leibnitz were not revolutionaries, but the mathematical method they discovered is recognised today as a scientific method; Mayer and Helmholtz were not revolutionaries, but their discoveries in the field of physics became the basis of science; nor were Lamarck and Darwin revolutionaries, but their evolutionary method put biological science on its feet. . . . Yes, *in this way* Messieurs the Anarchists will prove nothing but their own simplicity.

To proceed. In the opinion of the Anarchists "dialectics is metaphysics" (see *Nobati*, No. 9. Sh. G.), and as they "want to free science from metaphysics, philosophy from theology" (see *Nobati*, No. 3. Sh. G.), they repudiate the dialectical method.

Oh, those Anarchists! As the saying goes: "Blame others for your own sins." Dialectics matured in the struggle against metaphysics and gained fame in this struggle; but according to the Anarchists, "dialectics is metaphysics"! Proudhon, the "father" of the Anarchists, believed that there existed in the world an "immutable justice" established *once and for all* (see Eltzbacher's *Anarchism*, pp. 64-68, foreign edition) and for this Proudhon has been called a metaphysician. Marx fought Proudhon with the aid of the dialectical method and proved that since everything in the world changes, "justice" must also change, and that, consequently, "immutable justice" is metaphysical fantasy (see Marx, *The Poverty of Philosophy*). Yet the Georgian disciples of the metaphysician Proudhon come out and try to "prove" that "dialectics is metaphysics," that metaphysics recognises the "unknowable" and the "thing-in-itself," and in the long run passes into empty theology. In contrast to Proudhon and Spencer, Engels combated metaphysics as well as theology with the aid of the dialectical method (see Engels, *Ludwig Feuerbach* and *Anti-Dühring*). He proved how ridiculously vapid they were. Our Anarchists, however, try to "prove" that Proudhon and

Spencer were scientists, whereas Marx and Engels were metaphysicians. One of two things: either Messieurs the Anarchists are deceiving themselves, or they fail to understand what is metaphysics. At all events, the dialectical method is entirely free from blame.

What other accusations do Messieurs the Anarchists hurl against the dialectical method? They say that the dialectical method is "subtle word-weaving," "the method of sophistry," "logical and mental somersaults" (see *Nobati*, No. 8. Sh. G.) "with the aid of which both truth and falsehood are proved with equal facility" (see *Nobati*, No. 4. V. Cherkezishvili).

At first sight it would seem that the accusation advanced by the Anarchists is correct. Listen to what Engels says about the follower of the metaphysical method : "... His communication is : "Yea, yea; nay, nay, for whatsoever is more than these cometh of evil.' For him a thing either exists, or it does not exist; it is equally impossible for a thing to be itself and at the same time something else. Positive and negative absolutely exclude one another ..." (see *Anti-Dühring*, Introduction). How is that?—the Anarchist cries heatedly. Is it possible for a thing to be good and bad at the same time?! That is "sophistry," "juggling with words," it shows that "you want to prove truth and falsehood with equal facility! ..."

Let us, however, go into the substance of the matter. Today we are demanding a democratic republic. The democratic republic, however, strengthens bourgeois property. Can we say that a democratic republic is good always and everywhere? No, we cannot! Why? Because a democratic republic is good only "*today*," when we are destroying feudal property, but "*tomorrow*," when we shall proceed to destroy bourgeois property and establish socialist property, the democratic republic will no longer be good; on the contrary, it will become a fetter, which we shall smash and cast aside. But as life is in continual motion, as it is impossible to separate the past from the present, and as we are *simultaneously* fighting the feudal rulers and the bourgeoisie, we say: in so far as the democratic republic destroys feudal property it is good and we advocate it, but in so far as it strengthens bourgeois property it is bad, and therefore we criticise it. It follows, therefore, that the democratic republic is simultaneously both "good" and "bad," and thus the answer to the question raised may be both "yes" and "no." It was *facts* of this kind that Engels had in mind when he proved the correctness of the dialectical method in the words quoted above. The Anarchists, however, failed to understand this and to them it seemed to be "sophistry"! The Anarchists are, of course, at liberty to note or ignore these *facts*, they may even ignore the sand on the sandy seashore—they have every right to do that. But why drag in the dialectical method, which, unlike the Anarchists, does not look at life with its eyes shut, which has its finger on the pulse of life and openly says: since life changes, since life is in motion, every phenomenon of life has two trends: a positive and a negative; the first we must defend and the second we must reject? What astonishing people those Anarchists are: they are constantly talking about "justice," but they treat the dialectical method with gross injustice!

To proceed further. In the opinion of our Anarchists, "dialectical development is catastrophic development, by means of which, first the past is utterly destroyed, and then the future is established quite separately. . . . Cuvier's cataclysms were due to unknown causes, but Marx and Engels's catastrophes are engendered by dialectics" (see *Nobati*, No. 8. Sh. G.). In another place the same author says that "Marxism rests on Darwinism and treats it uncritically" (see *Nobati*, No. 6).

Ponder well over that, reader!

Cuvier rejects Darwin's theory of evolution, he recognises only cataclysms, and cataclysms are *unexpected* upheavals "due to *unknown* causes." The Anarchists say that the Marxists *adhere to Cuvier's view* and therefore *repudiate Darwinism*.

Darwin rejects Cuvier's cataclysms, he recognises gradual evolution. But the same Anarchists say that "Marxism rests on Darwinism and treats it uncritically," therefore, the Marxists *do not advocate Cuvier's cataclysms*.

This is anarchy if you like! As the saying goes: the Sergeant's widow flogged herself! Clearly, Sh. G. of No. 8 of *Nobati* forgot what Sh. G. of No. 6 said. Which is right: No. 6 or No. 8? Or are they both lying?

Let us turn to the facts. Marx says: "At a certain stage of their

development, the material productive forces of society come in conflict with the existing relations of production, or—what is but a legal
expression for the same thing—with the property relations. . . . Then
begins an epoch of social revolution." But "no social order ever perishes before all the productive forces for which there is room in it have
developed . . ." (see K. Marx, *A Contribution to the Critique of Political
Economy*. Preface). If this idea of Marx is applied to modern social life,
we shall find that between the present-day productive forces which are
social in character, and the method of appropriating the product, which
is *private* in character, there is a fundamental conflict which must culminate in the socialist revolution (see F. Engels, *Anti-Dühring*, Chapter II,
Part III). As you see, in the opinion of Marx and Engels, "revolution"
("catastrophe") is engendered not by Cuvier's "unknown causes," but
by very definite and vital social causes called "the development of the
productive forces." As you see, in the opinion of Marx and Engels,
revolution comes only when the productive forces have sufficiently matured, and not *unexpectedly*, as Cuvier imagined. Clearly, there is
nothing in common between Cuvier's cataclysms and the dialectical
method. On the other hand, Darwinism repudiates not only Cuvier's
cataclysms, but also dialectically conceived revolution, whereas according to the dialectical method evolution and revolution, quantitative and
qualitative changes, are two essential forms of the same motion. Clearly, it is also wrong to say that "Marxism . . . treats Darwinism uncritically." It follows therefore that *Nobati* is lying in both cases, in No. 6
as well as in No. 8.

And so these lying "critics" buttonhole us and go on repeating:
Whether you like it or not our lies are better than your truth! Probably
they believe that everything is pardonable in an Anarchist.

There is another thing for which Messieurs the Anarchists cannot
forgive the dialectical method: "Dialectics . . . provides no possibility
of getting, or jumping, out of oneself, or of jumping over oneself"
(see *Nobati*, No. 8. Sh. G.). Now that is the downright truth, Messieurs
Anarchists! Here you are absolutely right, my dear sirs: the dialectical
method does not provide such a possibility. But why not? Because
"jumping out of oneself, or jumping over oneself," is an exercise for
wild goats, while the dialectical method was created for human beings.

That is the secret! . . .

Such, in general, are our Anarchists' views on the dialectical method.

Clearly, the Anarchists fail to understand the dialectical method of Marx and Engels; they have conjured up their own dialectics, and it is against this dialectics that they are fighting so ruthlessly.

All we can do is to laugh as we gaze at this spectacle, for one cannot help laughing when one sees a man fighting his own imagination, smashing his own inventions, while at the same time heatedly asserting that he is smashing his opponent.

II

"It is not the consciousness of men that
determines their being, but, on the contrary,
their social being that determines their
consciousness."

Karl Marx

What is the materialist theory?

Everything in the world changes, everything in the world is in motion, but *how* do these changes take place and *in what form* does this motion proceed?—that is the question. We know, for example, that the earth was once an incandescent, fiery mass, then it gradually cooled, then the animal kingdom appeared and developed, then appeared a species of ape from which man subsequently originated. But how did this development take place? Some say that nature and its development were preceded by the universal idea, which subsequently served as the basis of this development, so that the development of the phenomena of nature, it would appear, is merely the *form* of the development of the idea. These people were called idealists, who later split up and followed different trends. Others say that from the very beginning there have existed in the world two opposite forces—idea and matter, and that correspondingly, phenomena are also divided into two categories, the ideal and the material, which are in constant conflict. Thus the development of the phenomena of nature, it would appear, represents a constant struggle between ideal and material phenomena. Those people are called dualists, and they, like the idealists, are split up into different schools.

Marx's materialist theory utterly repudiates both dualism and idealism. Of course, both ideal and material phenomena exist in the world, but this does not mean that they negate each other. On the contrary, the ideal and the material are two different forms of the same phenomenon; they exist together and develop together; there is a close connection between them. That being so, we have no grounds for thinking that they negate each other. Thus, so-called dualism crumbles to its foundations. A single and indivisible nature expressed in two different forms—material and ideal—that is how we should regard the development of nature. A single and indivisible life expressed in two different forms—ideal and material—that is how we should regard the development of life.

Such is the monism of Marx's materialist theory.

At the same time, Marx also repudiates idealism. It is wrong to think that the development of the idea, and of the spiritual side in general, *precedes* nature and the material side in general. So-called external, inorganic nature existed before there were any living beings. The first living matter—protoplasm—possessed no consciousness (idea), it possessed only irritability and the first rudiments of sensation. Later, animals gradually developed the power of sensation, which slowly passed into consciousness, in conformity with the development of their nervous systems. If the ape had never stood upright, if it had always walked on all fours, its descendant—man—would not have been able freely to use his lungs and vocal chords and, therefore, would not have been able to speak; and that would have greatly retarded the development of his consciousness. If, furthermore, the ape had not risen up on its hind legs, its descendant—man—would have been compelled always to look downwards and obtain his impressions only from there; he would have been unable to look up and around himself and, consequently, his brain would have obtained no more material (impressions) than that of the ape; and that would have greatly retarded the development of his consciousness. It follows that the development of the spiritual side is conditioned by the structure of the organism and the development of its nervous system. It follows that the development of the spiritual side, the development of ideas, *is preceded* by the development of the material side, the development of being. Clearly, first the external conditions change, first matter changes, and *then* consciousness and other spiritual phenomena change accordingly—the development of the ideal side *lags behind* the development of material conditions. If we call the material side, the external conditions, being, etc., the *content*, then we must call the ideal side, consciousness and other phenomena of the same kind, the *form*. Hence arose the well-known materialist proposition: in the process of development content precedes form, form lags behind content.

The same must be said about social life. Here, too, material development precedes ideal development, here, too, form lags behind its content. Capitalism existed and a fierce class struggle raged long before scientific socialism was even thought of; the process of production already bore a social character long before the socialist idea arose.

That is why Marx says: "It is not the consciousness of men that determines their being, but, on the contrary, their social being that determines their consciousness" (see K. Marx, *A Contribution to the Critique of Political Economy*). In Marx's opinion, economic development is the material foundation of social life, *its content*, while legal-political and religious-philosophical development is the *"ideological form"* of this content, its "superstructure." Marx, therefore, says: "With the change of the economic foundation the entire immense superstructure is *more or less rapidly* transformed" (*ibid.*).

In social life too, first the external, material conditions change and *then* the thoughts of men, their world outlook, change. The development of content precedes the rise and development of form. This, of course, does not mean that in Marx's opinion content is possible without form, as Sh. G. imagines (see *Nobati*, No. 1. "A Critique of Monism"). Content is impossible without form, but the point is that since a given form lags behind its content, it never *fully* corresponds to this content; and so the new content is often "obliged" to clothe itself for a time in the old form, and this causes a conflict between them. At the present time, for example, the private character of the appropriation of the product does not correspond to the *social* content of production, and this is the basis of the present-day social "conflict." On the other hand, the conception that the idea is a form of being does not mean that, by its nature, consciousness is the same as matter. That was the opinion held only by the vulgar materialists (for example, Buchner and Moleschott), whose theories fundamentally contradict Marx's materialism, and whom Engels rightly ridiculed in his *Ludwig Feuerbach*. According to Marx's materialism, consciousness and being, mind and matter, are two different forms of the same phenomenon, which, broadly speaking, is called nature. Consequently, they do not negate each other,[1] but nor are they one and the same phenomenon. The only point is that, in the development of nature and society, consciousness, i.e., what takes place in our heads, is preceded by a corresponding material change, i.e., what takes place outside of us. Any given material change is, sooner or later, inevitably followed by a corresponding ideal change. That is why we say that an ideal change is the form of a corresponding material change.

Such, in general, is the monism of the dialectical materialism of Marx and Engels.

We shall be told by some: All this may well be true as applied to the history of nature and society. But how do different conceptions and ideas about given objects arise in our heads at the present time? Do so-called external conditions really exist, or is it only our conceptions of these external conditions that exist? And if external conditions exist, to what degree are they perceptible and cognizable?

On this point we say that our conceptions, our "self," exist only in so far as external conditions exist that give rise to impressions in our "self." Whoever unthinkingly says that nothing exists but our conceptions, is compelled to deny the existence of all external conditions and, consequently, must deny the existence of all other people except his own "self," which fundamentally contradicts the main principles

---

1 This does not contradict the idea that there is a conflict between form and content. The point is that the conflict is not between content and form in general, but between the old form and the new content, which is seeking a new form and is striving towards it.

of science and vital activity. Yes, external conditions do actually exist; these conditions existed before us, and will exist after us; and the more often and the more strongly they affect our consciousness, the more easily perceptible and cognizable do they become. As regards the question as to how different conceptions and ideas about given objects arise in our heads *at the present time*, we must observe that here we have a repetition in brief of what takes place in the history of nature and society. In this case, too, the object outside of us precedes our conception of it; in this case, too, our conception, the form, lags behind the object, its content, and so forth. When I look at a tree and see it—that only shows that this tree existed even before the conception of a tree arose in my head; that it was this tree that aroused the corresponding conception in my head. The importance of the monistic materialism of Marx and Engels for the practical activities of mankind can be readily understood. If our world outlook, if our habits and customs are determined by external conditions, if the unsuitability of legal and political forms rests on an economic content, it is clear that we must help to bring about a radical change in economic relations in order, with this change, to bring about a radical change in the habits and customs of the people, and in the political system of the country. Here is what Karl Marx says on that score:

"No great acumen is required to perceive the necessary interconnection of materialism with . . . socialism. If man constructs all his knowledge, perceptions, etc., from the world of sense . . . then it follows that it is a question of so arranging the empirical world that he experiences the truly human in it, that he becomes accustomed to experiencing himself as a human being. . . . If man is unfree in the materialist sense—that is, is free not by reason of the negative force of being able to avoid this or that, but by reason of the positive power to assert his true individuality, then one should not punish individuals for crimes, but rather destroy the anti-social breeding places of crime. . . . If man is moulded by circumstances, then the circumstances must be moulded humanly" (see *Ludwig Feuerbach*, Appendix: "Karl Marx on the History of French Materialism of the XVIII Century").

Such is the connection between materialism and the practical activities of men.

*   *   *

What is the anarchist view of the monistic materialism of Marx and Engels?

While Marx's dialectics originated with Hegel, his materialism is a development of Feuerbach's materialism. The Anarchists know this very well, and they try to take advantage of the defects of Hegel and Feuerbach to discredit the dialectical materialism of Marx and Engels. We have already shown with reference to Hegel that these tricks of the Anarchists prove nothing but their own polemical impotence. The same must be said with reference to Feuerbach. For example, they strongly emphasise that "Feuerbach was a pantheist . . ." that he "deified man . . ." (see *Nobati*, No. 7. D. Delendi), that "in Feuerbach's opinion man is what he eats . . ." alleging that from this Marx drew the following conclusion: "Consequently, the main and primary thing is economic conditions," etc. (see *Nobati*, No. 6. Sh. G.). True, nobody has any doubts about Feuerbach's pantheism, his deification of man, and other errors of his of the same kind. On the contrary, Marx and Engels were the first to reveal Feuerbach's errors; nevertheless, the Anarchists deem it necessary once again to "expose" the already exposed errors of Feuerbach. Why? Probably because, in reviling Feuerbach, they want at least in some way to discredit the materialism which Marx borrowed from Feuerbach and then scientifically developed. Could not Feuerbach have had correct as well as erroneous ideas? We say that by tricks of this kind the Anarchists will not shake monistic materialism in the least; all they will do is to prove their own impotence.

The Anarchists disagree among themselves about Marx's materialism. If, for example, we listen to what Mr. Cherkezishvili has to say, it would appear that Marx and Engels detested monistic materialism; in his opinion their materialism is vulgar and not monistic materialism: "The great science of the naturalists, with its system of evolution, transformism and monistic materialism which *Engels so heartily detested* . . . avoided dialectics," etc. (see *Nobati*, No. 4. V. Cherkezishvili). It follows, therefore, that the natural-scientific materialism, which Cherkezishvili likes and which Engels detested, was monistic materialism.

Another Anarchist, however, tells us that the materialism of Marx and Engels is monistic and should therefore be rejected. "Marx's conception of history is a throwback to Hegel. The monistic materialism of absolute objectivism in general, and Marx's economic monism in particular, are impossible in nature and fallacious in theory. . . . Monistic materialism is poorly disguised dualism and a compromise between metaphysics and science . . ." (see *Nobati*, No. 6. Sh. G.).

It would follow that monistic materialism is unacceptable because Marx and Engels, far from detesting it, were actually monistic materialists themselves, and therefore monistic materialism must be rejected.

This is anarchy if you like! They have not yet grasped the substance of Marx's materialism, they have not yet understood whether it is monistic materialism or not, they have not yet agreed among themselves about its merits and demerits, but they already deafen us with their boastful claims: We criticise and raze Marx's materialism to the ground! This by itself shows what grounds their "criticism" can have.

To proceed further. It appears that certain Anarchists are even ignorant of the fact that in science there are various forms of materialism, which differ a great deal from one another: there is, for example, vulgar materialism (in natural science and history), which denies the importance of the ideal side and the effect it has upon the material side; but there is also so-called monistic materialism, which scientifically examines the interrelation between the ideal and the material sides. Some Anarchists confuse all this and at the same time affirm with great aplomb: Whether you like it or not, we subject the materialism of Marx and Engels to devastating criticism! Listen to this: "In the opinion of Engels, and also of Kautsky, Marx rendered mankind a great service in that he . . ." among other things, discovered the "materialist conception." "Is this true? We do not think so, for we know . . . that all the historians, scientists and philosophers who adhere to the view that the social mechanism is set in motion by geographic, climatic and telluric, cosmic, anthropological and biological conditions— *re all materialists*" (see *Nobati*, No. 2. Sh. G.). How can you talk to such people? It appears, then, that there is no difference between the "materialism" of Aristotle and of Montesquieu, or between the "materialism" of Marx and of Saint-Simon. A fine example, indeed, of understanding your opponent and subjecting him to devastating criticism!

Some Anarchists heard somewhere that Marx's materialism was a "belly theory" and set about popularising this "idea," probably because paper is cheap in the editorial office of Nobati and this process does not cost much. Listen to this: "In the opinion of Feuerbach man is what he eats. This formula had a magic effect on Marx and Engels," and so, in the opinion of the Anarchists, Marx drew from this the conclusion that "consequently the main and primary thing is economic conditions, relations of production. . . ." And then the Anarchists proceed to instruct us in a philosophical tone: "It would be a mistake to say that the sole means of achieving this object (of social life) is eating and economic production. . . . If *ideology were determined* mainly monistically, by *eating* and economic existence—then some gluttons would be geniuses" (see *Nobati*, No. 6. Sh. G.). You see how easy it is to criticise Marx's materialism! It is sufficient to hear some gossip in the street from some schoolgirl about Marx and Engels, it is sufficient to repeat that street gossip with philosophical aplomb in the columns of a paper like Nobati, to leap into fame as a "critic." But tell me one thing, gentlemen: Where, when, in what country, and which Marx did you hear say that "eating determines ideology"? Why did you not cite a single sentence, a single word from the works of Marx to back your accusation? Is economic existence and eating the same thing? One can forgive a schoolgirl, say, for confusing these entirely different concepts, but how is it that you, the "vanquishers of Social-Democracy," "regenerators of science," so carelessly repeat the mistake of a schoolgirl? How, indeed, can eating determine social ideology? Ponder over what you yourselves have said; eating, the form of eating, does not change; in ancient times people ate, masticated and digested their food in the same way as they do now, but the forms of ideology constantly change and develop. Ancient, feudal, bourgeois and proletarian—such are the forms of ideology. Is it conceivable that that which generally speaking, does not change can determine that which is constantly changing? Marx does, indeed, say that economic existence determines ideology, and this is easy to understand, but is eating and economic existence the same thing? Why do you think it proper to attribute your own foolishness to Marx?

To proceed further. In the opinion of our Anarchists, Marx's materialism "is parallelism. . . ." Or again: "monistic materialism is poorly disguised dualism and a compromise between metaphysics and science. . . ." "Marx drops into dualism because he depicts relations of production as material, and human striving and will as an illusion and a utopia, which, even though it exists, is of no importance" (see *Nobati*, No. 6. Sh. G.). Firstly, Marx's monistic materialism has nothing in common with silly parallelism. From the standpoint of materialism, the material side, content, necessarily *precedes* the ideal side, form. Parallelism repudiates this view and emphatically affirms that neither the material nor the ideal *comes first*, that both move together, parallel with each other. Secondly, what is there in common between Marx's monism and dualism when we know perfectly well (and you, Messieurs Anarchists, should also know this if you read Marxist literature!) that the former springs from *one principle*—nature, which has a material and an ideal form, whereas the latter springs from *two principles*—the material and the ideal which, according to dualism, mutually negate each other. Thirdly, who said that "human striving and will are not important"? Why don't you point to the place where Marx says that? Does not Marx speak of the importance of "striving and will" in his *Eighteenth Brumaire of Louis Bonaparte*, in his *Class Struggles in France*, in his *Civil War in France*, and in other pamphlets? Why, then, did Marx try to develop the proletarians' "will and striving" in the socialist spirit, why did he conduct propaganda among them if he attached no importance to "striving and will"? Or, what did Engels talk about in his well-known articles of 1891-94 if not the "importance of striving and will"? Human striving and will acquire their content from economic existence, but that does not mean that they exert no influence on the development of economic relations. Is it really so difficult for our Anarchists to digest this simple idea? It is rightly said that a passion for criticism is one thing, but criticism itself is another.

Here is another accusation Messieurs the Anarchists make: "form is inconceivable without content . . ." therefore, one cannot say that "form lags behind content . . . they 'co-exist.'. . . Otherwise, monism would be an absurdity" (see *Nobati*, No. 1. Sh. G.). Messieurs the Anarchists are somewhat confused. Content is inconceivable without form, but the *existing form* never fully corresponds to the existing content; to a certain extent the new content is always clothed in the old form, as a consequence, there is always a conflict between the old form and the new content. It is precisely on this ground that revolutions occur, and this, among other things, expresses the revolutionary spirit of Marx's materialism The Anarchists, however, have failed to understand this and obstinately repeat that there is no content without form. . . .

Such are the Anarchists' views on materialism. We shall say no more. It is sufficiently clear as it is that the Anarchists have invented their own Marx, have ascribed to him a "materialism" of their own invention, and are now fighting this "materialism." But not a single bullet of theirs hits the true Marx and the true materialism. . . .

What connection is there between dialectical materialism and proletarian socialism?

Akhali Tskhovreba
(*New Life*), Nos. 2, 4,
7 and 16, June 21, 24
and 28 and July 9, 1906
Signed: *Koba*
Translated from the Georgian

BIOGRAPHICAL CHRONICLE
(1879-1906)

1879

December 9
Josef Vissarionovich Djugashvili (Stalin) was born in Gori, Georgia.

1888

September
J. V. Stalin enters the elementary clerical school in Gori.

1894

June
J. V. Stalin graduates from the Gori school with highest marks.

September 2
J. V. Stalin enters first grade of the Tiflis Theological Seminary.

1896-1898

In the Theological Seminary in Tiflis, J. V. Stalin conducts Marxist circles of students, studies *Capital*, the *Manifesto of the Communist Party*, and other works of K. Marx and F. Engels, and becomes acquainted with the early works of V. I. Lenin.

1898

January
J. V. Stalin begins to conduct a workers' Marxist circle in the Central Railway Work shops in Tiflis.

August
J. V. Stalin joins the Georgian Social-Democratic organisation Messameh Dassy.

J. V. Stalin, V. Z. Ketskhoveli, and A. G. Tsulukidze form the core of the revolutionary Marxist minority in the Messameh Dassy.

J. V. Stalin draws up a programme of studies for Marxist workers' circles.

J. V. Stalin, V. Z. Ketskhoveli, and A. G. Tsulukidze raise the question of founding an illegal revolutionary Marxist press. This gives rise to the first sharp disagreements between the revolutionary minority and the opportunist majority in the Messameh Dassy.

1 8 9 9

May 29
J. V. Stalin is expelled from the Tiflis Theological Seminary for propagating Marxism.

December 28
J. V. Stalin starts work at the Tiflis Physical Observatory.

1 9 0 0

April 23
J. V. Stalin addresses a workers' May Day meeting in the region of Salt Lake, on the outskirts of Tiflis.

Summer
J. V. Stalin establishes contact with V. K. Kurnatovsky, a well-known supporter of Lenin's *Iskra*, who had arrived in Tiflis for Party work.

August
J. V. Stalin leads a mass strike at the Central Railway Workshops in Tiflis.

1 8 9 8 - 1 9 0 0

Under the leadership of J. V. Stalin, V. Z. Ketskhoveli, and A. G. Tsulukidze, a central leading group is formed within the Tiflis organisation of the R.S.D.L.P. , which passes from propaganda in study circles to mass political agitation. The group organises the printing of manifestoes and their distribution among the workers, forms underground Social-Democratic circles, and leads the strikes and political struggle of the Tiflis proletariat.

1 9 0 1

March 21
J. V. Stalin's lodgings at the Tiflis Physical Observatory are searched by the police.

March 28
J. V. Stalin leaves the Tiflis Physical Observatory and goes underground.

April 22
J. V. Stalin leads the workers' May Day demonstration in the Soldatsky Market Place, in the centre of Tiflis.

September
No. 1 of the illegal newspaper *Brdzola*, the organ of the revolutionary wing of the Georgian Marxists published on the initiative of J. V. Stalin, appears in Baku. The article "From the Editors," outlining the programme of the newspaper which appeared in that issue, was written by J. V. Stalin.

November 11
J. V. Stalin is elected a member of the first Tiflis Committee of the R.S.D.L.P., which followed the Leninist-*Iskra* trend.

End of November
The Tiflis Committee sends J. V. Stalin to Batum to form a Social-Democratic organisation there.

December
No. 2 -3 of *Brdzola* appears, containing J. V. Stalin's article "The Russian Social-Democratic Party and Its Immediate Tasks."

J. V. Stalin establishes contact with the advanced workers in Batum and organises Social-Democratic circles at the Rothschild, Mantashev, Sideridis, and other plants.

December 31
J. V. Stalin organises in the guise of a New Year's party a secret conference of representatives of Social-Democratic study circles. The conference elects a leading group, headed by J. V. Stalin, which acted virtually as the Batum Committee of the R.S.D.L.P. of the Leninist-*Iskra* trend.

1902

January
J. V. Stalin organises in Batum an underground printing plant, writes leaflets and organises the printing and distribution of manifestoes.

January 31 - February 17
J. V. Stalin organises a strike at the Mantashev plant which ends in the victory of the workers.

February 27 - beginning of March
J. V. Stalin directs the activities of the strike committee during a strike at the Rothschild plant.

March 8
J. V. Stalin leads a demonstration of strikers who demand the release of 32 of their arrested fellow-strikers.

March 9
J . V. Stalin organises and leads a political demonstration of over 6,000 workers employed in the various plants in Batum who demand the release of 300 worker-demonstrators arrested by the police on March 8.

Outside the prison where the arrested workers were confined, the demonstration was shot at by troops and 15 workers were killed and 54 were injured. About 500 demonstrators were arrested. That same night J. V. Stalin wrote a manifesto on the shooting down of the demonstrators.

March 12
J. V. Stalin leads a workers' demonstration which he had organised in connection with the funeral of the victims of the shooting on March 9

April 5
J. V. Stalin i s arrested at a meeting of the leading Party group in Batum.

April 6
J. V. Stalin is detained in the Batum jail.

April 1902 - April 19, 1903
While in the Batum jail, J. V. Stalin establishes and maintains contact with the Batum Social-Democratic organisation, directs its activities, writes leaflets, and conducts political work among the prisoners.

1903

March
The Caucasian Union of the R.S.D.L.P. is formed at the First Congress of Caucasian Social- Democratic Labour Organisations. J. V. Stalin, then confined in the Batum jail, is in his absence elected a member of the Caucasian Union Committee that was set up at the congress.

April 19
J. V. Stalin is transferred from the Batum jail to the Kutais jail, where he establishes contact with the other political prisoners and conducts among them propaganda on behalf of the Leninist-*Iskra* ideas.

Autumn
J. V. Stalin is retransferred to the Batum jail, whence he is deported under escort to Eastern Siberia.

November 27
J. V. Stalin arrives at the village of Novaya Uda, Balagansk Uyezd, Irkutsk Gubernia, his place of exile.

December
While in Siberia, J. V. Stalin receives a letter from V. I. Lenin.

1904

January 5
J. V. Stalin escapes from his place of exile.

February
J. V. Stalin arrives in Tiflis and directs the work of the Caucasian Union Committee of the R.S.D.L.P.

J. V. Stalin drafts the programmatic document entitled *Credo* dealing with the disagreements within the Party and with the organisational tasks of the Party.

June
J. V. Stalin arrives in Baku where, on the instructions of the Caucasian Union Committee, he dissolves the Menshevik committee and forms a new, Bolshevik committee.

Summer
J. V. Stalin makes a tour of the most important districts of Transcaucasia and debates with Mensheviks, Federalists, Anarchists and others.

In Kutais, J. V. Stalin forms a Bolshevik Imeretia-Mingrelia Committee.

September 1
Proletariatis Brdzola, No. 7, publishes J. V. Stalin's article "The Social-Democratic View of the National Question."

September – October
In connection with the disagreements within the Party, J. V. Stalin, while in Kutais, writes letters to the Georgian Bolsheviks abroad, expounding Lenin's views on the combination of socialism with the working-class movement.

November
J. V. Stalin arrives in Baku and leads the campaign for the convocation of the Third Congress of the Party.

December 13-31
J. V. Stalin leads the general strike of the Baku workers.

1905

January 1
Proletariatis Brdzola, No. 8, publishes J . V. Stalin's article "The Proletarian Class and the Proletarian Party."

January 8
The manifesto is issued entitled "Workers of the Caucasus, It Is Time to Take Revenge!" written by J. V. Stalin in connection with the defeat tsarism had sustained in the Far East.

Beginning of February
On the initative of J.V. Stalin, the Caucasian Union Committee dissolves the Menshevik Tiflis Committee, which had announced its withdrawal from the Caucasian Union of the R.S.D.L.P., and forms a new, Bolshevik Tiflis Committee.

February 13
In connection with the Tatar-Armenian massacre in Baku which had been provoked by the police, J. V. Stalin writes the leaflet entitled "Long Live International Fraternity!"

February 15
In connection with the successful demonstration of many thousands of people held in Tiflis to protest against an attempt by the police to provoke massacres among the different nationalities in that city too, J. V. Stalin writes the leaflet entitled "To Citizens. Long Live the Red Flag!"

April
J. V. Stalin speaks at a big meeting in Batum in a debate with the Menshevik leaders N. Ramishvili, R. Arsenidze, and others.

May
J. V. Stalin's pamphlet *Briefly About the Disagreements in the Party* is published.

June 12
J. V. Stalin delivers a speech at the funeral of A. G. Tsulukidze in which he outlines a programme of struggle to be waged by the workers and peasants against the autocracy, and subjects the tactics of the Mensheviks to devastating criticism.

July 15
Proletariatis Brdzola, No. 10, publishes J. V. Stalin's article "Armed Insurrection and Our Tactics."

July 18
In a letter to the Caucasian Union Committee, N. K. Krupskaya asks for copies of J. V. Stalin's pamphlet *Briefly About the Disagreements in the Party* and also for the regular delivery of *Borba Proletariata*.

July
J. V. Stalin speaks before an audience of 2,000 in Chiaturi in debate with the Anarchists, Federalists and Socialist-Revolutionaries.

August 15
Proletariatis Brdzola, No. 11 , publishes J. V. Stalin's articles "The Provisional Revolutionary Government and Social-Democracy" and "A Reply to *Social-Democrat.*"

October 15
Proletariatis Brdzola, No. 12, publishes J. V. Stalin's articles "Reaction Is Growing" and "The Bourgeoisie Is Laying a Trap."

October 18
J. V. Stalin addresses a workers' meeting in the Nadzaladevi district of Tiflis on the tsar's Manifesto of October 17.

October
In connection with the October all-Russian political strike, J. V. Stalin writes the leaflets "Citizens!" and "To All the Workers!"

November 20
No. 1 of *Kavkazsky Rabochy Listok* appears with a leading article by J. V. Stalin entitled "Tiflis, November 20, 1905."

End of November
J. V. Stalin directs the proceedings of the Fourth Bolshevik Conference of the Caucasian Union of the R.S.D.L.P.

December 12-17
J. V. Stalin takes part in the proceedings of the First All-Russian Conference of Bolsheviks in Tammerfors as a delegate of the Caucasian Union of the R.S.D.L.P. At this conference he became personally acquainted with V. I. Lenin.

1906

Beginning of January
J. V. Stalin's pamphlet *Two Clashes* is published.

March 8
J. V. Stalin's article "The State Duma and the Tactics of Social-Democracy" appears in *Gantiadi*, No. 3.

March 17-29
J. V. Stalin's articles "The Agrarian Question" and "Concerning the Agrarian Question," appear in Nos. 5, 9, 10 and 14 of the newspaper *Elva*.

End of March
J. V. Stalin i s elected a delegate from the Tiflis organisation to the Fourth ("Unity") Congress of the R.S.D.L.P.

April 10-25
J. V. Stalin takes part in the proceedings of the Fourth ("Unity") Congress of the R.S.D.L.P. in Stockholm a t which, in opposition to the Mensheviks, he substantiates and defends the Bolshevik tactics in the revolution.

June 20
No. 1 of *Akhali Tskhovreba*, directed by J. V. Stalin, appears.

June 21-July 9
J. V. Stalin's series of articles *Anarchism or Socialism?* appear in Nos. 2, 4, 7 and 16 of the Bolshevik newspaper *Akhali Tskhovreba*.

June-November
J. V. Stalin directs the work of organising the first trade unions in Tiflis (printers, shop assistants, and others).

July 13
J. V. Stalin's article "Marx and Engels on Insurrection" appears in *Akhali Tskhovreba*, No. 19.

July 14
J. V. Stalin's article "International Counterrevolution" appears in *Akhali Tskhovreba*, No. 20.

July-August
J. V. Stalin's pamphlet *The Present Situation and the Unity Congress of the Workers' Party* is published.

September
J. V. Stalin takes part in the proceedings of the Regional Congress of Caucasian Organisations of the R.S.D.L.P.

November 14
No. 1 of *Akhali Droyeba*, directed by J. V. Stalin , appears, containing his article "The Class Struggle."

December 4
Akhali Droyeba, No. 4, publishes J. V. Stalin's article "'Factory Legislation' and the Proletarian Struggle."

December 11
Akhali Droyeba, No. 5, resumes publication of J. V. Stalin's series of articles *Anarchism or Socialism?*

December 18, 1906 - April 10, 1907
Publication of J. V. Stalin's series of articles *Anarchism or Socialism?* is continued in the Bolshevik newspapers *Akhali Droyeba*, *Chveni Tskhovreba* and *Dro*.

www.ingramcontent.com/pod-product-compliance
Ingram Content Group UK Ltd.
Pitfield, Milton Keynes, MK11 3LW, UK
UKHW032310160125
4116UKWH00002B/42